The Care of the Elderly in Japan

The problems of an ageing population are particularly acute in Japan. With people living longer, many need more care; and this section of the population requires increasing support while there is a diminishing working population and a diminishing tax base.

This book, based on extensive fieldwork in a Japanese institution for the elderly, explores the problems associated with ageing and responses to it in Japan. By looking at the institution from the viewpoints of residents, staff and visitors, as well as from the policy point of view, the book carefully assesses how far the home succeeds in offering an acceptable quality of life to the residents. It gives insights into the life and work of long-term care institutions; discusses how people in Japan have changed their perceptions towards family responsibility, the institutionalisation of the elderly, and welfare rights; and examines how institutions for the elderly are run in Japan and how their management differs from that of those in the West.

Yongmei Wu is a Lecturer at the Beijing Centre of Japanese Studies, Beijing Foreign Studies University. She received her PhD in Japanese Studies from the University of Hong Kong. She was a research fellow at the Japan College of Social Work and a visiting researcher in the University of Tokyo. Her research interests include cross-cultural ageing research in Japan and China, Asian welfare models, gender and family.

Japan Anthropology Workshop Series
Edited by Joy Hendry
Oxford Brookes University

Editorial Board
Pamela Asquith, *University of Alberta*
Eyal Ben Ari, *Hebrew University of Jerusalem*
Hirochika Nakamaki, *National Museum of Ethnology, Osaka*
Wendy Smith, *Monash University*
Jan van Bremen, *University of Leiden*

A Japanese View of Nature
The World of Living Things
Kinji Imanichi
Translated by Pamela J. Asquith, Heita Kawakatsu,
Shusuke Yagi and Hiroyuki Takasaki
Edited and introduced by Pamela J. Asquith

Japan's Changing Generations
Are Young People Creating a New Society?
Edited by Gordon Mathews and Bruce White

The Care of the Elderly in Japan
Yongmei Wu

The Care of the Elderly in Japan

Yongmei Wu

Routledge
Taylor & Francis Group

LONDON AND NEW YORK

First published 2004
by Routledge
2 Park Square, Milton Park, Abingdon, Oxon, OX14 4RN

Simultaneously published in the USA and Canada
by Routledge
270 Madison Ave, New York NY 10016

Routledge is an imprint of the Taylor & Francis Group

Transferred to Digital Printing 2005

© 2004 Yongmei Wu

Typeset in Times by Taylor & Francis Books Ltd

British Library Cataloguing in Publication Data
A catalogue record for this book is available from the British Library

Library of Congress Cataloging in Publication Data
A catalog record for this book has been requested

ISBN10: 0-415-32319-3 (hbk)
ISBN10: 0-415-54605-2 (pbk)

ISBN13: 978-0-415-32319-2 (hbk)
ISBN13: 978-0-415-54605-8 (pbk)

To my son and my parents,
for their dedicated love and everlasting support

Contents

Illustrations

Series preface

Members of the Japan Anthropology Workshop carry out detailed and insightful research in Japan, and meet regularly to present papers about their work and to exchange views on the subjects of their study. This series aims to bring the best of their work into print, and to make it available as soon as possible. In this way we aim to offer a deeper understanding of contemporary Japanese society that records changes as they take place as well as illuminating the underlying continuity of Japanese ideas. Anthropologists specialise in digging beneath the surface, in peeling off and examining layers of cultural wrapping, and in gaining an understanding of language and communication that goes beyond formal presentation and informal frolicking. I hope that the series will open the eyes of readers from many backgrounds to the work of these diligent 'moles' in the social life of Japan.

Our series is open to the inclusion of translations of the work of Japanese scholars, collections of papers around particular themes, and monographs of ethnographic research on a range of different topics. The first book in the series was a translation of the work of the seminal Japanese anthropologist, Imanishi Kinji, who had profound ideas about the place of human beings in the living world. His ideas do not confirm theories that go almost unquestioned in the West, and we hope that the book will make readers rethink one or two of their long-held assumptions. The second book was a collection of papers about generational change in Japan, and presented the views of young people, Japanese and foreign, who had worked with young people. It gave a fresh picture of possibilities for the future.

The present volume is a monograph of ethnographic research, and exemplifies the method of participant observation that is a mainstay of anthropological field research. Here the aim is to get as far as is reasonably possible inside the lives of the people who are the focus of the study and thereby to gain deep insights into the way that they are organised. This method brings the reader most successfully into the heart of the subject in hand, and Wu has brought this aim neatly to fruition. She worked with the elderly in Japan to find out on the ground how society copes with the increasing numbers of people who are gradually losing the ability to care for themselves. By guiding the reader through the various circumstances of real residents of the large care home where she worked, as well as those of employees and volunteers who worked there, she depicts in fine detail the quality of life that they can expect, and relates it to their actual experience.

Joy Hendry

Foreword

The rapid ageing of the population and the subsequent concerns about care for frail older people can no longer be considered characteristics of only a few industrialised nations. Academic gerontology and clinical elder care institutions and practices which have developed in Western cultural contexts are now being studied, adapted and sometimes challenged as other societies face these demographic changes.

In Japan, as in all societies, most elderly who need assistance in daily living receive help from family members, friends and neighbours. Yet long life expectancies, small families, job mobility, increased participation of middle-aged women in the formal labour force, and changing definitions of family roles have combined to make it more difficult or less desirable to provide that care informally. Japanese policies for the last several decades have increasingly placed responsibility for the welfare of its oldest citizens on government, although the facilities and agencies offering the services may be local government offices, social service agencies, non-governmental organisations or for-profit corporations. Recent years have seen greatly increased 'demand' for institutional care for frail elderly, with which a 'boom' in long-term care beds cannot keep up. There remains a great deal of ambivalence about formal services, especially residential institutions. Yet the long-term care insurance programme that began operating in 2000 is based on the concept of a 'right' to such care, and after years of paying premiums into the system, demand can be expected to increase even more in the coming decades.

In this book, Dr Wu takes us inside such an institution providing elder care in suburban Tokyo. Japan represents an important case study, because it has both the world's most rapidly ageing population and notions of what it means to age and to care for others that are historically distinct from those typical of Europe and North America. Based on long-term ethnographic research, the book richly describes and illustrates daily life in Kotobuki, a long-term care institution comprised of three types of residential facilities, differentiated according to the health status and income levels of their residents. The author analyses the full range of roles and relationships that impact those who live, visit and work at Kotobuki, placing all in the context of the wider values, attitudes and policies of contemporary Japanese society.

Underlying this thorough study of a long-term care institution are critical questions about the applicability of Western gerontological assumptions to East Asian societies. Kotobuki shares many characteristics with long-term care institutions in other countries, and thus there are many parallels in the lives of residents and staff. Dr Wu finds that, contrary to expectations that old age in Japan is characterized by dependency, residents' satisfaction is partly derived from maintaining some degree of autonomy even in an institutional setting. Yet 'quality of life' cannot be defined by quantitative measures. Rather, it results from subjective experiences of setting, physical health and human relationships. By exploring the meaning of these experiences for people at Kotobuki, Dr Wu finds that various culturally grounded interpretations of such ideas as autonomy and dependency have significant impacts on the way that institutions operate, and thus on the 'quality of life' of the residents, staff and visitors.

Policy also shapes institutions and experiences, and Dr Wu foresees many changes following the implementation of Japan's long-term care insurance system that began in 2000. The twenty-first century will bring many more countries to deliberations about the need for policies and institutions to provide long-term care for frail elderly people. As a Chinese scholar well-versed in Western gerontology and deeply immersed in the study of Japanese society, Dr Wu raises crucial questions for policy-makers in her own country and others as they consider how to create culturally relevant institutions for a transformed society.

Susan Orpett Long
Department of Sociology
John Carroll University, USA

Acknowledgements

The present book originates from the PhD thesis I submitted to the University of Hong Kong. In the years of research leading to the publication of this book, I have obtained encouragement, information, advice and criticism from many people. Although words cannot fully express my feelings of gratitude, I would like to express my deep appreciation here to all those who have provided warm support and precious advice.

I am deeply indebted to my academic supervisor, Kirsten Refsing, who has provided steady support in my academic and personal life. Being an excellent mentor, Professor Refsing has given me tremendous encouragement and important academic advice throughout the various stages of my research, in the field, in the university and in the ensuing years of my graduation. Her expertise in all intellectual matters concerning topic development, fieldwork, thesis writing and linguistic amendment, and her warmth as well as consideration were invaluable assets to me.

I am also grateful to Dr M. Okano, who has played an important role in my academic development. Dr Okano provided a great deal of valuable advice and keen insight during the first stage, when I developed my research topic. Even after he left the university, he continued to provide me with valuable suggestions for my research.

My deep appreciation is due to Dr Jan van Bremen, who recommended that this study be included in the publisher's Asian Studies catalogue as part of the Japan Anthropology Workshop Series. Without his warm encouragement, this book would never have materialised. I am particularly indebted to Professor Susan Orpett Long, who has not only provided invaluable advice that greatly assisted me in revising this book, but also generously offered to write the Foreword for me. I am also very grateful to Mr Peter Sowden for his special interest in this work and I owe much to the staff at the Taylor & Francis Group, especially Sophie Richmond and Vanessa Winch for their editorial advice and help.

I must also thank Nelson Chow, Peter Cave and Jian Zhang for reading my manuscript and giving me valuable advice. Special thanks also go to Mark James McLelland and Andreas Christian Lützen who have helped to revise many chapters of the first version of this work. And my warm appreciation is due to Dr Catherine Weihong Ni, for her tremendous help in improving my English on the last version and saving me from many mistakes.

Essentially this is a study of a comprehensive institution for the elderly, the Kotobuki home, in Japan. I am greatly indebted to the home administration for offering me an opportunity to study Japanese institutional care and the lives of the residents. And my deepest thanks go to the people living and working in Kotobuki. I have changed the names and certain details of the 'home', its residents, staff and visitors in order to protect everyone's privacy. Although I cannot thank the people of Kotobuki directly, I owe them all a great deal of gratitude. Without their willingness to participate, their honesty and cooperation, I would never have been able to carry out my research smoothly and collect the necessary data. I sincerely hope that I have portrayed their stories in a way they recognise.

While in Japan, I was accommodated by the Social Work Research Institute of the Japan College of Social Work in 1998-9. I am grateful to Professor Hisao Satō for having introduced me to a number of welfare institutions for the elderly so that I could conduct a pilot research on Japanese facilities for the elderly. I am also grateful to Professor Daisaku Maeda, who generously introduced me to the institute. Without his help, my research plan would never have been carried out.

I would like to express my special thanks to Takashi Mochizuki, Professor of Taisho University. Not only did he introduce me to the Kotobuki home, he has also supported me continuously in both my academic and private life since 1993. Professor Sukehiro Hirakawa's support also deserves mention. His family dinner parties for graduates of the Beijing Centre for Japanese Studies during my two field-trips in Japan and his remarkable intellectual insights made all the difference. I also want to forward thanks to Hidekazu Araki and Mieko Araki, my life-long Japanese friends who treat me as their daughter. Their hospitality and loving care always let me feel at home.

I wish to acknowledge the various financial resources that supported different phases of the research. The Daiwa Bank Group Awards at the University of Hong Kong provided funds for a ten months' fieldwork in 1998-9. An additional follow-up field-trip in 2003 was supported by grants from the Japan Foundation, the Northeast Asia Council of the Association for Asian Studies. The generosity of these organisations is greatly appreciated.

My thanks also go to the several organisations that have provided support during completion of the work. The Beijing Centre for Japanese Studies granted me five months' leave so that I could be relieved from teaching and clerical load and concentrate on writing. The Graduate School of Arts and Sciences in the University of Tokyo provided a collegial environment in which I thought about many aspects of the book. The library at the International House of Japan rendered great help in obtaining the latest materials for my revisions of the manuscript.

For their warm support, comfort and inspiration at various stages of the research, I must express my gratitude to many special friends and colleagues.

Among them are Jing He, Sumei Chang, Jun Ma, Yan Yang, Sumyin Lau, Lily Choi, Shirley Chen, Sachiko Furudate, Masako Tsuzuki and Keiko Higuchi.

Finally, I owe a great deal to my family. This book would never have got off the ground without my supportive family. My parents have always believed that I could carry on my work to completion. They have given me enormous support by helping take care of my little son for almost two years so that I could have the time and energy to concentrate on my study. And my special thanks go to my dearest son, Kai Jiang, who has grown up with the book. He is the greatest source of hope and confidence in my heart. It is his bright smile and sweet voice that enabled me to persevere until the book reached a satisfactory completion.

Notes on language conventions and style

All Japanese words are romanised according to the modified Hepburn system used in Kenkyusha's New Japanese-English Dictionary (Masuda 1974). Long vowels, however, are indicated by a superscript bar. Long vowels are neither indicated in well-known place names such as Tokyo and Osaka, nor in the era names Taisho and Showa.

People's names are given in the English order, with the surname following the given name.

The exchange rates used are those of 1998 and 2000, that is, US $1 = ¥120 in 1998, and US $1 = ¥130 in 2000.

'Kotobuki' is a pseudonym, as are its four sub-institutions, Sazanka, Akashi, Aoba and Sakura. The names of the informants are also pseudonyms.

Abbreviations

QOL	quality of life
LTC	long-term care insurance
ADL	activities of daily living
PT	physical therapy
OT	occupational therapy
NGOs	non-governmental organisations

1 Introduction

The population in China is ageing rapidly. In a country where social security programmes have been scarce and care for the elderly has largely depended on the family, it remains a question whether younger generations will be able to take care of the increasing elderly population. China's one-child policy means that the number of children who can share the responsibility for caring for their elderly parents is decreasing, while the care burden is increasing because a young married couple have to take care of four old parents. Urbanisation and the nuclearisation of the family have made co-residence more difficult; financial difficulties as well as the scarcity of social services have also made it impossible for families to rely on social support. Under such conditions, what can we do for our old people?

To search for a solution, I turned my eyes to Japan, the only non-Western post-industrial country that is strenuously coping with the problems generated by population ageing and the side-effects of modernisation. The reasons for this were, first, because Japan became an ageing society earlier than China, and because its welfare systems and social services are more advanced than other Asian countries. Second, I think that although the nations are different, because the physical process of ageing is the same, and because the Confucian norm of filial piety is shared by both countries, there should be some common problems and challenges. Third, knowledge derived from Japan can help us build more relevant strategies and social policies for the aged in our own society.

This book, thus, is the first English publication of an anthropological study on Japanese institutional care for the elderly people by a Chinese researcher. Treating institutions for the elderly that Japanese refer to as 'homes' as a small-scale culture, I have explored both what constitutes good quality of life, and the reality of living and working in Kotobuki, a Japanese welfare institution for the elderly in suburban Tokyo. I attempt to answer questions such as: What has brought the elderly, their caregivers and outside visitors to the institution? How do these persons perceive their institutional experiences and adapt to the institutional world? How do these men and women think about institutional life and institutionalisation?

Based on the findings of the study, I examine how the Japanese general public think about ageing, institutionalisation and welfare, whether institutionalisation is a good option for family care for the elderly, what factors can affect the quality of life of the elderly residents, and what suggestions can be made for improving institutional care and work. Thus, the aim of this study is not only to further understanding of the cultural meaning of ageing and responses to it in another society, but also to discover whether there are any implications for other societies in general, and for practical institutional care in particular. The book is intended to contribute to the study of social gerontology, the anthropology of ageing, cross-cultural studies and social work for the elderly.

Background information on ageing in Japan

Demographic trends

Due to the decline of fertility rate and the extension of life expectancy, the population of Japan is ageing fast. The proportion of older persons, aged 65 or over, was 7.06 per cent in 1970 and increased to 12.05 per cent in 1990. In 2000 Japan moved past Sweden to become the world's 'greyest country', with its elderly reaching 17 per cent of the population. This trend will accelerate further in the future. The greying process will reach its first peak around 2020 when one in four Japanese will be elderly.

The average life expectancy in Japan is the longest in the world. After the war, as standards of hygiene improved and medical science and technology advanced, the average life span of Japanese people increased remarkably. In 1947, the average life span in Japan was 50.06 years for men and 53.96 years for women. In 1997, the average life expectancy had risen to 77.19 years for men and 83.82 years for women. Some of this increase is due to a drop in the child mortality rate. There are still 17.02 years and 21.75 years respectively left for a 65-year-old man and a 65-year-old woman to live (Sōmuchō 1999: 45).

Among the elderly persons aged 65 and over, the number of the 'old-old' (those aged 75 years or more) has significantly increased and will increase as follows: from 371,000 in 1950, to as many as 7.17 million in 1995, and to more than 17 million in the year 2020. Also it is supposed that among the elderly people aged 65 and above, half will be old-old by around 2015 (Japan Aging Research Center 1996; Maeda and Nakatani 1992; National Census 1997).

This increasing number of old-old persons also means that the elderly are more likely to suffer from disabling physical ailments. According to the 1995 Basic Survey of National Life, the percentages of elderly persons who answered that their health conditions had effects on daily life such as ADL,[1] doing housework, and sports, etc. were extremely high in the 74–85 years age group and the 85 years and above group (Kōseishō 1995).

Compared with other age groups, elderly persons, especially the old-old are more likely to have such diseases as cerebral arteries' diseases, cancer, heart ailments, hypertension, cataracts, arthritis and articulator rheumatism, etc. (Kōseishō 1996). Most of these diseases easily lead to the sufferers' being bedridden and developing senile dementia. Hospitalised elderly enter the hospitals mainly because of such diseases and other ailments such as broken bones and mental illnesses (Kōseishō 1996).

In 1993, there were about one million bedridden elderly, 0.1 million demented elderly and 0.9 million weak elderly in Japan. The figures were expected to reach 1.3, 0.2 and 1.2 million respectively in 2000, and the numbers will double again by 2025 (MHW 1998). Among these elderly who need care, 245,500 were living in special nursing homes (*tokubetsu yōgo rōjin hōmu*),[2] 137,200 in geriatric health care facilities (*rōjin hoken shisetsu*),[3] 296,900 in hospitals, and 861,000 in their own homes (Kōseishō 1995, 1996, 1997b, 1997c).

This means that the family and the society will shoulder the increasing burden of caring for the very old elderly, who are so vulnerable to debilitating illness that they have to depend on others totally. Because of the longer life expectancy of women, there will be more women in the category of 'old-old'. And there will be more mentally or physically disabled 'old-old' females than males. The care recipients are increasingly ageing women.

Social policy in an ageing society

Population ageing is viewed as a process causing the shortage of young labour, sluggish economic growth and higher tax burdens to support social security for the elderly. It is one of the most pressing issues in contemporary Japan. How does the Japanese government deal with problems caused by the ageing society?

According to John Campbell (1992, 2000), there are three periods of development of policy towards elderly persons from the 1950s to the 1990s. The first period, beginning from the first year after the Second World War to the early 1960s is characterised by the 'ageing problem' (*rōgo mondai*). Policy towards the elderly focused on the future security of the current workers. Pensions were the only old-age-specific public policies. Those already old were taken care of by their families and the marginal leftovers were covered by public assistance or in houses for the aged (*yōrō-in*). Although a significant old-age policy regulating welfare services for the elderly – including institutional services, community care services and recreational services – the Law for the Welfare of the Elderly (*Rōjin Fukushi-hō*), was enacted in 1963, it was only a compilation of existing services of the time.

From the late 1960s to the 1970s, is the 'old-people problem' (*rōjin mondai*) period. As Japan began to feel heavy demographic pressure, it started to take ageing problems into serious consideration. With the rapid economic growth and the arrival of the affluent society, both 'normal' elderly, who live in the same household with a child and 'left-out' old people, without family caretakers, were provided with many programmes such as pension benefits and free medical care. For the former, special loans were provided to add an extra room to their house, senior centres could accommodate the mother-in-law for a while, and various sorts of life-enrichment programmes were expanded. For the latter, programmes such as homes for the elderly, nursing homes, home-helpers and other services were provided.

From 1980s to the early 1990s, a period of moderate economic growth, the increasing number of elderly and the more expensive programmes began to become a burden on the society and the economy. This period, characterised as the period of 'ageing-society problem' (*kōrei shakai mondai*), shifted the main concerns to controlling current cost for social security and to worrying about how prosperity could be maintained in the future. Social policies regarding welfare and health care services in this period were mainly addressed to ordinary old people. For instance, the Law for Health Care of the Elderly (*Rōjin Hoken-hō*) was put into practice in 1983 to strengthen and expand the health and medical services for the elderly and to relieve the National Health Insurance System (*Kokumin Kenkō Hoken Seido*) from the serious financial deficits resulting from the lack of cooperation in the overall health care insurance system (Maeda 2000).

Many Japanese policy-makers and welfare specialists visited Sweden and other European welfare states to learn from their experience in order to solve the big problems of ageing faced by Japan. They suggested creating a 'Japanese-style welfare system' emphasising traditional Japanese values such as mutual dependency, obligation to the family and self-responsibility. It also promoted cooperation between central and local governments, and between the public and private sectors. With this framework, the government consecutively formulated several policies for the elderly during the late 1980s (Asano 1992; Nishio 1994; Shibata 1998). The governmental subsidy programme for the establishment of the Geriatric Health Care Facilities in 1988 to provide long-term care for elderly who are suffering from chronic diseases and need skilled care, is said to be the important 'starting point of recent changes in the Japanese elderly care service policy with regard to the legal responsibility of the family' (Maeda 2000: 44).

In 1989, the government began to address a comprehensive policy for long-term care for the elderly. The long-term care study group organised in the Ministry of Health and Welfare suggested developing in-home services to support family caretakers (Hashimoto 1998). In the same year, the 'Ten-year Strategy for the Promotion of Health and Welfare Services for the Elderly' (the so-called Gold Plan) was established with quantified goals to enhance the unification of community care and institutional care for the elderly. It is composed of an expansion of community care services and long-term care facilities, a campaign for the reduction of bedridden elderly, promotion of measures for the well-being of the elderly, a 10-year project for the promotion of research on ageing (Shimizu and Wake 1994).

In 1990 a consumption tax was introduced for the purpose of securing a new source of revenue necessary for the impending 'aged society'. The same year, with the revisions of the Law for the Welfare of the Elderly, the Law for the Health and Medical Services for the Elderly and eight other welfare related laws, the authority to decide the admission of an older person into a home for the elderly[4] or a special nursing home for the elderly was transferred from the prefectural government to the local government. It becomes local government's responsibility to plan and implement public health and welfare services for the elderly, from long-term institutional care to preventive, promotional and recreational services.

According to the plans for health and welfare of the aged drawn up by prefectures and local governments, the goals set in the Gold Plan were expanded substantially in 1994. This is referred to as the New Gold Plan. It intends to promote some new community-based in-home services, such as round-the-clock visiting care services, meals-on-wheels services, rehabilitation services, group-home services for the senile aged, etc. It propagates the development of educational facilities and training programmes for care workers, social workers and PT[5]/OT[6] professionals engaging in welfare enterprises for the elderly. The participation of private profit-making sectors in the social service delivery system is also encouraged (Maeda 1996a; Mineruva Shobō Henshūbu 1997). Table 1.1 compares the goals of the 1990 Gold Plan and the New Gold Plan.

Following the New Gold Plan, the most important reform of the social welfare system was the introduction of the Long-term Care Insurance (LTCI) scheme in 1996. This LTCI system aims at the collection of necessary revenue resources to expand social services for the elderly as was established in the Gold plans. It also aims to enhance cooperation of the welfare services system and the health/medical care system, to reduce the 'social hospitalisation'[7]phenomenon so as to relieve the burden of medical care for elderly on the health insurance system, and to balance the distribution of social security expenditure between pensions, health/medical care and welfare (Tochimoto 1999).

The LTCI system means a social services system in which, by contributing to the programme, all the needs for care of the elderly, including both institutional and in-home care, are met regardless of income (Kyōgoku 1996). Under the LTCI system, it becomes the right of the older persons to demand that the insurance body provide suitable care services to meet his/her assessed needs for care. It is a system in which the most suitable services are provided based on the self-determination of the elderly clients while referring to the advice of professionals, and in which the care cost is borne fairly by all of the citizens. The concept of care management is introduced into the system. In addition, the LTCI system also brings the market principle into the welfare service area: private profit-making enterprises will compete with the existing non-profit welfare providers to attract elderly clients. This is a thorough transformation of the former welfare system, which was traditionally thought to be one providing charity services for the needy. This LTCI policy started to be implemented in 2000. Appendix 1 shows the basic contents of the LTCI programme.

Table 1.1 Comparison of the Gold Plan (1990) and the New Gold Plan (1994)

	Gold Plan *(1990)*	*New Gold Plan* *(1994)*
(1) In-home service		
Home-helpers (persons)	100,000	170,000
Home-helper station (places)	—	10,000
Short-stay services (beds)	50,000	60,000
Day service/care centre (places)	10,000	17,000
Home care support centre (places)	10,000	10,000
Visiting nurse stations (places)	—	5000
(2) Institutional service		
Special nursing home for the elderly (beds)	240,000	290,000
Health care facilities for the elderly (persons)	280,000	280,000
Multipurpose senior centres in depopulated areas (places)	400	400
Care houses (persons)	100,000	100,000
(3) Manpower training		
Matrons and Care-workers	—	200,000
Nurses and Nurse's aides	—	100,000
Occupational therapists and Physical therapists	—	15,000

Mineruva Shobō Henshū (1997: 205).

Changes in the family

The Japanese family has long been regarded as a care institution that bears the main responsibility for looking after the elderly. This derives from the Confucian ethic of filial piety, the tradition of respect for the elderly and the ancient idea of ancestor worship (Benedict 1946; Palmore 1975). And the patriarchal *ie* system, which was firmly institutionalised during the Meiji period, is often cited as a system that entitles the aged to receive support from their children, especially the eldest son.[8]

Under the *ie* system, one must practice filial piety towards one's parents. Filial piety prescribes four responsibilities for the children: 'to show and feel respect toward one's parents, to promote the honour of one's family through achievements, to support one's parents in their old age, and to worship one's ancestors' (Kinoshita and Kiefer 1992: 49). With such legitimacy, an old person is able to reap repayment from many years of hard work and sacrifice invested in his or her children. And the most successful elderly person is thought to be the one who lives with his/her eldest son and his family, surrounded by beloved grandchildren and receiving attentive services and care from the daughter-in-law, who is supposed to be responsible for household management, and 'the welfare of the retired parents as well as that of their own children and other live-in relatives' (Long 1996: 159).

Although living with one of their children and receiving care from the younger generation is the ideal lifestyle for old people (Long 1987), it has gradually become difficult to practice due to the declining family role as a care institution for the elderly caused by the tremendous socio-economic, demographic and cultural transitions after the Second World War (Maeda and Nakatani 1992; Sodei 1994). Rapid economic development since the 1950s has drawn many young persons from rural areas to the cities to seek employment, leaving their parents at home. Housing for employees in big cities is usually not spacious enough for two generations to live together. These conditions have exerted a profound impact on the living arrangements of the Japanese elderly and made it difficult for them to live with their adult children.

Increased life expectancy means that more older persons will have serious physical and mental illnesses that need constant care. Due to the population itself ageing, there are many cases where the caretaking offspring are also elderly, so that they are not healthy enough to take care of their ageing parents. The continuously declining fertility rate also means that fewer children are available to look after their ageing parents.

Attitudes towards elderly persons living with children, and the norm of filial piety, have also been changing. Some studies indicate that the rejection of co-residence has been growing over time, and that the younger the generation, the greater the percentage of respondents who think it is better for elderly parents to live apart from their children. And there are more middle-aged women than men who prefer living separately from their old parents (Linhart 1997; Ogawa and Rethford 1990; O'Leary 1993).

Middle-aged persons have been seen as dependable family caretakers for older parents. However, their attitude towards elderly care has changed. Table 1.2 shows the results of a survey of the attitudes of middle-aged persons towards the care of their parents when they become bedridden. In 1992, more than half of the respondents answered 'should be cared for mainly by family' and 37.5 per cent chose 'family care supplemented by formal community care'. Only 5.1 per cent thought 'should be cared for mainly by formal care services including institutional care'. These results suggest that the majority of middle-aged persons in Japan still think it the children's responsibility to care for bedridden elderly parents. However, it is evident that the consciousness of family responsibility has weakened over time and that the expectations of formal services have risen during the past ten years (Sōmuchō 1992). In addition, middle-aged women's participation in the labour market has constrained the capability of the family to care for ageing parents.

Table 1.2   Plan of middle-aged persons aged 30–49 years for care of parents when they become bedridden (percentages)

Year	Should be cared for mainly by family	Family care supplemented by formal community care	Should be cared for mainly by formal care including institutional care	Don't know
1981	72.6	24.1	1.9	1.4
1987	62.2	32.2	3.7	1.9
1992	55.7	37.5	5.1	1.7

GMCA (1992) cited in Shimizu and Wake (1994: 229).

Today, the majority of Japanese elderly persons are still living with thier children (Table 1.3) and express a preference to be cared for by family members when they become physically impaired (Sōmuchō 1992). However, due to the reasons mentioned above, the three-generation family household has been declining, from 54.4 per cent of all households in 1975 to 33.3 per cent in 1995, while the percentage of single individual elderly households almost doubled from 8.6 per cent to 17.3 per cent. The percentage of households comprising just an elderly couple also increased from 13.1 per cent to 24.2 per cent (Table 1.4). This indicates a significant decrease in the capacity of families to care for ageing parents.

Table 1.3 Percentages of old persons living with children

Age	Total 65 and over	65 to 69	70 to 74	75 to 79	80 and over
Per cent	61.9	53.7	59.9	65.7	76.1

Ministry of Health and Welfare (MHW) 1989-nen Seikatsu Fukushi Kiso Chōsa (The 1989 Basic Survey of the Japanese Lifestyle) Tokyo: Kōseishō (1990), cited in Nishio (1994: 249).

Japanese elderly persons are less likely to be institutionalised than those in other industrialised countries. As of 1999, there were 396,338 old persons living in some kind of welfare institution (Shokuhin Ryūtsū Jōhō Sentā 2002: 520), accounting for only 1.66 per cent[9] of those aged 65 and above (Shimizu *et al.* 1994), while the corresponding figure was 5.5 per cent in United States (Campbell and Ingersoll-Dayton 2000: 233) and around 5 per cent in European countries (Martin 1989). The majority of the physically and mentally impaired old people are being cared for within the family.

Regarding family caregivers, the average age of them is 60.4. Most are middle-aged or early-aged (65–74 years of age) women who are becoming older and weaker (Kōseishō 1995). Under the massive stress of caregiving, some collapse and many complain of being too tired, not getting enough sleep or having no freedom to go out. And often the caregivers are forced to make changes in their lives such as quitting jobs, taking leave or changing jobs (Sōmuchō 1999: 77). Most of these family caretakers are caring for their old relatives with little outside assistance or trained help. Even though they want to utilise in-home services, such services are usually unavailable.

The declining family support and care for the elderly, together with the ever-growing number of elderly persons in the future, has inevitably led to an increasing demand for institutions for the elderly. In the 1980s, in order to relieve the enormous burden that medical and other welfare expenditure put on the economy, the Japanese government suggested a 'Japanese-style Welfare System' and promulgated that both the family and local community should shoulder the responsibility for caring for the elderly at home. Through several years of practice, the government has now realised the limitations of family care for the elderly, and has been trying to devise feasible policies and programmes to help the elderly and their family caretakers. The two main goals of developing 'community in-home services' and strengthening 'institutional services' established in the two Gold Plans have become the future orientation of social welfare and security programmes. The LTCI system has further enhanced this trend. If these two parts of the Japanese welfare system work successfully, then supposedly the government and the

Table 1.4 Trends in the percentage of households by family type containing at least one elderly person aged 65 and over, Japan, 1975–95

Year	Total households (1,000s)	One-person households (%)	Nuclear family households				Three-generation households (%)	Other related households (%)
			Total nuclear family households (%)	Married couple only (%)	Couple and unmarried children (%)	Single parent and children (%)		
1975	1,118	8.6	22.7	13.1	6.7	2.9	54.4	14.4
1980	8,495	10.7	26.7	16.2	6.7	2.8	50.1	12.5
1985	9,400	12.0	29.8	19.1	6.4	4.3	45.9	12.2
1986	9,769	13.1	29.3	18.2	6.6	4.5	44.8	12.7
1987	9,954	13.0	29.9	19.0	6.3	4.6	43.9	13.2
1988	10,225	13.7	31.5	20.0	6.7	4.8	41.7	13.1
1989	10,774	14.8	32.6	20.9	6.8	4.9	40.7	11.9
1990	10,816	14.9	33.2	21.4	11.8		39.5	12.4
1991	11,613	15.6	34.1	22.1	12.0		38.5	11.7
1992	11,884	15.7	34.9	22.8	12.1		36.6	12.8
1993	12,187	16.3	35.9	23.3	12.6		35.9	11.8
1994	12,853	16.4	36.4	24.0	12.4		34.9	12.2
1995	12,695	17.3	37.1	24.2	12.9		33.3	12.2

Source: Dept of Statistical Information, Ministry of Health and Welfare, Kokumin Seikatsu Kiso Chōsa no Gaikyō (Basic Survey of National Life), 1995, Tokyo (1996); before 1985, the survey was called Kōsei Gyōsei Kiso Chōsa (Social Survey for Health and Welfare Administration, cited in Kono (1996: 43).

family should be able to jointly take care of their ageing population in the aged society of the future.

Research on institutions for the aged and Quality of Life

Institutions for the elderly

Much research has been published on institutions for the elderly and the overriding theme is rejection and segregation. Goffman (1961) claims that nursing homes are a specific example of 'total institutions'. Nursing homes are 'total' because they share some features with mental hospitals, prisons, army barracks and nunneries. These features include the residents' loss of identity and control, their separation from the familiar community society, and institutional regulations taking precedence over individual needs. Both journalists and novelists have taken up topics of nursing home life. Books with such telling titles as *Nobody Ever Died of Old Age* (Curtin 1972), and *The Last Segregation* (Townsend 1971) exposed the inhumane aspects of institutional life in Western society. Savishinsky (1991) claims that there are prison-like geriatric facilities where older people end up in despair, and profit-making institutions where the elderly are treated as disposable commodities in both Europe and the United States. And a number of anthropologists and gerontologists have studied facilities for the elderly with an eye to documenting how people have come to live and work there, how the residents and staff adapt to the regime and life in institutions, and the quality of life and care there (Foner 1994; Gubrium 1975, 1993; Kayser-Jones 1981a, 1981b, 1981c; Laird 1979; Savishinsky 1991; Shield 1988).

The Japanese also tend to view institutions for the elderly negatively. As the family has been thought to be an institution for elderly care, institutionalisation is dissonant with the cultural norms of co-residence and filial piety. Institutions are commonly connected with the old legend of *Obasuteyama* (Fukuzawa 1964), the mountain where, long ago, ageing parents who no longer contributed to the family economy were taken by their eldest sons and left to die from starvation and cold. Facilities for the elderly are regarded as a modern *Obasuteyama* where old people are discarded by their children (Plath 1972). And most Japanese still have a dark image of welfare institutions, whose origins lie in the poorhouses for the destitute and the old people's homes (*yōrō-in*) for homeless or childless elderly in the pre-war period and just after the war, where the elderly received protection and custodial care from the government. So institutionalisation signifies the loss of prestige for the elderly and abandonment by the family, and it remains a social stigma for both the elderly and their families (Bethel 1992a, 1992b; Shimizu *et al.* 1994; Yamanoi and Saitō 1994).

Despite the social stigma attached to institutions, facilities for the elderly have become inevitable resources for security in later life. Recent increases in life expectancy mean that greater numbers of people will survive to an advanced age. Elderly persons who have Alzheimer's disease and other diseases that are incurable or beyond the scope of family caretakers to deal with, will spend some part of their later years in an institution. Even though most older people prefer living in their own homes, community-based services to assist the elderly and their families with home care are usually inadequate. Or family caretakers are unavailable because of the death of the spouse, childlessness, working adult daughters and daughters-in-law, and the separate living arrangements of the children. In other instances, the elderly have chosen to enter an institution to avoid becoming a burden to their families. These factors have led to an increase in the number of long-term care institutions as well as institutionalised elderly persons.

Besides hospitals for the chronically ill and long-term care wards in geriatric facilities and some new developed community facilities, the 1963 Law for the Welfare of the Elderly initially defined three types of welfare institutions: special nursing homes for the elderly (*tokubetsu yōgo rōjin hōmu*), homes for the elderly (*yōgo rōjin hōmu*), and homes for the elderly with moderate fees (*keihi rōjin hōmu*). I will use '*tokuyō, yōgo* and *keihi* homes' to refer to these three kinds of homes in later description.

The *tokuyō* homes provide nursing and personal care for those aged 65 and over who need constant care because of serious physical or mental impediments, and who cannot be cared for at home. There is no income requirement for entrance admission, but fees are set according to a sliding scale. The *yōgo* homes provide daily life assistance for those over 65 who cannot remain independent for physical, mental, environmental and financial reasons. The resident is usually entitled to national public assistance programmes or falls into the low-income category that is free from the municipality taxation. And the *keihi* homes are income-based boarding facilities provided for the functionally independent aged 60 and over who lack adequate housing for financial and environmental reasons. They are divided into two types: type A and type B. Type A homes serve meals, while type B homes require the residents to cook for themselves. With the enactment of the 1989 Gold Plan, *kea hausu* (care houses), a new type of home in this category, which provides both meals and care functions, has come into being and expanded rapidly. By 2000, all three types of institutions were receiving public subsidies for their establishment and operation.

As of October 1999, there were approximately 396,338 old persons living in these three types of welfare institutions. This is a seven-fold increase compared with the number of 48,186 in 1963. And the numbers of welfare facilities were 949 *yōgo* homes, 4,214 *tokuyō* homes and 1,272 *keihi* homes, while the total number was 690 in 1963 (Miura 1996; Shokuhin Ryūtsū Jōhō Sentā 2002).

In addition to these publicly funded institutions, there are a number of *yūryō rōjin hōmu*, literally homes for the elderly with charges. Most of these homes provide lifelong nursing care. They are established and run without any public grant or subsidy, therefore they are very expensive, and only those elderly who belong to the upper-income bracket can afford to use them. In

1999, there were about 298 such homes accommodating 23,079 older persons (Shokuhin Ryūtsū Jōhō Sentā 2002).

Although there are quite a number of quantitative studies on institutions, mainly contributing to policy-making and international comparisons, qualitative studies are rare. Ōkuma (1990, 1992), a journalist from *Asahi Shinbun*, has reported on the dismaying conditions in institutions such as mental hospitals, hospitals for the aged and *tokuyō* homes since the 1980s. He found that there are not only hospitals that treat the elderly inpatients as profit-making commodities, but also there are elderly persons being secluded in locked rooms or being confined to their beds. He strongly feels that modern Japan is abandoning its old citizens, that the public welfare services in Japan are lagging behind those in the Scandinavian countries, and that the Japanese social consciousness with regard to their own later lives and social welfare is weak. Yamanoi and Saitō (1994) drew similar conclusions after they had training experiences in facilities for the elderly all over Japan and visited nursing homes for the aged in European countries, the United States and some Asian countries.

Bethel (1992a, 1992b) depicts the lives of old residents in the Aotani home for the elderly in Hokkaido based on a 14-month participant observation study. Beginning with the legend of *Obasuteyama* and the dreadful image of institutions, Bethel focuses on how the residents, who initially felt mortification at being abandoned, managed to construct a home community by utilising various symbolic resources such as age hierarchy, friendship, and public and private space. She concludes that institutions for the elderly are alternatives to support from the biological family, although they tend to be impersonal and efficiency-oriented. Every institution structures and limits the freedom of those who live within it, yet it is the same structure that makes it possible to develop a community.

Serving as a volunteer in Kotoen, a pioneering age-integrated welfare facility that was constructed to accommodate both nursery children and older persons, Thang (2001) has investigated the possibility of whether intergenerational togetherness can be socially structured in an institutional setting by carefully observing the multigenerational living of the children and the elderly residents. She elucidates how the cultural ideas of large multigenerational household (*daikazoku*) and encounter between people (*fureai*) have been utilised in intergenerational interaction programmes to foster re-engagement among elders and positive attitudes towards ageing among children in contemporary Japan. However, the 'event grandparenthood' and 'collective grandparenting' defined in institutional settings, Thang indicates, have limited possibilities for developing intimate and lasting dyadic ties between the elderly and children.

A conceptual framework: Quality of Life

Since the 1980s, a sizeable body of research has been conducted in both the medical and social sciences about Quality of Life (QOL). As QOL is understood to be a multidimensional, value-laden concept with multiple methodological and measurement issues, there is no generally accepted definition yet. The quality of life of an individual is often determined by objective indicators such as income, health condition, quality of the environment, status in society and family integration as well as measures of subjective well-being, that is, life satisfaction, happiness and morale. Thus we may find a variety of definitions of QOL in the literature. These definitions often reflect the ideas and professional orientation of the authors. Clinically oriented researchers tend to define QOL in terms of health status or functional ability. Others take a broader view to include both physical and material well-being; relationships with others; social, community and civic activities; personal development such as learning and career; recreation and life satisfaction (Arnold 1991: 53).

Life satisfaction and other QOL measures have been of increasing importance in gerontology since the 1980s. In the 1990s, researchers and policy-makers have attempted to better understand the impact of elements such as disability, changes in health status, retirement, role loss, diminishing social networks, and modifications in involvement in activity on the QOL of the elderly. Critical questions concern how to provide programmes to enhance an older person's quality of life vis-à-vis their increasing potential for frailty and dependence.

According to Clipp (1996: 788–90), four different frameworks have been developed as ways of thinking about ageing and QOL. They are George and Bearon's (1980), Lawton's (1983, 1991), Ware's (1984, 1987) and the most recently developed framework of Stewart and King (1994). Each defines QOL in terms of multidimensional domains ranging from objective factors (interpersonal relations, health, socioeconomic resources and environment) to subjective factors (psychological well-being) and also disease/health-specific factors (pain and discomfort, energy/fatigue, cognitive, physical, social, sexual and ADL (activities of daily life) functioning), and they evaluate these domains by using specific measurement techniques and related psychometric properties.

The connection between psychological well-being and ageing has been a research focus in life-span developmental psychology. For instance, there are Erikson's (1959, 1970) model of the stages of psychological development, and Neugarten's (1973) description of personality change in adulthood and old age. Clinical psychology also offers multiple notions of well-being such as Maslow's (1954) concept of self-actualisation. And many researchers have developed scales that reflect psychological health and well-being based on personality and life-span theories developed by the above-mentioned psychologists. The typical model of well-being is a six-dimensional one that includes self-acceptance, positive relations with others, autonomy, environmental mastery, purpose in life and personal growth. Structured self-report scales with socio-demographic correlates such as age patterns, gender differences, class differences, cultural variation, life experience and interpretive mechanisms have been used to operate these six dimensions (Ryff 1995: 365–9).

In the field of long-term care, a number of researchers have written about the innovative programmes implemented in long-term care facilities in the United States and other countries in an effort to improve both the quality of care and quality of life of the elderly. Some issues considered have been the effects of the physical environment on the behaviour of residents, the importance of enabling the elderly to maintain the social roles that have brought them meaning and stability in their earlier lives, and the impact of staff attitudes and behaviours on the morale and moods of the residents. Others have investigated the effect of activity programmes on the well-being of the residents; the effects of management policies and practices in improving quality of life; and the effects of staff training methodology on how to provide a supportive environment and suitable care for the residents, give opportunities for the staff to demonstrate their talents and develop effective teamwork (Coons and Mace 1996; Cumming and Cumming 1962; Gubrium 1975; Koncelik 1976; Savishinsky 1991).

Thus, in the social sciences, the concept of Quality of Life has come to have an increasingly quantitative implication and there are specific tested scales to measure it. However, my intention here is not to test any specific instrument but to identify the factors related to QOL of the institutionalised elderly by qualitative methodology.

From my reading of Japanese books (Asano 1994, 1995; Asano and Tanaka 1993; Maeda 1996b), I find that fulfilment of an individual's desires is understood as a primary determinant of QOL in Japanese institutional practice. Asano provides a model concerning the needs of the elderly residents and welfare practices in welfare institutions based on Maslow's (1954) theory of human motivation and Cook's model (Cook 1981).[10] I found it reasonable to measure the QOL of frail elderly in nursing home by examining the extent to which their desires are satisfied. I believe that, except for some social or physical handicaps, old people in institutions are basically the same as ordinary people who need food, warmth, companionship and the opportunity to do what they want to do in order to get a sense of fulfilment, and that the QOL in long-term care facilities is largely determined by the extent to which these basic needs are satisfied. An individual's experience of life in an elderly institution is the result of the interaction between his or her ability to cope with the environment and the demands made by the surroundings. Not only the institutional environment, which is made up of physical features, the social environment such as rules, routines, regimes, etc., and the people and relationships, but also the individual's perceptions of his or her life constitute a whole picture of lifestyle in long-term care facilities. Based on such considerations, I decided to select the following eight dimensions as indicators of QOL in the light of the basic needs of human beings for observation and analysis.

Everyday functional ability and other aspects of daily life: Do residents' activities for daily living (ADL) function well? Does the home offer nutritional and tasty meals? Do the residents feel satisfied with the food, accommodation and other material provisions?

Building and facilities: Are the buildings designed to provide for the safety and convenience of residents? Do the homes provide comfortable ambient temperatures, daily life support facilities such as TV, laundry, refrigerator and other facilities? Can privacy of residents be ensured?

Income: What is the financial condition of the residents? Are they satisfied with their economic status?

Health care: Do the residents receive appropriate nursing care as well as medical care? Is there any indication of over-medication, especially among confused or awkward residents? Can the residents resort to staff for counselling when they have trouble? Are age-appropriate activities provided for residents according to their ADL level?

Autonomy: Are residents able to arrange their daily activities freely? Can they retain their own pension books and cash? Are they expected to attend various functions including club, occupational and recreational activities? Are residents and visitors free to come and go when they wish? Can residents choose their own companions such as room-mates? Is death talked about freely?

Interpersonal relations: Do residents have any communication and interaction with the world outside as well as the world inside? How are the relationships between the residents and the staff, their attitudes and behaviour towards each other? What about residents' interactions with their family members, friends and community? Do they feel satisfied with these relationships?

Role continuity: Do residents have opportunities to select new roles through hobbies, or hang on to old ones such as homemaker, worker, citizen and family member?

Life satisfaction: How satisfied do the residents feel with their lives? Do they feel their lives are worth living? Do they have any plans for their future?

After entering the field, I focused upon how the basic needs of the elderly residents were satisfied and how the dimensions of QOL could be explained in more specific ways. Through the involvement with the people in Kotobuki, I thought that rather than using quantitative scales to examine whether high QOL is achieved in institutions, the term could be better understood through the personal meanings people brought to and found in their experience of institutionalisation. Thus in later chapters the term is used in a general way, that is, describing the lives of the elderly people.

The culture of care: dependency and dependency on indulgence (*amae*)

In analysing people's experiences of institutional life and work, I found that the theoretical perspective of dependency could be helpful to explain elderly persons' status, their relationships with others and their related quality of life. It is also connected with the characteristics of Japanese institutional care. More importantly, it provides a basis for us to understand Japanese culture, to think about the relationship between culture and the practice of elderly care, and to raise a bigger question: whether dependency of the elderly and dependency on indulgence are ubiquitous phenomena in Asian contexts.

Many Western scholars think Japan is a paradise for older people because most of the Japanese elderly can enjoy increasing dependency as they age. For example, Benedict depicts the arc of a Japanese's life as follows:

> It is a great shallow U-curve with maximum freedom and indulgence allowed to babies and to the old. Restrictions are slowly increased after babyhood till having one's own way reaches a low just before and after marriage. This low line continues many years during the prime of life, but the arc gradually ascends again until after the age of sixty men and women are almost as unhampered by shame as little children are.
>
> (Benedict 1946: 177)

She attributes the reason why the Japanese elderly enjoy their great freedom in later life to the Confucian virtue and filial piety and the concept of obligation (*on*) a child owes to his/her parents.

In the traditional Japanese family system, dependency of the aged is tied to the institutional requirement of perpetuating the *ie* system. The elderly and retired parents depend on their successor and his family for security, comfort and emotional support. They also rely on the succeeding generation for funeral, family ancestor tablets, grave and memorial services for them and the ancestors. The successors are expected to be dependable and willing to satisfy their parents' dependency demands (Kinoshita and Kiefer 1992; Lebra 1976; Long 1996).

Amae is a term highlighted by the Japanese psychiatrist Doi (1962, 1971, 1992), which means 'to depend and presume upon another's benevolence or bask in another's indulgence' (1992: 8) and 'is generally used to describe a child's attitude or behaviour towards his parents, particularly his mother' (1962: 32). Matsuda (1959) indicates that it is primarily 'concerned with patterns of affiliation and interdependency that regulate the nature of intimate relationships'. Intra-psychically, *amae* represents a motive, drive or desire that yearns and expects to be held, fed, bathed, made safe, kept warm,

comforted emotionally and to be specially cherished. Through his therapeutic experience, Doi found that *amae* relationship is ubiquitous in
child–parent interaction, and can also bind two adults. The passive helplessness (*amae*) of a patient can solicit the active indulgence (*amayakasu*) of a
caretaker. Later he applied this concept of *amae* to all Japanese behaviour.
His study indicates that there is 'a social sanction in Japanese society for
expressing the wish to *amaeru* [be mothered]' (1962: 136). That is, *amae* is
not only dependency on the parent in the family context, but also operates
in a wider social context when an adult is permitted to behave like a baby in
seeking attachment to another adult.

Caudill (1961, 1962) observed that the Japanese were willing to go to bed
with mild illness and hospitalised patients liked to have an attached
(*tsukisoi*) caretaker (usually a hired sub-professional nurse or a female
family member). The sick person lying in bed usually draws the attention of
his family, friends and colleagues who come to visit him. The *tsukisoi* caretaker feeds the patient, sits and sleeps by the patient, so as to be available at
any time. Caudill thus concludes that sickness provides a social occasion for
emotional communication, for offering and accepting sympathetic care. He
suggests that the Japanese inclination towards total dependency necessitates
an overall caretaker.

Kiefer (1987, 1990) analyses the relationships between the elderly person
and his/her caretaker from a similar angle. In the patient–caretaker role set,
the caretaker tends to the elder's emotional as well as physical needs, while
the elderly person is expected to receive care passively or is encouraged to be
dependent on the caretaker. As care is usually done under the same roof, if
the old patient is to rehabilitate in an institution, the patient–healer role set
will be violated, which is abnormal in the eyes of ordinary Japanese. With
this cultural norm of dependency, the elderly are encouraged to remain
bedridden and be cared for by their families.

Lebra (1976) observes that *amae* can be commonly found in the relationships between mother and child, and the sick and elderly and their
caretakers. In her analysis of two films regarding elderly care in the 1980s,
Yakusoku (*A Promise*) and *Hanaichimonme* (*Grey Sunset*), Long (1996)
shows that the notions of dependency and selfless womanhood have created
ideal figures of mature daughters-in-law who totally nurture their senile old
parents. In her comparative study on Japanese and American perspectives
on ageing and social support in later life, Hashimoto (1996) claims that
Japan's protective approach to support, which relies on the cultural assumptions of reciprocity, dependency, entitlements and obligation, has allowed
the Japanese to regard filial ties as the most intimate and reliable social
bonds in self- sufficiency, and to sanction more vulnerability in old age than
in the United States.

Typified in the notion of dependency of the aged and *amae*, it is
suggested that Japanese elderly are able to totally depend on their caretakers.
Does this apply to the elderly residents in institutions? With this framework,

we can examine the relationship between the elderly residents and their care-takers as well as the nature of Japanese institutional care for the elderly. And we can contribute more to the understanding of the culture of care for elderly people in a wider Asian context. Also, we can give more considera-tion to the theory of dependency of indulgence (*amae*), which some have argued is a unique feature of Japanese culture.

Ethnographic methodology

This is an ethnographic study dealing with the realities of people living and working in a comprehensive Japanese welfare institution for the elderly, the Kotobuki home. Although the home setting is a small world, it extends outward to take in the experiences of residents, staff and visitors, their life and work in the home, the presence and absence of the residents' families, the operation of the home, and the connection with the outside community. Besides the people living there, there are facets such as the quality of institu-tional life, routines such as meals, baths and recreational activities, the voices of the elderly and their life histories, and their different status and profes-sions. There are also interpersonal interactions, confrontations and conflicting feelings hidden behind the harmonious surface, the shifting mood and morale of care staff, and visitors' self-evaluation towards their involvement as well as their feelings towards old age. Thus a multi-faceted approach to the complexities of institutional life is necessary.

Furthermore, due to the unique capabilities and limitations of the subject population in hearing, vision, writing, energy and memory, many traditional methods are not viable in this setting. Keith (1988) advocates the use of anthropological methods that allow maximum discoveries over an extended period by utilising non-intrusive techniques such as participant observation, in-depth interviews and so on. I therefore chose to use anthropological methods in my research, adopting a contextual, system-specific and emic-etic[11] perspective. I carried out 10 months' fieldwork in Japan from October 1998 to July 1999.

Through the introduction of Professor Hisao Sato, director of the Social Work Research Institute at the Japan College of Social Work, and Professor Takashi Mochizuki in Taisho University, I conducted preliminary research by visiting six welfare institutions for the elderly in Tokyo area during the first four months. I decided to choose Kotobuki as my intensive fieldwork setting because it fitted my needs perfectly: it is an unusual facility in which all three types of welfare institutions for the elderly are operated at the same site, and some newly developed community care programmes such as day care services, visiting home help service and counselling for in-home care, etc. are also provided. By studying the single institution of Kotobuki, I should not only attempt to understand the nature of institutional care for the elderly, but also gain a glimpse of the community care programmes that are being developed in Japan.

From February to July 1999, I became a daily commuter travelling 45 minutes from my home to Kotobuki by bicycle four to five days a week (for about eight hours a day). To understand the real conditions of Japanese institutional welfare services and obtain an insider's view of the realities of institutional lives and working, I chose to work as a trainee for 40 days and then as a volunteer. And the fundamental technique I used was participant observation.

As a field trainee during the first 40 days, it was arranged for me to do daily staff jobs in four different sections of Kotobuki, two weeks in Sazanka[12] and Akashia[13], nine days in Sakura[14] and two weeks in Aoba.[15] During the first two weeks, I was assigned to the third and fourth floor of Sazanka and Akashia. My duties included cleaning toilets, delivering meals, cleaning residents' rooms, and attending a variety of club activities and other recreational activities. After my duties were done, I stayed in the anteroom (*ryōbo-shitsu*), listening to the explanation of the director of the matrons (*ryōbo shunin*)[16] about the responsibilities of the care workers and the daily operation of the floors. I observed how the matrons dealt with the residents. During the breaks in the day, I drank tea with the staff and had informal conversations with them. Besides the interaction with the staff, I observed activities and conversations carried out by the residents in spaces such as the day room, washroom, dining hall and recreation hall. And I made small talk with the residents there. After office hours, I stayed late (usually an hour or so after office hours) to study individual case files and meeting records, in order to make myself familiar with the background of the residents. And I spent about three hours keeping a diary based on the brief field notes I had written down during the daytime.

For the next nine days, I switched to the Sakura Centre. Corresponding to the goals of developing 'community in-home services' and realising the integration of community care and institutional care in local communities that are set up in the 1989 Gold Plan, Sakura was established as an annex of Aoba in November 1991. It provides day care services for senior citizens in local community who are bedridden, have senile dementia, live alone or who are prone to shut themselves indoors. It has two kinds of day services: C type and E type. The C type is one providing services that range from recreation activities, counselling, health checks, class for family caretakers, lunch service to bath service, and rehabilitation (OT and PT training). The E type provides day care services for mentally impaired elderly persons. Except for exercises for rehabilitation purposes, services are the same as those of the C type.

My daily responsibilities at the centre included picking up and seeing off the elderly, helping with baths and rehabilitation, communicating with the elderly and taking part in recreational activities. I had opportunities to ask the clients why they came to the day service centre and whether they were satisfied with the services. Also, I was able to learn about the general conditions of the elderly who lived in the local community through conversations with the staff and by accompanying the director of Sakura when he went to have face-to-face interviews at clients' homes.

For the next two weeks of my field training, I went to work on the third floor of Aoba. My duties included: changing diapers, guiding the demented elderly to the toilet, delivering water to the residents, answering nursing calls and feeding the elderly. Every morning, I attended the morning greeting or the contact meeting. Besides daily responsibilities, I went to visit the kitchen, nurse station, rehabilitation hall and laundry room, and I had conversations with the staff there. I attended study classes for staff, and I was on the night shift twice. I took part in case meetings and care conferences concerned with individual elderly. And I had lunch with other trainee students from professional welfare schools and listened to their impressions of institutional life. After work hours, I stayed late to read individual case records and take notes.

When I started working in Kotobuki, all directors in the four sections introduced me as a Chinese student who was enthusiastically studying the welfare conditions for the elderly in order to apply the lessons learned in Japan to China. Because many of the elderly had experienced living in China during the war, some as wives of company men in Manchuria, others as soldiers, we had some common topics regarding China to share. Quite a number of staff had travelled to China or Hong Kong. So to both the staff and the residents, I was not a total alien from Mars. Another advantage was that I could speak Japanese fluently. This made us grow familiar with each other quite quickly.

After the 40 days' field training, I conducted two-months' focused research. At this stage there was a shift in research activity from general exploration to a more specific investigation of institutional life, the focus of which was to determine the quality of life. However, I found my research target to examine the 'Quality of Life' of the residents impossible to achieve when I started to work in Aoba, because of all the 50 residents on the third floor, only five could express themselves clearly. The care staff worked as if they were on a battlefield, so they seldom had time to talk with me. In Sakura, I also found that it was difficult to establish a lasting relationship with the clients because they were frequent commuters rather than permanent residents. The residents in Sazanka and Akashia, compared with those in Aoba, were higher in ADL ability, less confused and hence more independent. In addition, I had become relatively familiar with both the staff and the residents so that conversations were more easily carried out. Considering all of this, I decided to continue doing participant observation in Sazanka, Akashia and Aoba, the three long-term care sections, so as to hear different accounts of life experience and different perceptions of institutional life.

My main task was to establish good relationships with both the staff and the elderly residents. I narrowed my observation spaces to the dining hall, the day room and recreational/club activities, mainly observing the human relationships and activities there. I began to visit residents in their private rooms. And I started to identify the factors that comprise QOL in the home. I found that some aspects I formerly had not incorporated were also related to QOL, that is, religious belief, the issue of how the home dealt with the death of an individual or how a resident prepared for his/her own death. I thought it necessary to broaden the dimensions of QOL. And because all the people involved in the home had their own unique backgrounds, their perceptions of institutional life could hardly be the same. As a result, I decided to use personal interviews. A set of open-ended questionnaires incorporating the dimensions of QOL was prepared for in-depth interviews, one for the residents and the other for the staff. With regard to the elderly informants, I wanted them to recall their life histories: significant experiences in their childhood, during the war, after the war and after entering the home. I also asked how they thought about their current status, whether they were satisfied with the material aspects of their lives, interpersonal relations with peers, staff and significant others, and what the most worrying things were for them. Regarding the staff, I asked why they had chosen to work in Kotobuki, how they thought about the residents and about institutionalisation, how they planned for their own old age, and whether they were satisfied with their current job and so on.

From June to July 1999, I was busy interviewing both the residents and staff. Only volunteering on restricted floors in the homes, I was unable to make myself acquainted with all the staff. On a work day, the staff was so occupied with nursing care that they were unable to take a couple of hours off just to talk with me. In addition, as all care workers were working on rotation, if I wanted to interview a staff member, I had to schedule a day convenient for both of us. The above reasons made it difficult to interview the staff, so I decided to ask them to answer my questions in open-ended questionnaires. But I did manage to interview staff such as matrons, rehabilitation staff and dieticians in different departments. For instance, I chose to work on the night shift in order to interview a chief matron. Sometimes I caught up with a matron who was on early duty (*hayade*)[17] before he/she went back home. I felt it more effective to have in-person interviews with the staff rather than using the questionnaires. Interviews with staff were usually carried out in the meeting room or in the matron's anteroom.

Regarding the interviews with the residents, apart from some elderly persons who were unwilling to recall their past (usually recipients of Livelihood Protection [*seikatsu hogo*][18] who were formerly homeless), most of them were cooperative. Some interviews were done in the resident's room while most were carried out in public areas such as the dining hall or reading room. When we were talking, I was always served a cup of tea and some Japanese cake. Talk proceeded in a relaxed way with much joking and laughing.

Family members, volunteers in charge of club activities and trainee students from welfare schools are the main source of outside visitors. During my stay in Kotobuki, I did not meet many relatives of the residents. In Sazanka and Akashia, few family members came to visit their relatives. If they did pay visits to the elderly, they tended to meet them outside. In Aoba, family visitors tended to come to the home on the weekends when I was unavailable. As a result, I only came across seven family members of the elderly residents when I was in Kotobuki. I had chances to talk with two sons and two daughters of the residents when they came to visit, asking them what they thought about the institutionalisation of their mothers.

Among the volunteers, two were the daughters of former residents, some were teachers of recreational clubs, and some were local residents. I asked how and why they became involved in volunteer activities in Kotobuki. Also I asked them about their image of old age institutions, their perspective about life in institutions, the meaning of welfare in Japanese society, and their future plans for their own old age and so forth. Another kind of outsider was the students who were doing field training in Kotobuki. They usually compared the real institutional life to the knowledge they were taught in classes. Since I shared the rest room with them, I was able to ask them about their attitudes towards ageing and institutional life during lunchtime.

By the end of July, 24 residents (20 from the third and fourth floor of Sazanka and Akashia, 4 from Aoba),[19] 14 staff[20] and a couple of volunteers had responded to my interviews. Also, I received 21 open-ended questionnaires from staff. All the interviews were taped and various kinds of recreational activities and events were photographed. During the second brief field trip in 2003, some more interviews were carried out to supplement the data I collected in the previous study. In order to protect the privacy of the informants, the name of the institution and personal names in this study are all pseudonyms.

Organisation of this book

Organised and centred specifically on identifying factors that affect the quality of life of elderly people living in a Japanese welfare institution, the book is divided into eight chapters. Chapter 1 begins with the purpose of this research, the background of ageing in Japan, followed by review of the research regarding institutionalisation and QOL and discussion about my reflections on QOL for the institutionalised elderly, and concludes with theoretical framework of this study and methodology.

Chapter 2 provides the general information on Kotobuki, such as history, location, physical layout of the home, the socio-demographic background of the residents and the administrative operation of the home. It also presents a daily routine through the author's eye as a participant observer. Two different scenarios are given for the understanding of institutional life and work in Japanese welfare homes for the elderly.

Chapter 3 presents an account of how some of the institutionalised elderly visualise their past and current lives. The narratives of five residents show how these elderly persons describe their life experiences and evaluate their whole life; how they came to the home; how they coped with interpersonal relationships; how the issues of autonomy and privacy were interpreted; how they developed distinctive styles for adapting to daily life; and what they thought of their impending death.

Chapter 4 deals with institutional work of the staff. Four staff members from different departments speak about the rewards and frustrations of their job, about their views of the residents and institutional life and about their plans for their own later lives. Three major issues related to institutional work and life are discussed. The first is the working culture of the staff members: why employees choose to work in a welfare institution, how they deal with stress and difficulties in their jobs, what affects their emotions, expectations and sense of impartiality, and what are the effects of gender and institutional organisation on their work. The second issue is staff members' image of the institutional life of the residents, their attitudes towards institutionalisation and social welfare. Employees' reflections on the quality of life of the residents are discussed as the third issue.

Chapter 5 shows how volunteers, families, students and other visitors speak of their experiences in the home and what they think about institutional life. It examines how visitors of Kotobuki see their involvement with the residents.

Chapter 6 deals with two kinds of conflicts (confrontational/ non-confrontational) in the interactions of the residents by illustrating how they were initiated, extended and terminated. Through the analysis of problematic cases, the chapter discusses how the limitations of the home, such as the lack of a therapeutic environment and privacy, affected the quality of life of mental patients as well as the ordinary elderly.

In Chapter 7, a new social policy for the welfare of the aged, the Long-term Care Insurance plan, is examined. This chapter intends to explain what employees in Kotobuki thought about the LTCI scheme before and after its enactment. It also deals with how the enactment of this system has affected the operation of the home and the people in it in terms of quality of life of both the residents and the staff members.

The concluding chapter summarises findings from major issues developed in the previous chapters, discusses theoretical aspects regarding dependency of the elderly and the disengagement/activity dichotomy theory, and offers some reflections on the implication of the study.

Notes

1 Acronym for Activities of Daily Living. These activities include getting up, dressing, walking, eating and bathing.
2 Please refer to the explanation of this kind of home on p. 12.
3 A government-subsidised programme implemented in 1988 under the Law for the Health Care of the Elderly (1982). The purpose of this kind of institution is to provide long-term institutional care for the elderly who are suffering from chronic diseases and need skilled care, but not hospitalisation. Unlike *tokuyō* homes, where health and medical care services are limited and means-testing as to the amount of income or the availability of family care is required, a geriatric

health care facility is a health care institution that any older person can utilise, regardless of his/ her income.

4 Please refer to the explanation of this kind of home on p. 12.

5 PT is the acronym for physical therapy, a dynamic care profession. Physical therapists plan, organise and direct programmes for individuals of all ages, using physical means to promote health, prevent physical disability, or alleviate pain or disability resulting from disease or injury.

6 OT is the acronym for occupational therapy. Occupational therapy is a health treatment that helps people who have been affected by accident or injury, disease, ageing, developmental delay or psychological disability make the necessary lifestyle changes for better self-sufficiency and independence.

7 Elderly persons who are in need of nursing care or with dementia have to be hospitalised in general hospitals to receive long-term care due to the lack of adequate welfare facilities and home care services.

8 The 1898 Civil Code prescribed the *ie* as a legal family system. Under the patriarchal *ie* system, only the eldest son could inherit a house. He had the responsibility of taking care of his old parents and other family members. Other non-inheriting children were not supposed to shoulder the responsibility of caring for old parents.

9 It is sometimes suggested that if the numbers of elderly in *rōjin byōin* is also included, the percentage of institutionalised elderly is not in fact very different from that in the United States or northern European countries (Campbell 2000: 89). Considering the 'social hospitalisation' problem in *rōjin byōin* and the number of the elderly living in health care facilities, the percentage of elderly people in institutions in Japan should be higher than 1.66 per cent. But as the Japanese statistics show that the majority of the elderly are still living with their children (see Table 1.3), I do not think the rate of institutionalisation will reach that of Western countries.

10 Cook thinks that Maslow's theory of human motivation or hierarchy of human needs has provided a useful operating framework for professionals working with residents of long-term care institutions. He says that it is the legal responsibility of nursing homes to meet the basic physiological and safety needs of the residents. For the continued enjoyment of life, persons working in long-term care facilities should promote an environment that permits freedom, provides stimulation, encourages self-respect, and maintains a sense of fairness, honesty and order for the residents.

11 A pair of notions originally proposed by the American structural linguist Kenneth L. Pike (1954) in his Tagmemics Theory. Pike suggests that the differences between phonemic and phonetic in phonology can be applied to both verbal and nonverbal behaviour, or cultural phenomena.

Emic and *etic* derive from the words 'phonemic' and 'phonetic'. An emic unit, according to Pike, is 'a physical or mental item or system treated by insiders as relevant to their system of behaviour' (Pike 1990: 28). So 'emic statements refer to logic-empirical systems whose phenomenal distinctions are built up out of contrasts and discriminations significant, meaningful, real, accurate, or in some other fashions regarded as appropriate by the actors themselves' (Harris 1990: 48). An emic perspective simply means an insider's view of his/her own cultural system.

On the other hand, *etic* denotes an approach by an outsider to an inside system, in which the outsider brings his own structure or emics to interpret his observation on the inside system (Pike 1986). So etic statements depend on phenomenal distinctions judged appropriate by the scientific observers. As ethnographic studies usually deal with villages, regions, races and languages, an emic–etic perspective which combines the two approaches is required.

12 Sazanka: camellia, the name of a *yōgo* home.

13 Akashia: acacia, the name of a *keihi* home.
14 Sakura: cherry tree, the name of a day service centre.
15 Aoba: green leaves, the name of a *tokuyō* home.
16 In Japanese welfare institutions for the elderly, a matron (*ryōbo*) is a person who tends to the personal care of the residents. His/her function is similar to that of the nurse-aide in an American nursing home.
17 A staff member on this shift works from seven o'clock in the morning to three o'clock in the afternoon.
18 A kind of Japanese welfare policy that is similar to public assistance in Western welfare states. Based on the principle of Article 25 in the Japanese Constitution, the Law of Livelihood Protection was established in 1950 in order to protect poverty-stricken citizens. Its purpose is to ensure minimum standard of living and to promote the independence of poor people. According to this law, there are seven kinds of aid to the destitute: (1) an allowance to meet the needs of daily life; (2) subsidy for compulsory education; (3) housing subsidy; (4) medical allowance; (5) aid for child delivery; (6) subsidy for operating a business; and (7) aid for funeral (Mineruvā Shobō 1997).

  In Kotobuki, a recipient of Livelihood Protection receives about 20,000 yen pocket money per month, free articles for daily life, free medical treatment and aid for funeral when he /she dies.
19 Since I normally worked and volunteered on the third and fourth floor of Sazanka and Akashia, and the third floor of Aoba, the informants I chose were mainly from these three floors. During my stay in Kotobuki, the number of residents on the third and fourth floor of Sazanka and Akashia were 63 and 50 respectively, while 50 frail elderly were living on the third floor of Aoba.
20 Forty-five staff members were working in Sazanka and Akashia, while 48 were working in Aoba. Informants were equally chosen from among the three sections of Kotobuki distributed on different occupations.

2 The setting: Kotobuki

The origin of the welfare corporation Airin-kai[1] can be traced back to 1946. By the end of the Second World War Tokyo had been totally destroyed: hundreds and thousands of people were roaming around the streets searching for food, clothing and shelter. With subsidies from the Tokyo Metropolitan government, an old barrack in Nerima ward was refurbished by Mikaeri[2]to take in the homeless, which marks formal birth of the institution. At that time, as the institution was operated under emergency measures, impoverished persons, whether single, married, orphaned, elderly or handicapped, all were living cheek by jowl.

In subsequent decades, Mikaeri's programme expanded with the development of welfare administration to become a private, non-profit corporation governed by a board of directors. In 1957, a part of the old institution was set aside to house 30 elderly persons. Entitled the Yayoi Dorm, this was the beginning of the first long-term care institution for the elderly in Mikaeri. In the 1960s, with the revival of the economy, old buildings in metropolitan areas had to be torn down to meet the needs of newly established businesses, as a result of which a number of welfare institutions had to be moved to suburban areas. Consequently Yayoi Dorm was moved to a neighbourhood of Higashimurayama City and started its new life as the Kotobuki Home for the Aged, housing 236 older persons under the Law for the Welfare of the Elderly.

The 1970s saw the 'Golden Age' of welfare for the aged in Tokyo. Under the radical metropolitan administration of Minobe, the governor of the Tokyo Metropolitan government, a range of social security measures were enacted. These included the expansion of old-age pensions, a construction boom in welfare institutions, free medical treatment for the elderly over 75 years of age and a salary boost for those who worked in welfare institutions. It was during this period that the old terraced houses of Kotobuki were razed to make way for a five-storey concrete building and two additional new sections, Akashia and Aoba. The section containing the *yōgo* home in the new building was renamed Sazanka, while by that time Kotobuki had become a comprehensive home consisting of three different kinds of homes for the elderly, Sazanka, Akashia and Aoba.

In 1992, with support and funds from the city of Higashimurayama, Sakura, a two-storey day service centre was added on to the Aoba wing to provide both short-stay and day care services for the elderly citizens of the city. In 1998, the Kotobuki Home Care Support Centre (*zaitaku kaigo shien sentā*) was opened to provide in-home care, counselling, home help and visiting nursing services for local residents. After the LTCI scheme was enacted in 2000, a Home-help Station was established to supplement Kotobuki's in-home care services. This station and Sakura now comprise the two pillars of the new Kotobuki In-home Care Support Facility (*kyotaku kaigo shien jigyō-jo*). As a result, Kotobuki has now become a complex welfare institution combining long-term care facilities with day care facilities that provides both institutional care and in-home services for the elderly.

Location and the physical layout

The Kotobuki home is located in the south-western part of Higashimurayama City, a city lying 20 to 30 kilometres west of central Tokyo. As a residential city, Higashimurayama City has a population of roughly 140,000 with the number of elderly aged 65 or over reaching as many as 21,585. The percentage of elderly persons aged 65 and above has increased continuously in recent years, from 12.7 per cent in 1995 to 15.4 per cent in 1999. The city has the third-highest rate of ageing among all cities of metropolitan Tokyo (Higashimurayama-shi Kaigo Hoken-ka 1999). Despite its weak financial situation, the city spends one-third of its general budget on public welfare, and is thus regarded one of the leaders in promoting the well-being of its citizens. It has more than 140 facilities, including various kinds of hospitals, the city health care centre, nurseries, schools, libraries, cultural centres, and institutions for the handicapped and the elderly. Map 2.1 shows the location of the Kotobuki home, an example of these institutions.

Kotobuki is well known in the local community. Lying on the corner of two main roads, the home has Sunshine, a big food supermarket that the residents use a lot; Fujiya, an inexpensive clothes shop into which the residents' subsidies for clothes mainly flow; and a number of restaurants, convenience stores, a drug store and a post office in the vicinity. Next to Kotobuki are schools whose students sometimes come to visit the residents. The Higashimurayama Central Park, where a lot of outdoor activities such as birthday parties, gateball club (gateball is a form of croquet, also known as 'ground golf') and group work are held, is about 10 minutes' walk north of Kotobuki. In addition, there are two polyclinic hospitals and ophthalmologic clinics not far away from the home. Thus, the residents in Kotobuki live in a favourable surrounding.

Kotobuki is a large home for the elderly, with five floors and three residential sections. Though physically the three facilities are placed within a single building, they are not all under the same administration. The residents of Sazanka and Akashia are under the same administration and receive the same

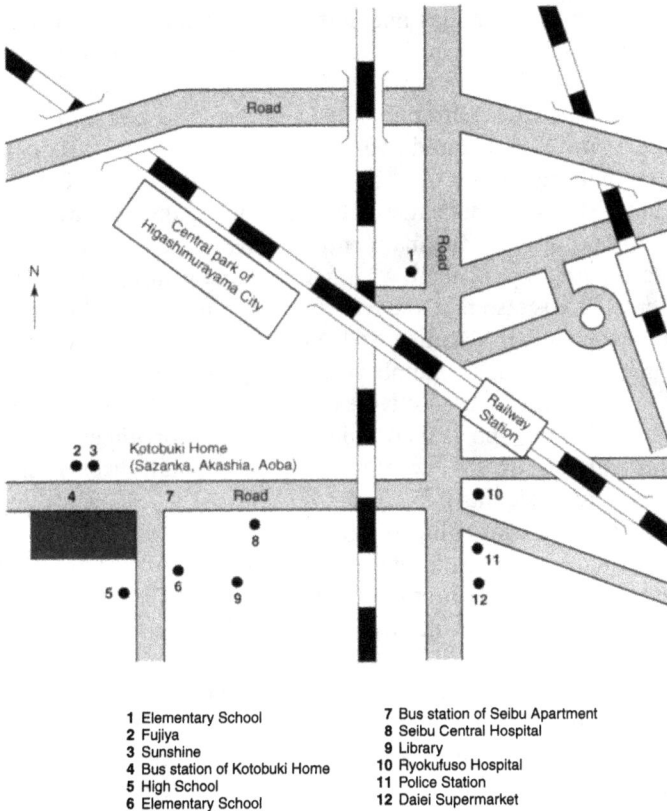

Map 2.1 The location of Kotobuki Home

1 Elementary School	7 Bus station of Seibu Apartment
2 Fujiya	8 Seibu Central Hospital
3 Sunshine	9 Library
4 Bus station of Kotobuki Home	10 Ryokufuso Hospital
5 High School	11 Police Station
6 Elementary School	12 Daiei Supermarket

treatment, except for financial issues, entrance qualifications and procedures. Basically, the elderly of Akashia live in the southernmost rooms of the building with one private room per person. There are 15 such rooms on each of the first and second floors, and 10 each on the third and fourth floors. On the first floor of Akashia, every resident has a small patch of yard in front of his or her room, where he/she can hang out clothes to dry, cultivate some flowers or even grow vegetables. The other rooms (36, 26 and 23 rooms on the second, the third and the fourth floor respectively), are occupied by the residents of Sazanka. Every room has accommodation for two persons. The three-storey east wing of the building is the Aoba nursing home. Here 100 elderly persons live in 27 rooms, with four elderly sharing a room in most cases. In addition to living space, the building has a hall for cultural and recreational activities, Buddhist memorial services for the dead and art exhibitions, etc. on the fifth floor, and a floor for administrative services.

Appendix 2 shows the physical arrangement of the building.

In addition to residential rooms and administrative offices, other spaces include kitchens (one for Sazanka and Akashia and the other for Aoba), bathrooms, a lounge, a laundry and linen room, a rehabilitation hall and some washrooms. The food is made and delivered to each floor by a special lift three times a day from the kitchens. There is a washing machine and a hot water boiler in each washroom. The whole building has four elevators, two in Sazanka and Akashia and two in Aoba. It also has four stairways, at the end of the hallway or near the elevators. Officially these are fire escapes. And there are additional emergency exits at the end of the hallways.

There is a parking lot at the main entrance of the home. Cars and buses belonging to Kotobuki park there when picking up or dropping off the residents or clients.[3] Taxis also take the residents who are going out or returning to the home. Residents in Sazanka and Akashia cross it to get to the clinic on the premises. Every day a number of elderly persons could be seen on their way to or from the clinic. Activities in this area would show who was in the home at that time, and display evidence of past or impending events, such as a funeral held for the recently deceased or a stall display on a cool summer evening for residents (*nōryō taikai*).

The residential rooms are officially considered to be a private domain. All rooms in Sazanka and Akashia are of the same size, each with a window and a small veranda. Every room has a wardrobe for clothes. In Sazanka, each room is separated from the hallway by a sliding door. Due to space constraints, residents are unable to bring in many of their possessions. The residents are provided with beds, a TV set, two small cabinets with drawers, two low folding tables and two chairs. All of their personal articles are kept in the closet and the cabinet. Most residents furnish their rooms with pictures, mirrors, radios, bedspreads and plants. Each bed also has an alarm cord connected to the matron's station.

In the rooms in Akashia the elderly can bring in their own furniture, use their own telephones, refrigerators and TVs, but they need to pay additional fees for electricity and telephone. The rooms in Aoba are much more spacious because they house four elderly persons. Privacy is maintained by pulling the curtain in the middle of the room. Each elderly person is provided with a clothes cabinet, and a nightstand where they can put books, a TV set or a Buddhist altar. A resident has to bring in his/her own TV set to watch TV. Each bed has an alarm cord to the matron's room and a bed-height control in the headrest. Because of the physical and mental disability of the residents, the rooms are bare of furnishings.

Socio-demographic background of the residents

Average age and length of residence

Currently 150, 50 and 100 elderly persons live in Sazanka, Akashia and Aoba, respectively. Among the three facilities, the elderly in Aoba are the longest lived, with an average age of 80.1 years for males and 85.6 years for females. In Sazanka the average age of males and females is 76.4 and 79.5 years, respectively, and in Akashia it is 75.8 and 78.0 years. Since the age limit for entering a *keihi* home is lower than for the other two types of homes, the residents in Akashia tend to be younger. In all three facilities, the female elderly outnumber their male counterparts and tend to be older than the males.

In Sazanka and Akashia, the largest groups of the elderly have resided in the home for 5–10 years and 1–3 years, respectively, while in Aoba the higher rotation rate of beds has caused two groups of concentration in residence, the less-than-one-year group and the 1–3 years group.

ADL and health condition of the residents

In Aoba, almost every resident had some form of disability that interfered with what is technically called ADL, the 'activities of daily living'. These consist of the basic abilities to eat, walk, dress, visit the toilet and bathe themselves. About half of the residents can eat and walk by themselves. In other ADL categories, more than 70 per cent of the residents need assistance, either from a matron, other staff or sprecial equipment. Over 50 per cent have been diagnosed with some form of dementia, 20 per cent are being spoon-fed, 36 per cent have handicap certificates,[4] and 3 per cent are on an NG[5] tube. Illnesses causing such physical and mental incapability run the gamut of osteoporosis, diabetes, cerebral infarction, cerebral haemorrhage, subarachnoid haemorrhage, arthritis, emphysema, arterio-sclerosis, stroke, heart ailments, malnutrition, depression, neurosis, vascular dementia and Alzheimer's disease.

Regarding the ADL conditions and psychological state of the residents, Sazanka and Akashia have recently carried out a survey based on the forms for *yōgo* homes and *keihi* homes designed by the Tokyo Metropolitan Social Welfare Council. In Sazanka, the items reporting the highest rates of independence, or 'no help', are excretion, meals, dressing and bath, with 96 per cent, 95 per cent, 87 per cent and 80 per cent, respectively. About three-quarters of the residents can walk without any aid, do laundry, go shopping, look after money and change the sheets by themselves. About 40 per cent of the residents need assistance with cleaning, medication, going to hospital and regulating personal possessions. Many have illnesses ranging from hypertension, diabetes to heart ailments, asthma and rheumatoid arthritis.

Regarding mental condition, about 46 per cent of the residents have some form of dementia or psychological disorders such as schizophrenia, alcoholism, epilepsy, etc. Ten persons have Certificates for the Mentally Retarded and 18 elderly have Certificates for the Physically Disabled. Some 13 persons have problematic activities such as abusive actions, wandering and playing with their excreta. It is said that compared to previous years the ADL ability of the residents is worse or declining, and the number of people requiring help in daily life is increasing.

In Akashia, in general, the residents' ADL ability is better than for residents in Sazanka. Except for the items of administrative procedures, cleaning and meals which are lower than 90 per cent in independence, most residents can manage by themselves in bathing, excretion, money, laundry, medication, shopping and so on. With regard to psychological aspects, about 10 per cent of the residents have some kind of disorder.

Reasons for institutionalisation

Why do these elderly people come to Kotobuki? Based on the case records and personal interviews, I found that in Sazanka, except for some cases such as protecting a homeless elderly, most elderly came from their own homes. A large number, especially of women, came to the home because of inability to manage personal care: they had difficulties in cooking a hot meal or going shopping. Exposure to risks had made it impossible for them to live by themselves at home. Some had no children or relatives to depend on. Some came because of intra-familial tensions, especially a bad relationship with their daughters-in-law; some others were forced to come because of eviction or other economic reasons. The number of elderly choosing to live in the home is small. In most cases, the elderly were persuaded by their district welfare commissioners (*minsei iin*),[6] officials in the welfare offices, relatives or friends to apply for entrance.

In Akashia, nearly half entered the home for family reasons and because of housing conditions: some because of the death of family caretakers, or bad relations with sons or daughters-in-law, or the lack of sons to depend on and their unwillingness to burden their married daughters; others could not live with their children for shortage of living space. Most of them came to the home unwillingly or were encouraged by their families.

The most common reasons for institutionalisation in Aoba are severe physical or psychological impairment, and the impossibility of family care due to the lack of equipment and caretakers. Currently the numbers of persons on the waiting list of Sazanka, Akashia and Aoba are 213, 11 and 198, respectively.

Some figures

Some figures convey information about the scale and character of the home. According to Mr Satō, the warden (*enchō*) of Aoba, it costs about $24,500, $27,000 and $35,200 per year to keep a person in Sazanka, Akashia and Aoba, respectively, while the institution's annual budgets of $3,680,000, $1,346,000 and $3,520,000 respectively, support 300 residents and 94 staff ($1 = 120 yen in 1998; the figures are based on the annual budget for 1998). During the period of research, there were about 240 residents who were paying fees according to their income with tax and social premium deducted, which mainly came from National Pension and Welfare Pension, and the rest

– mostly residents of Sazanka – were on Livelihood Protection. Currently the residents in Sazanka are paying fees ranging from nothing to 140,000 yen a month ($0 to $1,167); the payment range in Akashia is from the lowest of 24,400 yen to the highest of 98,580 yen a month ($203 to $822); and the elderly in Aoba need to pay from nothing to as much as 240,000 yen ($2,000) a month. Due to the continuing economic depression in recent years, and the LTCI scheme, all three facilities are facing subsidy cuts from the central as well as metropolitan government. As a result, Kotobuki is limiting its wages bill by hiring part-time care staff and other workers, for most of the costs of running the homes (about 70 per cent) go into salaries.

Organisation and administration

Staff and their duties

The home is largely a female world: women outnumber men, not only among the residents but also among the staff. Of the 94 staff employed, only the wardens, directors of the nursing departments, staff in the welfare department and some workers in the dietary department are male, the rest (about 77 per cent) are predominantly female. Of the female staff members, more than half are middle-aged women who became employees after they finished the task of childrearing. In recent years, many new employees in Kotobuki are young matrons who have just graduated from welfare profession schools or colleges. The youngest female matron in Kotobuki is only 19 years old. Some male care workers in their early 20s are also hired in Aoba.

The administration management in Kotobuki home is divided into two teams, one in charge of Sazanka and Akashia, and the other administering Aoba. Figure 2.1 shows the organisation of personnel in the homes.

The largest department at Kotobuki is nursing. There are 27 employees in Sazanka and Akashia and 38 in Aoba, including two directors, a section chief, eight welfare supervisors (*seikatsu shidōin*),[7] 48 matrons (including six male staff), eight nurses and two rehabilitation staff. Qualifications are required for the occupations of welfare supervisors, nurses and dieticians. In recent years, a certificate in Care and Welfare Work (*kaigo fukushi-shi*) or Home-help is required to become a matron. The department of general affairs is responsible for financial management and administration of the homes, building and repairs, and other affairs of the corporation. The largest division in it is the dietary section, employing 13 and 7 workers in the two sections. The housekeeping and maintenance is in the hands of part-time workers or a contracted company.

The nursing department deals with the residents directly. It is responsible for (1) administering the treatment of the residents, which includes admission, daily routine, contact and coordination with outside institutions, other departments and subsections, and financial administration for the residents who have entrusted their property to the office; (2) making, implementing

The warden of *Sazanka* — General Affairs Department (16 persons)
- General officer (1 persons)
- Accountant (2 persons)
- Dietary section (13 persons)

The warden of *Akashia* — Nursing Department (27 persons)
- Welfare supervisors (5 persons)
- Matrons (19 persons)
- Nurses (3 persons)

The warden of *Aoba* — General Affairs Department (10 persons)
- General officers (2 persons)
- Accountant (1 persons)
- Dietary section (7 persons)

Nursing Department (38 persons)
- Welfare supervisors (3 persons)
- Matrons (30 persons)
- Nurses (3 persons)
- PT/OT staff (2 persons)

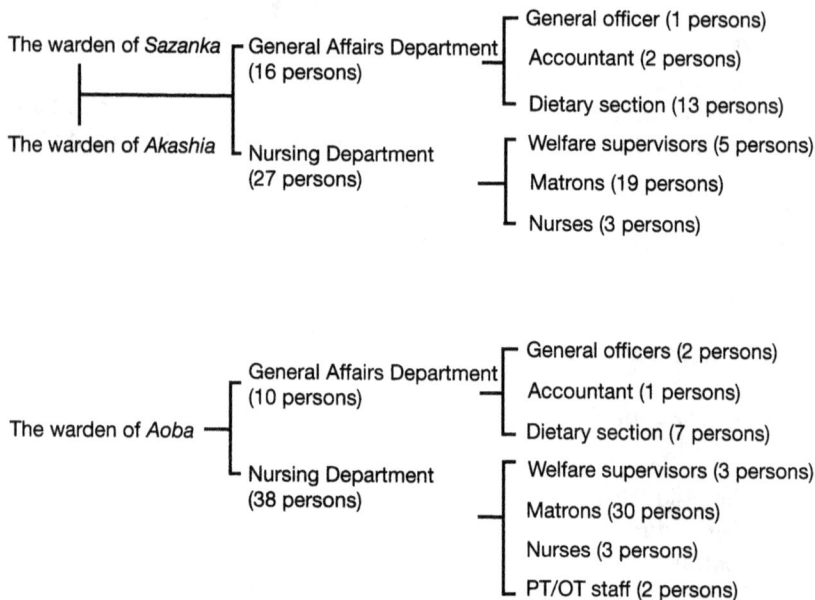

Figure 2.1 Organisation and numbers of staff

and evaluating care plans including various events and activities for the residents, individual care plan, rehabilitation, medical care, nursing care, and funeral services, etc.; (3) dealing with necessary entrance and discharge procedures, hospital visits and other contacts for those who are hospitalised; (4) receiving and organising trainee students, volunteers and other visiting groups; (5) cooperating in surveys organised by welfare-related institutions; (6) promoting integration of the home by taking part in activities organised by local community and inviting local citizens to participate in the events initiated by the home; (7) organising the work schedule for the staff; and (8) arranging affairs related to in-service training, etc.

The director is in charge of the overall supervision of the above processes. Welfare supervisors also do their share in maintaining inter-institutional and inter-departmental contact and coordination, planning events and activities, counselling, overseeing money for the residents, communicating with the families of the residents, organising voting in local and national elections, etc.

The nurses share the responsibilities of daily care for the residents ranging from nurse care, rehabilitation, counselling, recreation, coordination with medical institutions and record-keeping to health administration for both the residents and staff members. The matrons are required to assist with daily life of the residents directly. Their tasks include counselling, nursing care, assisting in club and recreational activities, case work, group work, medical barometer check, helping with cleaning and laundry, record-keeping and so on. Based on the assessment and individual training plan made by the PT/OT professionals, the rehabilitation staff are in charge of implementing the training plan, communicating with other sections, counselling, assisting in various recreational activities and keeping records.

The head of each section is responsible to the director of the nursing department and needs to attend various meetings regarding care of residents. He/she is responsible for conveying opinions or decisions regarding the treatment of the residents between his/her supervisors and subordinates, and training new employees. In order to enhance communication among staff members in different sections and improve efficiency of teamwork, contact and coordination meetings are held by staff members of particular occupations.

The principals or wardens are in charge of the general operation of the home and communication with outside organisations. They are responsible not only for decision-making as to general treatment measures for the elderly but also for personnel administration. They, in turn, are responsible to a board of directors whose membership includes the founders of Airin-kai, local government officials, scholars, health care professionals and family members of the residents. Since the home is a private, non-profit one, its operation largely depends on this board. Half of the formal employees are members of a union (*kumiai*) that safeguards the well-being and rights of the employees. The union works together with the corporation, Airin-kai, to improve work conditions for the staff so that they can continue the job as long as possible.

There are also some committees that require attendance by the residents. These include the management committee, and general informal gatherings for the residents. During these regular meetings or gatherings opinions are exchanged with respect to the daily operation of the home, events and activities, demands from the residents and on-going policy changes, etc. Since no resident has volunteered to become a representative on the management committee in recent years, every year ten elderly residents take turns to serve on it.

Coming to the home

The Kotobuki home serves the elderly population from Higashimurayama City and other wards and cities of Tokyo, but it also accommodates residents from other prefectures who have moved to Tokyo to live near their families. Since 1999, the application procedure and assessment for a *tokuyō* home and a *yōgo* home have been dealt with by the welfare office in the local government where the elderly applicant is registered.

As the process of determining whether or not an elderly applicant is eligible for institutionalisation is administered by government organisations, it is officially called '*sochi*' (measure). The necessary level of institutional care is determined by 'the Screen', an assessment form used by the Entrance Determination Committee in the welfare office whose members include a welfare manager for the elderly in the ward welfare department, an official in charge of welfare for the elderly in the local government, the director of the health care centre, doctors and the principals of the institutions. They make decision based on their judgement of an elderly applicant's health condition, mental state, economic condition, living conditions, family care capacity, medical condition, and ADL capability. If an elderly person is judged to be eligible for institutional care, the welfare office assigns a welfare institution for the elderly to take care of him/her. Based on the Transfer Standard of the State Liability for the Subsidy of Elderly Protection, the welfare institution receives public funds known as Measure Fees (*sochi-hi*) for its operation and the living expenses of the elderly (Shimizu *et al.* 1994). However, in 2000, the *tokuyō* home began to be operated on public funds and insurance premiums collected under the LTCI scheme, which replaced the old '*sochi*' system. Elderly clients who want to receive long-term care services in a nursing home no longer need to apply to the welfare office and wait for assessment of admission eligibility by the government. He/she can choose a facility freely. But the *yōgo* home is still under public administration.

An elderly person aged 60 or over and unable to live with his/her family because of housing and/or other social problems, is eligible for a *keihi* home. He/she must apply directly to the principal and sign a contract if accepted. A guarantor is needed when signing the contract. The elderly person can live in a private room because he/she pays for the fees.

Institutional care

Once admitted, an in-person interview and an in-advance visit are arranged for an elderly person by the home. The individual's family can accompany him/her for the interview. When a new resident moves into the home, he/she is discussed at the floor case meeting and the monthly case meeting directed by his/her matron in charge. And an individual care plan is drawn up according to the resident's life experience, family relations, former medical treatment, professionals' advice, taste for food, hobbies and his/her living condition after entering the home, referring to staff opinions from other sections. After this plan has been tried out for three months and the daily living condition of the resident has stabilised, the plan is presented by the matron in charge at the monthly 'Tuesday Treatment Meeting'.

This is a regular staff meeting at which an individual's 'care plan' is established and periodically reviewed. During the meeting, information about the resident's life, their physical and mental conditions and their family relations after they entered the home are widely discussed among the director, welfare supervisor, rehabilitation staff, dietician, nurses and matrons. Care plans specify what kind of rehabilitation activities a resident should get, indicate what food and medication should be given, and identify other supportive needs such as interpersonal relations and recreation activities.

Once the plan is formalised, a formal Resident Case Record is developed for each resident. This becomes a running record of all the treatments, consultations and activities that each person is involved in every day. Disagreement over a person's care plan often exists among staff in different occupations. If there is disagreement in a specific aspect of care such as whether or not to use a soporific, the professionals' opinions are usually respected. During the enforcement of the care plan, if there is further disagreement among staff members in different occupations, suggestions are usually put forward first to the section chief, then to the director. Through the coordination of the director, further discussion is carried out at another meeting and the plan is revised.

In Kotobuki, the staff members regard keeping records as of the utmost importance because they have the lives of the residents in their hands. The Resident Case Record itself is a compilation of the records kept by each section in different departments. For instance, Mrs Kobayashi, a matron on the third floor of Sazanka, commented 'on Tuesday Mr Shiraishi attended the Japanese chess club for the first time ever since the death of his wife'. Mrs Murakawa, another matron in *Aoba*, put a '+' symbol in Mr Ueda's record, which meant he had not excreted for three days, so he was made to take a purgative. In PT, Mrs Okada made a plan to have certain persons do 'range of motion' exercises to enhance the flexibility and movement of their limbs. One of her primary tasks was 'ambulation', which meant helping the elderly recover their ability to walk. Mrs Kuroda, as a nurse, made a note when she treated someone for a decubitus sore (*tokozure*) or replaced a NG tube. She also had the responsibility to keep up-to-date medicine sheets for all the residents. These records detailed the medicines and dosages each resident received, and furthermore she had to write down who had been taken to see a doctor. Each matron cared for four to six residents and had to learn a variety of procedures, including how to change a diaper, bathe an elderly person and do a proper 'transfer', the term for moving a resident from one position to another, such as from bed to wheelchair, or wheelchair to toilet. They also needed to learn a lot about materials and technologies, such as 'catch',[8] diaper, body suit,[9] catheter, respirator, machine bathtub and a 'geri-chair'.[10] Besides the individual care plan, many group care plan and general treatment measures such as recreational and club activities, birthday parties, trips and various annual events are carried out in the homes in order to assist the residents in living a fulfilling life.

Daily lives in Kotobuki

In order to let my readers get a glimpse of the life and work in Kotobuki, this section presents a description of the daily routines through my eyes as a participant observer. The day portrayed here is a composite day derived from separate events during the first stage of observation. Thus the day is somewhat fictive because it is not a particular calendar day in the home. It is based on observations conducted around the clock, and my own experiences of involvement in care practice and conversations with the residents and staff are the main sources used to typify the daily routine of the home. Descriptions interweave activities of the residents and duties of the staff members in a chronological order in accordance with the staff timetable. Because of different levels of ADL ability, the residents in Sazanka and Akashia lead more leisured and autonomous lives than those in Aoba, who are mostly confined to their beds or wheelchairs. And the jobs of the staff also differ in purpose: for the residents of Sazanka and Akashia, daily assistance is provided to maintain the autonomy of the residents, while for residents of Aoba, nursing care is predominant to maintain a dignified human life for the seriously disabled elderly. Here I shall present the two different scenarios separately, hoping that the sounds, sights, smells and feelings of life in Kotobuki will shed light on institutional life.

A day in Sazanka and Akashia

5:30 a.m.

The only visible movement this early in the morning is the staff member on night duty[11] on each floor who walks through the hallway to turn on the mini-boilers in the washroom. After that, she plugs in the socket to get the washing machine ready and goes to unlock the linen storage room.

6:00 a.m.

Mrs Takahashi, the matron, goes around to knock on the residents' doors and greets them with a 'Good morning. It's time to get up.' Residents who have been awake for at least half an hour come out of their rooms, walking towards the nearby washroom to wash their faces. An early arrival switches on the washing machine, and others queue up to do laundry by putting their buckets with nameplates on to reserve a place on the iron table beside it. Those already finished begin to clean their rooms and mop the hallway in front of their rooms. The person on newspaper duty goes to pick them up at the entrance and deliver them to the reading room. Mrs Takahashi helps to clean the rooms of those who are demented.

7:00 a.m.

Mrs Takahashi puts on her apron and a hood, and makes her way to the dining hall with a huge kettle of hot Japanese tea. 'Good morning. Many thanks for your help', she greets the four residents who are on this week's dining hall duty.[12] Since only one staff member on each floor is on duty in the early morning, the residents are required to help with laying the tables for breakfast. Chatting with the elderly standing behind the hatch waiting for food to come up, Mrs Takahashi pours the tea into teapots and a resident delivers them to the tables.

As soon as food and eating utensils arrive, everyone takes his/her share. While handing out the dishes, one has to pay attention to the coloured cards stuck on the table which indicate who is served with cereal, minced dishes and small helpings. Mrs Takahashi is responsible for checking whether all the food is delivered correctly and putting the pills the residents need to take on their tables. During the process, four or five residents using sticks, walking frames or carts get seated on their chairs.

7:30 a.m.

A small queue has already formed in front of the matron's station. With a sign of 'please' from Mrs Takahashi, Takako Hosoda, the meal announcer, puts on the speaker switch and informs the residents on the floor: 'Dear everybody. The meal is ready. Please wash your hands and go to the dining hall.' Then the people in the queue march towards the dining hall, with some others coming directly from their rooms. There is a succession of greetings between staff and residents.

As soon as everyone is seated, Mrs Takahashi says 'Enjoy your meal.' Then the elderly begin to consume the food on their trays: rice, miso soup, fried onion or a cooked dish with seaweed, pickled vegetables, and milk. The residents sit at three to four long tables in each dining hall. Each table has 8 to 20 persons and everyone has his/her name card stuck on the table. Except for the occasional remarks exchanged by people who sit near each other, the meal is fairly quiet. Eating quietly was said to be good manners in pre-war Japan and the residents were trained under strict home discipline in their childhood.

During the meal, Mrs Takahashi stands before the notice board, observing the scene and ready to serve a second helping if anyone wants one. It takes only 5 minutes or so for quick eaters to finish their meals. They rise and carry their trays to the handcart, throw away the leftovers, put the dishes in order and go. Others finish off their meal, talk, take medicine and queue up to put away their trays. Unfinished milk or fruit is wrapped in tissue or cellophane so that it can be put in the refrigerator for later consumption. Some help their feeble female peers to clear away the dishes.

8:00 a.m.

Unable to wait till the last one has finished his/her meal, Mr Baba begins to clean the hall floor with a mop. Mrs Yamada sweeps up crumbs on the floor with a broom and dustpan. Miss Nagaya, a nice but mentally retarded old woman, volunteers to accompany Mrs Kikuchi, an old woman with medium dementia, in the elevator to take the damp towel bucket to the laundry in the basement for cleaning.

Most residents make their way back to their rooms; some go to the smoking corner or the day room where benches are placed for smoking. And those on duty for cleaning the sinks or sorting and collecting rubbish or cleaning the ashtrays start to assume their responsibilities.

9:00 a.m.

At the main entrance, Mrs Ōkubo is taking a taxi, heading for the Seibu Central Hospital to have a heart check. Mr Shimada, a 70-year-old mentally retarded man with a crippled right leg, is starting the day's journey to Higashimurayama Central Park. 'My target is 5,000 today', he unfastens the pedometer from his belt and pushes his cart in the direction of the park. 'Oh, master (*danna*),[13] where are you going?' the stooped Miss Nagaya greets Mr Ishii, whose goodwill she sometimes tries to buy with some candies from Wednesday's stall. They make their way together to the clinic on the premises, Mr Ishii to have his blood pressure checked, and Miss Nagaya for an electric massage for her back.

With notebooks in their hands, all employees hurry to the activity room on the second floor where the daily morning assembly is held. No sooner has everyone been seated than Mr Itō, the director of the Nursing Department, begins to ask persons on night shift to report the situation on each floor the night before. After that, the wardens convey some information about meetings they attended outside; the head nurse mentions whose medication needs to be attended to and who will be discharged from a hospital, etc.; the welfare supervisor gives the schedule for the day, especially the events planned such as a birthday party, going fishing or gathering for cherry-blossom viewing, etc; and the dietician announces the menu of the day. The meeting lasts about 10 minutes.

9:30 a.m.

The music for callisthenics is heard throughout the home. Four to six elderly people step out to do exercises in the middle of the hallway in front of their rooms. In the meantime, the matrons put on working clothes, change into rain boots and start to clean the toilets. 'The women's toilet on the west side is soiled with faeces again. I don't understand how the handrail and the wall were stained. It must be Mrs Yanagi. She has been declining so tremendously recently. I have to post a notice in the toilet to remind the residents.' A young matron steps into the matron's station with her brows frowning. A few minutes later, a notice saying 'One more step forward! Your back will get dirty' is seen on the wall inside the toilet and another one on the door going out saying 'The person who has soiled the toilet may make the next user feel bad. Should the toilet be soiled, please contact the matron as soon as possible.'

In the washroom, an old lady is picking up her clothes from the washing machine and is going to hang them out on the veranda in her room.

Another lady is rinsing some red cherries. Two or three are reading newspapers in the reading room. In the day room, four to six residents are watching TV while smoking; one is already dozing. Some stay in their rooms, have a cup of tea or watch TV or chat with their room-mates. Other people go downstairs to make a phone call, or sit in the lobby to watch the flow of people.

In the activity room on the second floor, seven to nine residents, mostly women, are making flower arrangements with marguerites, white lilies, spireas and rape blossoms. 'The rape blossoms here seem a bit lonely, let's add some more.' The volunteer teacher goes around to give advice, pulling the twigs from the *kenzan* (pin holder) and cutting them to adjust the length and balance. The work of the residents is later exhibited at the entrance of each dining hall. On the fifth floor, more than 10 residents are playing cards or mah-jong. Sometimes Mr Katō from the administrative office is seen mingling with the residents.

10:30 a.m.

Ms Shinozaki, the director of the matrons, announces on the loudspeaker: 'Those who ordered articles[14] for this month, please come to pick them up. The bank service[15] is now available in the administrative office, those who want to withdraw money, please go downstairs to do so. And the pocket money[16] from the metropolitan government for this month is available, those eligible for the allowance please come to pick up at the matron's station.' At this news, residents come to the matron's room now and then to pick up what they need and sign for it.

The matron who is in charge of making case records is sitting at her desk taking notes. One lady gives the matron at the desk a box of cakes, saying that it is a gift from a visiting family. Some residents are watching *A Detective Story*, a favourite TV series in which the late Ishihara Yūjirō, brother of the current governor of the Tokyo Metropolitan government, played the lead.

11:30 a.m.

A matron is boiling water to make barley tea on a small gas stove in the matrons' station. Two other matrons walk towards the dining hall. Mrs Noji has prepared the damp towels and seasoning sets for each table and left.[17] A nurse is distributing medicine according to her notes.

Ms Shinozaki looks at the menu on the notice board and checks the kinds of diets some residents are required to eat. As soon as the food arrives by the lift, the matrons start to set the tables. There is an occasional foul-up where some dishes have been taken to the wrong persons. A staff member jokes with Mrs Yanagi, the one who was supposed to have soiled the toilet in the morning. 'Mrs Yanagi, I heard that you are going to elope with a young man, aren't you?' she asks. 'Yes, I am going to marry a 24-year-old young man tomorrow. In order that he will not discover that I am old, I am going to put two small balloons in my brassiere.' Mrs Yanagi speaks seriously. Laughter is heard and some more questions are asked about the details of how Mrs Yanagi succeeded in eloping with her lover when she was in her 20s.

12:00 p.m.

Nearly everyone is sitting at the tables. Two are absent – they have not come back from the hospital. Ms Shinozaki reserves the lunch for them by wrapping the trays with cellophane. There are noodles, fish broiled with soy sauce, vegetable salad and banana. A man stands up to have a second helping; another woman does not eat much because she hates noodles. Some get up to leave, some take their medicine, others help the feeble ones put away the dishes, and the persons on dining hall duty remain to clean the hall.

12:45–13:30 p.m.

It's lunchtime for the staff. A junior matron sets up a small table in the middle of the staff room at the matrons' station. She serves everyone with a cup of Japanese tea. Everyone takes out her lunch box while a senior distributes soup that she has reserved from the dining hall a moment ago; dishes are sometimes shared. Conversations centre on things that happened during the morning. Other topics concern private issues such as one's naughty but bright grandchildren, a recent bargain, education of one's children and a forthcoming staff trip. Most of the time the junior staff members just listen to what the seniors are saying with occasional comments. On days when the senior staff are absent, and all the matrons on duty are of similar age, or with a trainee student present, some discontent is heard concerning teamwork and the hierarchical system.

At this time, many residents in the rooms have settled in their armchairs. Several are in their beds. The TV is on in some rooms. Two or three who want to stay overnight in a relative's home or want to go out of the city to meet a friend come to the matron's station to register as absent.

13:30 p.m.

Some residents walk into the elevator with a washbowl and a plastic bag of clean clothes, going downstairs to have a bath,[18] the so-called *ichiban-yu* (first bath) of the day. One or two residents stand in front of the door to the bathrooms which have a blue or red shop curtain with a big Japanese character '[Yu](hot water)'. More are waiting on the sofas in the lounge. In the bathroom nearest to the elevator, a matron is helping the residents get dry and sort out the clothes in the small changing room outside the bathtub. Another matron is bathing an elderly person. Two people are soaking in the hot bathtub.

In the nurses' station, Mrs Watanabe, the head nurse, is calling the welfare supervisor to say that she is ready to go with him to pick up a resident who has been discharged from the hospital. A nurse is giving advice to a resident who has a headache. Another nurse is preparing medication for the residents.

'I am going to the *shogi* and *go* club', Ms Shinozaki says to the matron left at the station and steps forward to the activity room on the fifth floor with a box of cakes and a teapot in hand. Two volunteers, both about 60 years of age, are already seated at the table playing Japanese chess with some male residents. Mrs Yanagi is now playing *gobang* with Mrs Ōmori, a 91-year-old lady who always says that '*gobang* is a good exercise for the brain to prevent senility'. And in the recreation hall, a group of old ladies are dancing a folk dance; some wear Japanese *kimonos*.

The matron at the station keeps the case records for the residents. Occasionally she looks up and talks to the residents who come to the station. And she calls the names of 10 residents to pick up the tallies (*futa*) (equal to 1,500 yen) for a haircut tomorrow. A local barber comes to the home once a week to provide services for the residents, charging a fee less than an ordinary beauty shop does.

16:00 p.m.

Mrs Kobayashi comes up to the home bar on the fifth floor to open the business. For those who like alcohol, the home permits them to drink a cup of sake or a beer per day. Some bottles are stored in a refrigerator; others are put in the closet on the wall. The prices are written on a blackboard. Five to six residents are sipping *takara shōchu*, a brand of sake, with relish.

17:00 p.m.

Ms Shinozaki brings the Matrons' Record to the activity room on the second floor. She and the other two staff on duty tonight exchange information about the residents on each floor and mention some issues that need to be taken care of. Other matrons go to the dining hall to set the tables. There are announcements from the administrative office now and then.

17:30 p.m.

Dinner time. The pattern is similar to the other meals. Today's meal is ordered from outside restaurants according to residents' wishes. This is called '*kibō-shoku*' (a desired meal). There are bowls of sea urchin and rice (*uni-don*), bowls of eel and rice (*una-don*), bowls of roast meat and rice (*yakiniku-don*), omelettes, seaweed seasoned with vinegar, pickles and *miso* soup. 'Yours seems very delicious', the residents look into each other's bowls. The atmosphere is more pleasant.

18:00 p.m.

Some go to the lavatory to wash their faces and brush their teeth. Two are still doing laundry before the closing time at 7:00 p.m. Six to eight are sitting on the benches in the day room watching the summer sumo wrestling match on TV. The hot topic is 'whether Takanohana or Akebono will win the match'.[19] More are turning on the TV sets in their rooms. Two demented female residents are singing songs while tapping on their legs. A couple of old ladies who both dislike their room-mates are going to the lounge on the first floor to relieve each other's gloom. Several of those who still want to have a bath before 8:00 p.m. (the ending time) enter the bathroom. Two are calling friends or families at the public phone corner.

Ms Shinozaki is having for her dinner what the residents have had. It is called 'a test meal', the only meal the home provides for its staff for the purpose of checking the taste of the dishes. She has already cleaned the matrons' room and is going to check whether everyone has come back at 7:00 p.m.

20:00 p.m. – 21:00 p.m.

The residents who have psychological disorders come to the station to take medicine. Ms Shinozaki speaks softly while handing over the pills, paying attention to the emotions of these persons. She also puts away the articles for cleaning up for the senile residents and takes care of their dentures.

There are still one or two persons in the day room. The music of TV programmes is flowing through the hallway. Occasionally a cough is heard.

The main entrance is closed at 8:30 p.m. The guard turns off the lights in the lobby and the boilers on each floor. Everyone goes to bed at nine o'clock.

A day in Aoba

4:00 a.m.

The metallic creak from the wheels of the diaper cart is heard from the dim southernmost hallway. Mrs Suzuki starts the first round of diaper changing in the morning. Opening the closed curtain and turning on the light at the head of the bed, she calls out to Mrs Ōshima, a bedridden 76-year-old widow, in a soft voice that it is time to check her diaper, while the latter nods slightly with sleepy eyes, saying that she dreamed she was going to deliver a baby. Smiling quietly, Mrs Suzuki helps Mrs Ōshima's neighbour, who has been awake for a while, to get on to the portable toilet at her bedside.

Mr Nagaoka, a bedridden old man next door, who has had a cerebral infarction, is snoring soundly with his right hand resting on his chest clenching a *bunkobon*-size novel when Mrs Suzuki comes to his bed. When she unfastens the buttons of the body suit and uncovers the cotton diaper, he lets out a 'oh, that hurts' reflexively, his right hand stretching to touch his hipbone. 'Sorry to make you hurt. I will finish in a minute,' Mrs Suzuki apologises and quickly replaces the wet napkin. Mr Nagaoka smiles a pleasant smile after the changing is over. A somniloquy of moans issues from the bed across from Mr Nagaoka's.

With the help of a soporific, Mrs Kondō, who frequently called the nurse to ask for toilet assistance last night, has now fallen asleep peacefully. Nearly half of the residents on the floor have wet their diapers. It takes Mrs Suzuki about an hour to replace the diapers for 16 persons.

5: 30 a.m.

Mrs Suzuki puts a basket of hot towels on the drinks trolley, and prepares for the round, handing out water and waking up those who need to be dressed. Mrs Nakamura has been awake for a while because of a painful bedsore on her back. Although she has just recovered from a recent leg operation and is not supposed to get up without assistance, by the time Mrs Suzuki comes to her bed, she has already wheeled herself back from the lavatory, even having had time to wash her face and comb her hair. Mrs Suzuki smiles and asks her whether she needs help with the toilet, while admonishing Mrs Nakamura for her independence.

Mrs Nakamura's room-mate, Mrs Nishimura, is lying on her bed motionless. 'Mother (*okāsan*)',[20] Mrs Suzuki calls in her right ear and feeds her some Pocari Sweat (a sport beverage, used for salinity replenishment and rehydration of residents). Then she checks the almost filled reservoir for her urinary catheter and replaces it with a new one. And she continues feeding water to the bedridden residents and washing their faces. Now and then she hands over the towels to those who are awake and able to wash themselves.

Mrs Nakamura wheels over to open the curtain that separates her from Mrs Nishimura. She picks up the plastic cup in front of her family ancestor tablet on the nightstand, and wheels herself towards the washroom to fetch a new cup of water. She wants to begin today's morning service for her ancestors.

7:00 a.m.

It's time for meal guidance. A part-time staff member arrives in the dining hall to prepare tea for the residents and then she goes downstairs to fetch the breakfast cart in the kitchen. Mrs Suzuki does a second round to dress and transfer those who can eat in the dining hall to their wheelchairs, while using the bed control to adjust the height of the beds so that those who eat on their beds can maintain a comfortable position. As soon as the meal tray is attached, Mr Nagaoka puts on his glasses and begins to read his favourite novel.

Mr Nomura, who is physically disabled from polio, comes to report that Mrs Minezawa has urinated again beside the sofas in front of her door, a place she seems to regard as her toilet. Mrs Suzuki hurries to clean the place with a dry towel.

7:30 a.m.

Mr Sodei is on early duty. After wheeling the elderly to sit at their seats and putting aprons on some residents, he begins to distribute their medicine. For those who need to take the medicine before the meal, he tears the small pouch and drops the pills directly into their mouths.

Mr Nomura asks repeatedly why breakfast has not come yet. 'How can you forget my name? I told you a minute ago, didn't I?' Mrs Tanabe, an old lady who sometimes says that her name is Tanabe, but at other times says Murakami, her family name before her marriage, is very angry with her neighbour. Mrs Kondō, who sits to the left of Mrs Tanabe, turns her eyes to Mr Sodei asking whether she may use the toilet in her room, although she has just been there. She has problems with her bladder, but much of her concern about urination is psychological. Hearing her, Mrs Tanabe turns around to scold Mrs Kondō, 'What's wrong with you? Didn't you just go?'

The metallic crack of the breakfast cart is heard from the elevator. Meals have already been set on trays. Standard breakfast with some variation: cereal, a steaming egg, pickles, soup and milk or milky coffee. After delivering the trays to everyone, the staff members begin to feed those who cannot eat by themselves. Medication is taken care of as well. The TV set is turned off during the meal. Nobody gets second helpings. Those who have finished wait for the staff to clear up the leftovers and the trays. Mrs Aoki, who was a housekeeper for more than 40 years, helps by putting the utensils in order. Those who are relatively independent eat in the northern dining hall on the third floor.

After the meal is over, Mr Sodei wheels Mrs Ōshima back to her bedside and lowers Mrs Nishimura's bed to a more comfortable reclining position. Then he guides Mrs Miura, a resident with Alzheimer's disease, to the toilet, having her sit on it. During the time Mrs Miura is sitting on the toilet, Mr Sodei transfers Mrs Ōshima from the wheelchair to her bed, the latter now telling how she had her currently 12-year-old son when she was 71. Mrs Miura is later taken back to the hall and seated in her wheelchair, fastened with a belt.

The TV has been switched on with four or five people watching. Mrs Kudō is smoking a cigarette on the sofa before the matron's station. She is going to help fold the cotton diapers in the linen room on the first floor with her friend.

9:00 a.m.

In the rehabilitation room the daily morning assembly is taking place. The pattern is similar to that of Sazanka and Akashia. After that, some staff members are required to attend a case conference for a resident, usually one of those who have their birthday in this month, while other staff members go back to start their jobs. A meeting discussing the past year's conditions for the elderly is held in the conference room presided over by a welfare supervisor, with the matron in charge of that resident, a nurse, the dietician, a staff member in charge of PT training and the principal also in attendance.

9:15 a.m.

Mrs Suzuki says goodbye to her colleagues and leaves. The diaper cart is seen at the door of a residential room. The matrons are changing the diapers for the first time of the day. A strong smell of urine and faeces spreads in the air. Seeing Mrs Minezawa, who is about to pull down her trousers to urinate in her usual place, Mrs Miki, a matron who is going to interview a newcomer together with a welfare supervisor, cries out, 'Mrs Minezawa, please wait a moment. That is not your toilet', and leads her to the toilet.

Meanwhile two matrons in charge of moving the residents who need special baths come to pick up Mr Nagaoka, who has had his diaper changed and lies undressed in his bed. After the big old man is transferred to a mobile bed in a bath towel, a part-time staff member makes the bed and puts clean clothes on his bed. The special bathrooms on the second floor are separated by a curtain in the middle. A trainee student and a matron are helping dry those who have finished their baths. Afterwards, they undress the ones in wheelchairs. Inside four matrons are bathing the residents, two using the machine bathtub for bedridden elderly, and the other two using the one for those who can sit. Soaked in hot water, the elderly people occasionally let out an 'I feel good.'

Mrs Kondō is pushed in her wheelchair down to the rehabilitation room by Mrs Okada, from the PT staff. More than 10 people are already there. Three are having their legs electrically massaged; two are exercising their arms with pulleys; one is doing a puzzle. Another PT staff member is massaging an old lady's shoulders. Mrs Okada parks the chair at the end of the row of people who are waiting for electric massage and is about to leave when Mrs Kondō stops her by asking 'Doctor (*sensei*), can I go to the toilet?' Mrs Okada patiently promises that she will push her to the toilet when she is back.

In the nurses' station, a nurse has just picked up the medicine for the residents from the clinic and is about to distribute it. One is preparing the medical cart for the round. The other is accompanying the psychiatric doctor who comes once a week to see his patients.

11:00 a.m.

The drinks trolley is taken round. Most of the tea and other drinks in the cups remain untouched. A start is made on getting some residents ready for lunch. They are taken to the toilet or helped along to the dining hall. Two or three are arranged in 'geri' chairs. Three are watching TV in the dining hall, one is dozing off. Mrs Nishimura's son is sitting beside his mother whose eyes open slightly when her son clutches her bony hand. One elderly man is telling a trainee student to 'call 927188 to let my wife know that I am going to have lunch outside.' A matron is helping a resident who has mistaken his room for another return to his own bed.

12:00 p.m.

Lunchtime. The pattern is similar to that of breakfast, but more hands are available to feed the residents. Meals are made into kinds of paste, cut into very small pieces, cut into larger pieces or not cut up at all. Also there is rice and cereal. A staff member from the kitchen observes the residents while they eat. Mrs Kondō is absent from her table. She is being cared for by the nurses who are carrying out the new care plan they suggested at the case conference. The idea is to keep her out of bed and let her urinate once every four hours. Mrs Minezawa hides some tissue paper in her clothes. Mr Sodei is taking a rest in the matrons' station while his colleagues tend to the residents.

13:30 p.m.

The second round of diaper changing begins. Baths and rehabilitation continue. Mrs Nakamura wheels herself along the hallway several times, saying that this is her daily exercise. Mr Morita is making a new crate from newspapers on a table near the matron's station. Various samples of his works are displayed here.

14:30 p.m.

Club activities are going on in the big dining halls on the second and third floors. Nine to 15 elderly people are practising calligraphy or arranging flowers under the supervision of volunteer teachers. Such activities are similar to those in Sazanka and Akashia, but more assistance is needed here. Several residents who have looked forward to viewing the hydrangeas[21] are wheeled out for fresh air. Taking some candy, cakes and dishes from the cupboard in the dining hall, Mr Sodei prepares the refreshments for the afternoon tea at 15:00 p.m. His shift is over when the tea is finished.

Mrs Kondō, in the nurses' station, begins pleading, 'Please take me home. Have I done something wrong? Why can't I go to the toilet?' over and over. A nurse explains the sudden change in her life and insists that they are doing so for her sake. Later Mrs Kondō is found dozing in her chair, her head falling forward to her chest.

16:45 p.m.

The third round of diaper changing is finished. A part-time staff member begins her duties by assisting with the dinner. The matrons start dressing and transferring residents, and setting up meal trays in the residents' rooms. Mrs Kudō, who is taking a rest from her folding job in the linen room in a sofa near the matrons' station, is now chatting happily with Mrs Minezawa while smoking a cigarette, although it is obvious to everyone that the two cannot understand each other. Seeing the matrons push other residents to the dining hall, Mrs Kudō stands up saying that she is going to wash up for dinner.

Dinner begins at 17:15. The pattern is similar to the other two meals. Mrs Kondō is back in her seat. Mrs Ōshima says that she would like to be served by the male staff member (*oniisan*) who had changed her diaper. During the time when her colleagues are serving the residents, the matron in charge of keeping case records does her job. Mrs Suzuki is ready for the night shift. She prepares the cups, toothpaste and tooth brushes for teeth cleaning after dinner.

19:00 p.m.

The staff members on day duty have gone back home. Mrs Suzuki pushes the drink trolley into the rooms to replace tea or water, now and then answering the nurse calls. Most residents are already in their beds. One wheels herself to the lavatory to wash her face, with a washbasin on her lap. Three or four watch TV in the dining hall. Mrs Nakamura replaces the cup of water in front of her ancestors' tablet and puts a cup of rice that she reserved during the meal next to the water, thus beginning the night service to her ancestors. Mrs Kondō is calling for help. She fell down when she was trying to hold on to the handrail of the portable toilet by her bedside, but her voice is so weak that no one notices it. It is not until Mrs Suzuki enters her room that she can be transferred back to her bed, after having wet the floor.

20:00 p.m.

When Mrs Suzuki is about to take care of the medication for some residents, Mrs Kudō appears at the station asking for a cigarette. She comes again with a purse claiming that her money is missing. Hearing that her money is administered by the office, Mrs Kudō leaves satisfied. At this time of the day, she is haunted by a state called '*madara boke*' (sporadic senility). In the dining hall, Mrs Aoki, Mr Morita and two other residents are folding the clean towels for the back and hanging out the aprons. They volunteer to do this job at this time every day and are rewarded with a piece of cake and a cup of tea each.

After finishing her 'test dinner', Mrs Suzuki brings the records up to date and starts to prepare the diaper cart for the night changing round at 21:45. She continues answering the nurse calls here and there. After putting away the ashtrays and turning off the lights in the northern wing, she also turns off the lights in the hallway. By this time in the evening, nearly everyone has fallen asleep.

The life in Sazanka and Akashia is a prelude to that in Aoba. Living in the facilities on the same premises, witnessing the decline, senility and death of their peers, experiencing a life moving from autonomy to constraint, how do the residents think about the provisions in the homes, their roles and status, their relations with others, and the control of their lives in institutions? The next chapter will discuss some aspects that constitute QOL in the home from the viewpoint of some of the residents.

Notes

1 *Airin-kai* means 'an association for loving your neighbours'. It was so named after the Christian motto, 'Love your neighbours as you love yourself'. In addition to Kotobuki, the Airin-kai runs other two welfare institutions for the elderly in the Tokyo Metropolitan area.
2 *Mikaeri* means security in Japanese. It is the forerunner of Airin-kai.
3 For instance the elderly who utilise the Sakura Day Service Centre.
4 Physically handicapped persons aged 15 and over can apply for this kind of certificate to a prefectural governor with a medical certificate from an approved doctor. If accepted, the person is eligible for various kinds of medical and welfare services. The other kinds of official certificates for handicapped persons include 'Health Care and Welfare Certificate for the Mentally Disabled' (*seishin shōgaisha hoken fukushi techō*) and the 'Certificate of Love' (*ai no techō*) for mentally retarded persons.
5 Acronym for 'naso-gastric' tube (*bikō keikan*).
6 The general tasks and concerns of district welfare commissioners are summarised in the 1948 Law Concerning Volunteer Workers (*Minsei iin-hō*). The post of a welfare commissioner (*minsei-in*) is an honorary one. Recommended by the prefecture governor, a *minsei-in* is commissioned by the Minister of Health and Welfare. So he is called a 'governmental volunteer' (*kansei borantia*). A *minsei-in* is supposed to undertake matters of protection and guidance in the local community and make efforts to promote social welfare based on voluntarism. His duties include conducting investigations frequently to find out the real living conditions of the citizens in his district, making suitable provision for families who need public assistance, keeping close contact with the local welfare office and helping with its functions. As an influential member of the voluntary social services, he is usually active in various community projects and programmes. He is a respectable citizen who know the actual conditions of the wider society and who has the right to be elected as a member of the local city, town or village assembly. The term of his service is three years (Ōhashi 1999).
7 Welfare supervisors must be university graduates with qualifications of welfare manager (*fukushi shuji*) or social welfare worker (*shakai fukushi-shi*). Welfare manager was the only qualification for those who worked in welfare institutions in charge of advisory and guidance affairs before 1988. Since the enactment of the Law for Social Welfare Workers and Care Welfare Workers (1988), someone

newly employed as a welfare supervisor in a welfare institution generally requires a qualification as a Social Welfare Worker. A Care and Welfare Worker (*kaigo fukushi-shi*) is someone who has professional knowledge and techniques in nursing care for those who are too physically or mentally impaired to lead their daily lives by themselves.

8 A kind of napkin similar to those used for menstruation. It is put under the diaper to prevent wetting during the night.

9 It is also called a '*tsunagi*' pyjama; it is a kind of underwear with buttons or fastener at the back and the inside legs so as to prevent the resident from playing with his/her faeces.

10 A chair which is specially equipped with wheels and a tray across the armrests to provide both a restraint and a surface for meal trays and other articles.

11 In Sazanka and Akashia, the night shift is a team of nurses and matrons, while in the Aoba, there are no nurses. Thus there is some criticism among the staff that the lives of the residents in *tokuyō* homes are not really regarded as important.

12 Except for those who are senile or physically disabled, the residents in Sazanka and Akashia are assigned small duties such as dining hall duty, lavatory duty, rubbish duty, day room duty, newspaper delivery, etc.

13 Miss Nagaya likes to call all men in the home, both the residents and staff, 'master' (*danna*), so she is nicknamed '*danna*' by some male residents. She is supposed to have been brought up in an urban servant family.

14 In Kotobuki, the homes provide daily living articles such as tissues, soaps, toothbrushes, bath towels and batteries, etc. according to the needs of the residents. The homes also provide tokens for purchasing garments up to the value of 20,000 yen per person a year. Most residents use the tokens to buy clothes in the Fujiya shop.

15 Primarily, money is administered by the residents themselves. For the convenience of the residents, clerks from two local banks come to Kotobuki to provide cash and saving services twice a week. For those who cannot manage their money, the homes look after it. Generally, the personal seals of the residents are administered by the office and the bankbook is kept in the matron's station.

16 Recipients of Livelihood Protection live free of charge in Kotobuki. In addition, they receive 20,000 yen pocket money from the Tokyo Metropolitan government per person per month.

17 Mrs Noji is a 76-year-old lady with a speech disorder. She regards putting the damp towels and the seasoning sets on the tables before each meal as her daily job.

18 Since early modern times, it has been a custom for Japanese people to bathe communally. It is normal for them to go to a public bath in local communities or in Japanese inns at resorts.

In Sazanka and Akashia, baths are communal. There are two public bathrooms on the first floor, one for the male residents and one for the females. They are opened from Monday to Sunday from one o'clock in the afternoon to eight o'clock in the evening. There is no restriction on how many people can enter at once. On Sundays, showers are provided instead of baths.

19 Two famous sumo wrestlers.

20 Mrs Nishimura only responds when she is called '*okāsan*'. She is said to have raised seven children and have good relationships with all of her children.

21 In Japan the hydrangea is a flower symbolic of the rainy season. Although it may not be as common as cherry blossom viewing, a number of Japanese go hydrangea viewing in June or July.

3　The residents

Just as each musical instrument has its own voice in an orchestral performance, each elderly person in Kotobuki has his/her unique life story and view of institutional life. At the individual level, each resident spoke only for himself or herself and did not claim to represent all the residents in Kotobuki. Yet, the three common features of age, declining energy and institutionalisation had brought them all to the same situation in life. Thus they also had a great deal in common with their peers in terms of how they felt about and dealt with life and social interaction in the institution. In this chapter, Mrs Matsumoto, Mr Gotō, Mrs Sugiyama, Mr Aoki and Mrs Yamaguchi recount their past life trajectories. Drawing on their memories and their own words, each brings a unique feeling to the discourse about what it is like to spend one's residual life in *Sazanka*, *Akashia* and *Aoba*.

The narratives of these five elderly residents are brought together to illustrate some important themes in institutional life with respect to QOL: religion, homelessness, connections with the local community, mental illness and previous career. The stories also show us how these people described their life experiences and evaluated their whole life; how they came to enter the home; how they coped with interpersonal relationships; how the issues of autonomy and privacy were interpreted by them; how they developed distinctive styles for adapting to daily life; and, finally, what they thought about their impending death. The insights presented here are those of five articulate residents who were able to put their thoughts and feelings into words. I chose these five persons because I became involved with them the most and knew them better than other residents. And to some extent, I thought that they represented the different lifestyles I found in Kotobuki.

Narratives of five residents

Toshiko Matsumoto

'I leave my destiny to my Goddess (*kamisama*).'

With a fair complexion and dark hair, Mrs Matsumoto looked at least ten years younger than her real age of 76. Having entered Kotobuki at the age of 52, she had been living in Sazanka for about 24 years, a period long enough to make her a senior resident at the home and easygoing with the staff members. She was often seen to joke with both the matrons and her fellows, receive or give gifts in the hallway, attend various club activities and knit while chatting with others. She regarded washing the teapots after each meal as her daily duty and said that she would continue doing that as long as she was healthy.

Mrs Matsumoto was born into a big family in Hokkaido, where she lived with her grandparents, parents and three siblings. When she was very young, her grandparents often told her and her brothers to help others as much as they could. They said, 'by doing so, even if the favours are not returned to yourself, they will be returned to your children or grandchildren'. As she was raised in such circumstances, she liked to look out for others.

After graduation from a girls' school, she worked in a foil factory for a while. Then she stayed at her aunt's home in Tokyo for four years, and fell in love with a university student who lodged in her aunt's home. When the air raids worsened in the later part of the Second World War, she went back to Hokkaido, and got married ten days later after an *o-miai*[1] at the age of 24. Although she was unwilling to marry the man her father had arranged for her, she had no choice, for at that time a daughter was not allowed to offend her father. After that she lived in her husband's home for 22 years until she got tired of having to run their home-shop alone for seven years after her husband died of tuberculosis.

Mrs Matsumoto did not think her marriage a happy one. She thought she would have been happier if she had married the man she loved. 'It was my fate', she said. Her husband hoped for a boy to inherit his shop, so she had to keep on producing children until she finally got a boy seven years after marriage. She was awfully busy because she had to raise six children while running the shop at the same time. She could never sleep more than four hours for over 10 years.

Not a bad person, her mother-in-law helped to take care of the grandchildren. However, her three sisters-in-law were very spiteful. Mrs Matsumoto was called 'a rotten bride' (*kusare yome*) when she could not get up because of severe morning sickness when she was pregnant for the first time. Sometimes when she opened the *fusuma* door of their bedroom, she found one or two of them standing at the door eavesdropping and spying. She tried her best to restrain her rage until one day she could not bear the piercing pain in her stomach because of an ulcer.

Her husband was a gambler and a playboy. As Mrs Matsumoto took care of the bills of their home-shop, her husband could not take out money freely. He had property such as a mountain and other land inherited from his father. But he sold all of them gradually to pursue personal pleasure. Mrs Matsumoto did not know that until, one day after the death of her husband, a man in her village proved it to her. She lost her temper: how could her husband do that, without any consideration for their children? But anger was of no use: what was sold could not come back again. She worked day and night to run the shop and to support her six children, her mother-in-law and a shop helper.

Mrs Matsumoto moved to Tokyo to live with her son after she closed the shop. There was no problem as long as her son was single. However the situation changed after he got married. The daughter-in-law wanted her husband to concentrate only on her and was jealous when her husband showed kindness to his mother. At the same time, Mrs Matsumoto took it for granted that she could presume on her son's goodwill (*amaeru*) because it was she who had brought up all the six children. So the presence of Mrs Matsumoto became the source of quarrels between the couple. She felt sorry to put her son in the position of being pressured between mother and wife. She said:

> It was because of me that the two could not get along well. I thought it would be better for me to leave, so I moved to live with my eldest daughter who was then in Tokyo. Because I am the mother of the wife in the household, it's unusual for me to live there.[2] I felt restrained and embarrassed (*enryo*) towards my son-in-law. He was also reserved towards me. And my daughter, because I am her mother, she felt indebted to her husband. After a while our relationships became strange. As a result, I began to think of living separately. I went to consult with the welfare commissioner in our district. She suggested that I go to the welfare office directly. There I was told that about 300 persons were waiting for vacancies in the homes for the elderly and that I needed to wait for 5 to 10 years. I was disappointed at that moment, but I applied for entrance that day. Upon returning home, I prayed to this god, my goddess (*kamisama*) Tomomaru-hime.[3]

Mrs Matsumoto pointed to a picture of a middle-aged woman which she had put in front of a tablet on which was written the characters for 'Ōyamanezu no Mikoto' on her old dressing table. According to her, Ōyamanezu no Mikoto is a goddess of the heart. One's prayer will be answered if one prays genuinely from one's heart. Mrs Matsumoto entered this religious group some 20 years ago after she went to listen to the teachings with one of her daughters, who was then suffering an unhappy marriage. She did not believe in the goddess until some miraculous things happened to her children. For example, her son was in a traffic accident once when he drove his boss and a female colleague to a villa near Mount Fuji. The car was severely damaged and both the boss and the woman were seriously injured. However, her son was not hurt at all! He was a believer in the religious group and had prayed to the goddess every time before he went out. Another case was her second daughter. She was diagnosed with ovarian cystoma after she became pregnant. She was told to give up the baby because she needed an operation to remove the cyst. But as she had married after the age of 30, she wanted the baby very much. So she prayed to the goddess every day to keep her baby and for the tumour to disappear. On her next visit to the hospital it was found that the tumour had become smaller, and eventually it disappeared. Her daughter has since delivered a second child. Impressed by these miracles, Mrs Matsumoto became a follower of this religion. She said:

> I was totally convinced of the existence of the goddess – Ōyamanezu no Mikoto. I entered the church and went to Yokohama three to four times a month to listen to Tomomaru-hime's teachings. After I applied for admission to the old-age home, I prayed to Tomomaru-hime every day: 'Oh, my *kamisama*, I want to live separately from my daughter. If there is a good place supported by welfare, please let me in.' Then when I went to the welfare office several days later, the officer thought I was in a hurry, so he put my application form ahead of the others. I continued praying to Tomomaru-hime and was told that there was a vacancy in Sazanka three days after my second visit to the office. So it was owing to the goddess that I was able to live a comfortable life here in Sazanka.

Mrs Matsumoto thought it was better living in Sazanka than being with her children, since by living separately from her children, and thereby graduating from the role of a mother-in-law, she felt relieved of many worries and much anguish. She also thought she had been relieved through faith healing (*kaji*) from her *kamisama* many times since she joined the church. After she moved to Sazanka, she had been operated on twice. Each time, before the operation, she prayed to the goddess 'Dear Tomomaru-hime, please change the doctor's hands into your hands. Please guard me.' Both operations were very successful. She was told by the doctors that their hands were extraordinarily dextrous when operating. She knew that it was the goddess who had helped her.

Mrs Matsumoto also felt she had been redeemed by her religion. At the time she came to live in Sazanka, she could not adjust to the world of the home, that was so different from her former life. She had to follow the regulations and pay attention to others, especially her room-mate. It was stressful adapting to the new environment and human relationships in her old age. She said if she had not had Tomomaru-hime with her, she would have become strange. It became her habit to greet the goddess at six o'clock every morning and night. She would do everything Tomomaru-hime told her. If she was unsure about something, she would pray to the goddess for directions. According to her, the goddess understands that human beings do not know how to choose the right way, and how to follow the rules. Therefore she guides her followers in the heart, and she saves people who are trying their best to obey rules. Mrs Matsumoto believed that her goddess was showing her the right way and protecting her from illness as well. She spoke placidly, 'I have given my life to my *kamisama*, so I fear nothing, not even death.'

When talking about her current life in Sazanka, Mrs Matsumoto said that she was quite satisfied. As she had been busy making a living for her families when she was young, she had no time to think about hobbies. She had dreamed of living a leisurely life in which she could enjoy her hobbies and do the things she liked while keeping an orderly schedule in eating, bathing and sleeping. Although there were times when she felt uncomfortable because of the limitations of her privacy, troublesome interpersonal relations and disagreeable matrons, the environment and schedule in general met with Mrs Matsumoto's expectations. 'Except for the human relationships, this is a paradise', she said.

> I feel at home here. The food is not bad. I can't comment on the quality of the meals because everyone has his/her own taste. Every day the staff members in the kitchen do their utmost to prepare the menu and make the dishes for us, so I am obliged to them. Besides, we can bathe any time we want; we can get some exercise by sweeping the floor or the like. In an ordinary family, the children are usually the focus of attention. However, this is a place where many elderly gather to lead a group life. So we are the centre of the world and the staff here are all working for us. That's very good. We also have recreational and club activities. Each year the home arranges something for us. Another good thing about living here is that when our health deteriorates, we can move to Aoba or another *tokuyō* home. This makes me feel secure.

Mrs Matsumoto was grateful to the home for the services it provided, and she thought residents should not demand too much. She did not like those who kept complaining about this and that and speaking ill of others. She said, 'As the life here is a group life, everyone cannot have his/her own way. And since everyone is different, one should not expect others to share the same ideas as oneself. One should learn to compromise.' She thought it important to tune in to others in order to lead a harmonious group life. In fact, her relations with other residents were quite good. She was called 'everybody's friend' (*happōō bijin*)[4] in secret because she had a lot of friends, not only women but also men. She thought that since both she and other residents had had a hard life, they should have fun during the last stage of their life. 'We should be considerate with each other and enjoy our lives here with our peers', she said, 'those who only think about themselves or act like a god will not get along well here.' And she exemplified:

> I once lived with a person who had never married. As she had long lived a self-centred life, she didn't care about others as long as she herself was OK. People who have never married or who have no children do not

understand the importance of interpersonal relations, and they don't know that they should consider others' situation before thinking about their own. That's why some people feel isolated from others.

Mrs Matsumoto was very active in club activities. The clubs she attended were calligraphy, handicrafts, card playing, table tennis and mah-jong. She was good at paper folding and knitting. She was pleased to be one of the representatives of Sazanka to provide something for the yearly handicraft exhibition held in the City Cultural Centre. She liked to keep herself busy and was willing to continue participating in recreational and club activities as much as her health permitted. But she was thinking about quitting the table tennis club, because she thought her declining energy was not up to playing twice a week. Also, she did not want to be involved in the complicated interpersonal relationships caused by the problem of who would be responsible for club duties. It seemed that her philosophy of life was to avoid conflicts and maintain peace as far as possible.

Mrs Matsumoto missed her children, but she stated that she would not live with them, because she thought of Sazanka as her own home. She could go to visit her children or call them when she missed them. But she did feel lonely sometimes, especially at dusk. Even if she was talking to somebody, she felt somewhat lonely at heart. 'I think everyone here has the same feeling as I do', she said, 'It's miserable to be old. But you have no choice.'

Having lived in Sazanka for more than 20 years, Mrs Matsumoto thought it easier for her to ask a favour from a matron than it was for newcomers. 'I can make fun of the matrons', she said, 'it is advantageous if you can make fun of the matrons.' She preferred to talk to the older matrons rather than the young staff because 'they give you a sense of reliability. The young matrons sometimes don't understand the feelings of us old people.' Although she thought the staff members were good to her and she could joke with them, they were not her family and she could not always depend on their goodwill. She would like to leave her destiny to her *kamisama* and ask her to keep her healthy and protect her from being a burden to others. Her wishes now were to devote herself to her goddess and to live harmoniously with her peers.

Kazuo Gotō

'I am carrying a heavy loneliness on my back.'

Deeply inhaling the fumes of a cigarette, the 77-year-old Mr Gotō began to narrate his life story. He was paralysed on the left side of his body because of a cerebral infarction five years ago. After receiving rehabilitation in a hot-spring hospital for nearly a year, he had an operation to remove cancer in the colon. Since then he had lived in Sazanka and received monthly pocket money from the Tokyo Metropolitan government. He was a recipient under the Livelihood Protection scheme.

Mr Gotō was born as the second son in a wholesaler's family in 1922 in Bunkyo-ku, Tokyo. The family came from a well-known tea-producing centre in Shizuoka Prefecture, and a lot of relatives were engaged in growing tea, so his mother ran a tea wholesale business. He was brought up in a family whose economic condition was quite stable. He was the boss of the children in the neighbourhood because he had the money to make other children follow him. He hated study and often skipped school. Because of his bad scores, he was unable to enter a public middle school, so he went to the private Waseda Vocational School to learn to be a barber. But he did not do well there either. His parents worried that he would become a delinquent so they enrolled him in the army. He was 19 years old that year. With the beginning of the Great East Asia War (*daitōa sensō*), Mr Gotō was sent to Manchuria to fight against the Chinese army.

Ten months before the war ended, he was dispatched to the Pacific battlefield. Since the American army already dominated in the air, the soldiers of his unit were forced to enter the jungles in the Philippines. About one month after the war ended, he became a captive, interned in the camps for Japanese captives in Manila. He stayed in the camp for almost two years.

Mr Gotō returned home in 1947 when he was 24 years old. His eldest brother had already been killed in a battle against the Soviet Army and his other two brothers had been back home. Tokyo was then in turmoil and black markets were brimming with vitality everywhere. As the companies and factories were not reconstructed yet, there was nowhere for him to work. Moreover, his parents had sold nearly everything they had to get food. He had no choice but to join the black market business. 'As we had just returned from the battlefield, we had plenty of guts to do that', he said.

In order to be dutiful to their parents, Mr Gotō and his brothers went to Niigata, a rice-producing district, to lay in provisions. Half of the rice they bought was for consumption at home, the other half was sold on the black market. Mr Gotō and his friend also produced soy sauce by using the thick base of the sauce and salt. They made a big profit by selling the product to restaurants and hotels. However most of his money went on gambling which he enjoyed.

With increasing social stability, Mr Gotō began to think about getting a proper job. However, according to an order from the General Headquarters of the Allied Occupation Forces, no former military officer above the rank of non-commissioned officer (*kashikan*) was permitted to work in public offices. Since Mr Gotō was an officer on probation, he had to wait for two years to apply for a position in the city office of Yokohama City. He was employed as a barber in the welfare department in 1949. As the welfare department was in charge of the welfare of staff members and their families, there were many chances to get hold of goods such as clothing, food, charcoal, etc., as well as chances to do bad things. Five years later he was demoted to a ward office on account of his questionable conduct in the department. Considering that he would be unable to get promoted any more, he was angry and began to think about doing business with his friend in Tokyo. He eventually did so, leaving his second wife and an apartment in Yokohama. Mr Gotō recalled his old days,

> I was 29 that year. I did the same thing three times. Every time when I said good-bye to a wife, I only took with me a suitcase with the necessary clothes. To think about it now, it was pitiful for my wives. My first wife was forced to leave me because of her inability to have a child. Though we had married for love, my parents didn't look kindly upon her because of her sterility. As a result, we could not get along and had to separate from each other. The second one was divorced by mutual agreement. I left everything to my wife and came to Tokyo alone.

He helped a good friend with his real-estate business in Setagaya-ku. There was a time when the Taiwanese had to leave Japan, so Mr Gotō and his friend bought a lot of houses owned by the Taiwanese in Shinjuku and Ikebukuro at low prices, refurbished the houses and sold them at good prices. It was during his 30s that Mr Gotō was the most successful. He made big money, opened a beauty parlour and built a three-storey house in Ikebukuro. It was during that period that he came across his third wife, a cosmetician 12 years younger than him. Despite her parents' strong objections, they got married. The marriage came into being because Mr Gotō was powerful: he bought his wife a beauty parlour to run her business. Soon a daughter was born to them.

One never thinks about the future when one is at one's peak. That went for Mr Gotō, too. His friend died soon after the Olympic Games in Tokyo in 1964. Without a good partner, he lost his direction and his business gradually collapsed. He liked gambling for big stakes. In addition to horse racing, he crazily invested some tens of millions of yen in stocks, which eventually made him bankrupt. He lost everything: three shops, house, wife and daughter. After that, he worked as a driver to make a living. As he advanced in age and fell ill several times, he became unable to do physical jobs so for some time he did day labour, delivering bills in Ginza and waiting for orders in the golf practising fields, for example. If there was no job, he begged, too. He slept in corrugated cardboard inside the stations of Shinjuku and Ikebukuro when he had no place to go. Finally he found himself in Sazanka.

Obviously Mr Gotō was nostalgic about his golden age in his 30s. He had never thought he would end up in a home for the elderly; the only knowledge he had of such homes was that they were places for group living. He was obliged to the welfare office of Tokyo Metropolis. And he seemed to be quite satisfied with the treatment he had received from the government. He said:

> ... My fate was decided on the day when I was taken to the hospital for a cerebral infarction and the officer came to investigate my background.

I was sent to a great rehabilitation hospital with a hot spring. When I became better, the welfare office again took the whole responsibility of looking after me. I received the best care from the welfare office: entering expensive hospitals free of charge and receiving pocket money every month. I am really very lucky. So I think the welfare in Japan is good.

When talking about his life in Sazanka, he said he was living in ease and comfort. He did not need to worry about food and a place to sleep, and he did not need to work to make a living for himself. Also he did not have the obligation (*giri*) to socialise with his neighbours. Even if there was some socialising in the home, since all residents were in similar circumstances, it was not worth mentioning. Since everything was done for the residents, Mr Gotō thought he could live an easy life without thinking much. But, he commented:

It is a good thing that I have become detached after I was put into such an environment. However, without the necessity to use my brain and survive, I am afraid I will get dotty quicker than those who live by themselves. You see, even a chicken or a bird has to feed itself! Here one needn't think about survival and ambition, so one's capability keeps on declining. Since I am handicapped by my leg and arm, I cannot move about freely. All I do every day is sleep, eat, smoke and watch TV. I have become gradually isolated from the life of ordinary people, so I become senile little by little.

People are strongest when they have the ability to work. Since the cells of my brain are sleeping, I cannot make any progress. This is the end of my life. There is no necessity to speak ill of politicians because old folks like me haven't any power to change the world. It is really sad to become old. What I hope now is to live peacefully with my roommate, not to be a burden to others, and to keep my independence as long as possible. I am not the type to presume on other's goodwill so I rarely ask for help from the matrons.

As Mr Gotō explained, there was not much socialising among the residents, especially among the men. So except for his room-mate, Mr Gotō had no close friends on the floor. He never spoke to the female residents since he had come to dislike women after he was divorced by his wife. He was willing to teach the tacit rules of the home to newcomers. On the whole, he kept a distance from both his peers and the matrons. The only duty he did in Sazanka was to bring the bucket of washing to the laundry. He had done that for three years. Sometimes he felt it was not worth doing because nobody appreciated him doing it. But when occasionally someone said 'Thank you very much', he felt very rewarded. He said he would continue doing it for it was necessary to get some exercise.

When I asked him whether or not he missed his daughter and his wife, he became gloomy. 'It's difficult to talk about my feelings towards my family', Mr Gotō said, inhaling a mouthful of smoke.

I have neglected my family for a long time. When I was young, it was a tradition for an adult man to marry a woman, so I took it for granted that I should get married when I attained manhood. You know, a man is inconvenient without a wife, because he needs a wife to do the washing, cooking and so on for him. A wife is a kind of security in life. Figuratively speaking, a wife is a side dish to have with one's rice.

I miss my daughter. But how can I dare to ask her to meet me? So I pull back. To tell you the truth, I want to beg my daughter's forgiveness, even though this would be a disgrace for me. Do you think an apology will help? I don't think so. I cannot work any more, neither do I have any money. If I still had enough deposited in the bank in addition to the money for my own funeral, my family might be glad to accept me. Nobody will take care of a relative without a penny.

Mr Gotō felt fortunate that old people like him still had public institutions to depend on. He could not understand why, recently, elderly people who had families also came to live in an institution. His explanation was that the younger generations were neglecting their responsibility for caring for their old relatives. At the bottom of his heart, he missed his daughter and wished she would forgive him. Since he separated from his last wife 15 years ago, he had been to see his daughter several times in secret. Once in a while, when he happened to think about her, he went to see her, from very far away, for he did not want to interfere with her and his former wife's life. His daughter never knew he was there. Mr Gotō guessed that she might have got married and had children. He thought she had forgotten him, for if she really thought about her father, she would have looked into the family register[5] and found him.

He had not had any information about his siblings since his bankruptcy, either. He did not know whether his brothers were still alive, and he did not think they would come to see him even if they were. 'There is something strange in Japanese families', he said, 'they do not want to show bad things or defective relatives to strangers. In the old *ie* system, there were humane feelings (*ninjō*) to some extent. But there is none in modern families. Everyone is selfish: one only thinks about one's own life.' He did not think there were good points in the current family system. He was sad when talking about his family and his future.

When I think in the dark, I feel miserable. I have no future except to wait for death. Though I have relatives, I cannot enjoy their company. I have to do everything by myself. Do you understand the feeling of loneliness? You may find I am cheerful on the outside (*omotemuki*), but I am carrying a heavy loneliness on my back. It cannot be helped even if I cried out loudly with regret. So I would rather hide my feelings deeply. You cannot imagine how heavy the loneliness is! I attribute my misery to the sins I have committed in the past. By doing so, it becomes tolerable to think about why I am unable to eat delicious food, why I cannot move about freely and why I have to end up here. I am eating the punishments for what I have done long before! When one approaches Buddha, one will understand naturally. So now I can accept my fate honestly.

However, Mr Gotō never thought about death. He wanted to die in his sleep, or abruptly with little pain. As he did not think he would have any connection with his family when he was alive, he thought he would become a *muen-botoke*[6] when he died. He planned to have the home to do a funeral service for him. Among the 20,000 yen monthly pocket money he received, 12,000 yen was spent on cigarettes, and the remainder was for his funeral fee. As he could save 60,000 yen every year, he thought he would have enough money for his funeral, that would probably cost 250,000 yen.

'Possibly this will be the place where I die', Mr Gotō sighed with a sad smile and ended his story.

Haruko Sugiyama

'My hobbies and extensive friendship outside bring me a happy life in the home.'

Mrs Sugiyama was a senior (*furukabu*) who had resided in Akashia since it was opened. With a head of silver hair and a pair of still brightly shining eyes, she looked different from other residents. Yet, what made her even more special was that she was the only female member of the gateball club. Despite her age of 76, she was actively engaged in various cultural activities organised by both the home and outside elderly groups. She was an active person and good at many things. The Western and Japanese clay figures of varied shapes, and the photos, medals and cups on display in her room showed the vast range of her hobbies: making figures in clay, painting, playing table tennis and travelling.

Mrs Sugiyama was born the youngest child of six siblings in an artisan's family in 1923 in Nagaoka, Niigata prefecture. Since she was the only girl in the family, she was brought up indulgently. So she called herself a self-willed person. After she graduated from middle school, she went to work as a sales clerk in a draper's shop in Ginza in Tokyo. The manager was a childhood friend of her mother.

The two years and a half working in that shop were the happiest period in her girlhood. Business was good when she entered the shop, however, it gradually stopped making a profit because all clothing was rationed when the war became serious. So she went back to Nagaoka where she later met a young man who promised to marry her. But he was conscripted and left saying 'I will not fail to come back.' He never returned because he soon died on the transport ship in a disaster at sea. She was sad at the news and swore that she would never get married.

However, she did marry, at the age of 19, following a meeting arranged by her eldest brother and his boss, whose nephew became her husband. Since her brother and her husband-to-be were in the same occupation, Mrs Sugiyama said that her marriage was a 'strategic marriage'. With money sent by her husband's eldest brother, they set up a house. One month after their marriage, her husband was drafted to work at a military base. As he was sent to a secret place, she did not receive any letters from him for three years. She raised their first child with the help of her mother.

In the evening of 1 August 1945, Mrs Sugiyama witnessed the disaster of Nagaoka: numerous incendiary bombs trapped the whole city in a sea of fire. Carrying her daughter on her back, she escaped to the field at the side of Shinano River. When she came back home the next morning, she was astonished:

> My home had burned to the ground. All my dowry and the beautiful dressing table my father had made for me from our family sandal tree were burned so completely that I could not help crying out. Oh God, it was too cruel! This was the first time that my home was destroyed.

Mrs Sugiyama's husband did not come back straight after the war, so her family thought he was dead. Both her mother and brothers persuaded her to remarry. The eldest brother said that as it was pitiful to be a woman with a child; she could leave her daughter with him and he would take the responsibility of bringing her up. Mrs Sugiyama disagreed. Several months later her husband came back with a surprised question 'Whose child is she?' when he saw their daughter. He did not know he already had his own daughter. After that they went to her husband's birthplace in Mie prefecture, but they soon moved to Nagoya because there were no jobs in the rural district.

In Nagoya, Mrs Sugiyama delivered two more daughters at the age of 25. When her children became older and she did not need to take care of them constantly, she began to work as a warehouse keeper in a factory that produced tyres for cars. Thanks to her 18-years career in a big company she was able to enrol in the Welfare Pension scheme. After she retired, she also joined the National Pension Scheme. As a result she was able to receive a reasonable pension allowance each month.

Her husband was quite a skilful craftsman, who could earn several times as much as the monthly salary of an ordinary salary-man by working. They were financially well off when they were in Nagoya. They wanted to build a home of their own, so they worked hard and soon realised their dream.

However, hardly had they breathed a sigh of relief when their home was destroyed by a typhoon. That was the second time Mrs Sugiyama's home was destroyed. She did not cry for she thought that maybe she was doomed to be unable to possess her own home.

Since the compulsory retirement age in her company was quite low, Mrs Sugiyama retired at the age of 52 and then went to work for another company for two years. At the age of 58, she and her husband moved to live with their eldest daughter, who was then living near the Higashimurayama station with her husband and two children. They put in a lot of money to help their daughter construct a new house and in return they were assigned a ten-mat room to live in. Her son-in-law was a highly motivated person but he was not good at management. Eventually his business collapsed and their new home had to be taken in return for liabilities. So Mrs Sugiyama and her husband lost their home for the third time and had to live in cramped conditions with their daughter and her family in a rented 3 DK[7] apartment.

Their grandchildren had grown up, so it was quite inconvenient to live together. Mrs Sugiyama began to think seriously about entering a home for the elderly. Precisely at that time there was a campaign of donating mops and nightwear, etc. at the women's association in the community she lived. She bought many new towels, and made cushions wholeheartedly. Soon she received a letter of thanks that indicated where her donations had gone. It contained the name of Kotobuki.

The housewife next door told her that a five-storey building had been newly constructed for Kotobuki, and she offered to go for a look with her. During the visit to the home, Mrs Sugiyama found out that an applicant could choose either a single room or a double room. In addition, the facilities were well equipped; the fee was not so expensive; and the home would consider her first because of the contribution she had made, so she applied on the spot. However, both her daughter and her husband objected strongly. Mrs Sugiyama persuaded her husband that it would be better for them to try living in the home for a while, and if he really did not like it, they could move out. He agreed and they moved into Akashia. She recalled:

> That year I was 60 years old and my husband was 69. Unfortunately my husband died eight months later. According to the regulations at that time, a husband or wife had to move out if his/her spouse died. So I began to live with my daughter again shortly after the death of my husband. The warden told me that I could move back to Akashia if I liked when he came to attend my husband's funeral. Thanks to his kind invitation, I have been able to live comfortably in Akashia ever since.

Mrs Sugiyama chose Akashia out of economic considerations. Sixteen years ago, if she had rented a small apartment with her husband, their savings would have run out quickly. But in Akashia, she did not need to use a lot of money: the fees for accommodation, meals, water, baths and so forth are all included in the monthly charges. Compared to the rent for an elderly person living in the community on his/her own, the fee, in her case about 49,200 yen a month, was inexpensive. In addition, in contrast to the residents in Sazanka who had to share a room even though they might be paying more than her, Mrs Sugiyama had her private room so she could do anything she liked there. When she thought about this, she considered herself lucky. She thought that she had made the right decision 16 years ago. She said:

> When an old person reaches this age, it's unreasonable for him/her to cook meals and travel about by him/herself without the care of the family. Here everything is done for us and we also have a health check regularly. It is very safe to live here. So I would say that there are good points in the Japanese welfare system. Some people may criticise that we healthy elderly persons are clever ones who know how to depend on welfare. I don't think so, for I am paying the fee. However, I do not intend to become a user who exploits welfare. You see, I am now taking part in all the clubs that require physical exercise for I want to keep fit and maintain my autonomy. I don't want to live till I am 90 years old and have my diapers changed by others. And I would not like to be indebted to the country or the staff members here.

Mrs Sugiyama thought her hobbies and extensive links with friends in the outside community had made her life in Akashia worthwhile. She became interested in figure-making in clay after she befriended Tetsuko, a neighbour two years older than her. Born as the daughter of a notable doctor in Higashimurayama City, Tetsuko never married because of her poor health, but she was refined and had a lot of hobbies. She invited Mrs Sugiyama to learn figure-making in a handicraft class in Shinjuku. Enchanted by the figures, the two ladies paid for the classes out of their pocket money and made a lot of figures. Mrs Sugiyama gave them to her grandchildren as presents when they entered school. Through these works of art that could be preserved for a long time, she thought they would be able to remember her. She also presented them to friends. She felt a particular feeling of satisfaction when she saw how her grandchildren and friends appreciated receiving the figures.

While they were making the clay figures, Tetsuko suggested holding an exhibition. They went to talk with the welfare commissioner in the community, who advised that it would be better to hold an exhibition in the city cultural centre in the name of Kotobuki rather than personally. Then the welfare commissioner talked about the issue to the first principal of Kotobuki, and the exhibition was later held successfully. This was the origin of the Elderly Handicrafts Exhibition in Higashimurayama City. Mrs Sugiyama exhibited her works for more than seven years until she became unable to make small things due to her failing eyesight.

It was under the influence of Tetsuko that Mrs Sugiyama felt herself to have grown up. Tetsuko introduced her to a local cultural and recreational group for the elderly. There they went mountain climbing regularly, attending various activities and classes with old people in local communities, and making friends who formed a meaningful social network for her. Tetsuko was the best friend and teacher she had ever had. However, regretfully, she had passed away 10 years before. Mrs Sugiyama was nostalgic about the days when she was with Tetsuko.

> For six or seven years after I entered Akashia, I went out nearly every day. So both the residents and the matrons were not familiar with me for quite a long time. To associate with friends outside is the last pleasure in my life, and I have more friends in the community than in the home. I still maintain contact with the friends I made in the women's association and in the elderly group I mentioned before.

After Tetsuko died, she continued commuting to the city cultural centre to participate in the activities of the community elderly group. It was there that she fell in love with a man who has left her with many beautiful memories. At first, they went mountain climbing and took part in various cultural activities with other friends. It was their common interest in travel and art that made them feel close. The man was an honest man who had formerly worked in a big bank. He had devoted most of his life to supporting his family, paying for his children's education in first-class universities, and for his wife's wardrobe. However, when he retired and began to think about his own life, he found himself already an old man. In order to live a meaningful later life, he asked Mrs Sugiyama to go out with him in public, but she could not because he had his wife. However, they enjoyed many outings together.

> We love travelling, so we went on trips around the country. We strolled on the beach, painted at the foot of the hills and drank under the cherry blossoms. It was the happiest period in my life when I was together with him, even though love came late in our twilight years. I usually applied to stay out overnight whenever we went for a trip, and I was careful to avoid troubling others so I do not think I have done anything that tarnished the name of Kotobuki.
>
> Our secret love was maintained until he died of cancer three years ago. Two weeks before he passed away, he called to tell me that he was unwilling to let me see his haggard figure. 'I am dying. I had hoped I could enjoy life with you longer, but it is impossible. I was lucky to come across you at the time when I had finished my life long duty of serving my family and wanted to have my own way of life. Because of you I have had a good time in the last stage of my life. Thank you very much.' What he said moved me to tears.

Recounting her story, Mrs Sugiyama could hardly hold back her tears. She had deep feelings beneath her solid expression.

> I am a lucky person. Since I came to Akashia, I have enjoyed my hobbies, toured around the country, made a lot of friends, and I have a beautiful memory of romance in my twilight years. I have had nothing tedious and no regrets in my life. Here is my last paradise. I am really grateful to Kotobuki for having brought me all this.

Mrs Sugiyama expressed her overall satisfaction with living in Akashia.

At the same time, she also mentioned some unpleasant points about the home. Primarily, since the home was composed of homogeneously elderly persons, it lacked vigour and hope. She said, 'It makes you feel depressed when the people around you die one after another, especially those who you know well. You have to always think that next time it might be yourself. There is no future here.'

The other thing was gossip. Unlike Mrs Sugiyama, the residents in Akashia tend to confine themselves to the small world of the home.

> Their world is so small that they have nothing to do but to speak ill of others and quarrel with others over tedious things such as who should eat first, do the laundry first, and enter the bathtub first. And the residents seldom feel gratitude.

Mrs Sugiyama suggested they should be more modest, try to live the group life harmoniously and be more open-minded in enjoying the limited time available to them.

Mrs Sugiyama was satisfied with all the service the home offered. The only desire she had at present was to die suddenly. She hoped to look after her own affairs as long as possible while she was alive. She did not want to stay in a hospital too long because she was unwilling to become a burden to others.

Chinseki Aoki

> 'I still have an ambition: to become a scholar.'

With a Japanese-language dictionary, several notebooks, and a box of pastels arranged in meticulous order on a table in the reading room, Mr Aoki started to do his lessons for the day: classical Japanese, mathematics and civic studies for middle school second-year students, and painting. He was a 78-year-old resident of Akashia. Except for going out to see his doctor and going shopping, Mr Aoki spent most of his time studying. He wanted to realise his dream of becoming a scholar.

Born the eldest son in a politician's family in Tokorozawa City, Mr Aoki was called a 'grandmother's child' (*obāsanko*) by his relatives in his childhood. He was so timid that he was often ill-treated by his two younger sisters and brother. 'Maybe I was too mild and my sisters were stronger in character; my mother always said that I should change places with my sisters', Mr Aoki recalled his childhood. His father was mayor of the city and too busy to care about the son. The only one of the siblings raised by his grandmother (all the others were raised by his mother), Mr Aoki felt somehow alienated from his mother.

Mr Aoki had long known that he was not a strong-minded person. In primary school, he got good grades but was said to be incapable of leading his classmates. In middle school, he was very eager to become a soldier. But his uncle said 'A serviceman needs the ability to rule over others. You are not suitable to enter the army. You are the type of a scholar.'

Eventually he was unable to go to the army, because he contracted tuberculosis when he was about to graduate from middle school. He was hospitalised for three months in 1943 and later stayed at home for convalescence. Since he had nothing to do at home and his ears were ringing severely, he became irritated and offensive. He did not obey his mother and lay in his bed all the time. Maybe it was because of this unstable psychological state that his mother decided to send him to a mental hospital in 1946, to which he stayed connected for nearly 30 years.

After he was discharged from the hospital in 1949, he was admitted to the high school of his alma mater. He had planned to go to university, but was forced to enter the mental hospital again because he was unable to find a job during the period after he was discharged. He said that if he had not been hospitalised for the second time, his life would have been different. He commented:

> In Japan, especially a long time ago, people had prejudice against mental patients. One's future ended if one was diagnosed as a mental patient. So no one would like to employ a person like me who had been discharged from a mental hospital. Even if such a person was employed, he could not work for long. He would be forced to quit because of the intolerance of others. I couldn't understand why my family, especially my mother, wanted to put me into the hospital again. Apart from not looking for a job and occasionally opposing my mother, I did nothing wrong and I had never thought I was a mental patient. I was just weak in mind! She cared much more about appearances (*sekentei*) than about the future of her son.

Mr Aoki became a real patient during his second stay in the hospital. The continuous treatment with electro-shocks destroyed his physical health to such an extent that he finally became a schizophrenic. Although disgusted with the electro-shock treatment, he had no power to refuse. He thought he must have been very sick at that time.

Normally one lives a life without contact with culture and characters if one enters a mental hospital. Mr Aoki felt strong sympathy with the saying 'Free time without literature is death' because he had nothing to do during the day. Fortunately he was able to share a room with a former university student who suggested that he write and read without wasting time. He borrowed textbooks from the student and began to learn algebra, geography, history and English, to write essays and keep a diary. Also he took part in clubs, wrote for the bulletin of the hospital and held a personal exhibition of watercolour paintings. He did his best to study hard. He took people who had refined hobbies and lived a human life such as Winston Churchill and MacArthur as his models, and he encouraged himself to study hard with proverbs such as 'Study is just like pushing a car on a slope, the car will go back again if you are careless', 'Piling up small particles of dust will eventually create a mountain', and 'Rome was not built in a day.'

During the 21 years of his second hospitalisation, he had learned the algebra for middle school twice, and the English several times. He had finished reading *Makuranosōshi* and *The Analects of Confucius* (*Rongo*), kept 70 notebooks and read more than 300 books. Besides, he had spent six months getting a distance-learning certificate in proofreading while working outside the hospital. He enjoyed distance learning. And he had long had an aspiration to become a scholar, one indifferent to riches and honours.

Around the age of 49, Mr Aoki was discharged for the purpose of 'outside participation' (*gaibu sanka*).[8] Before that, in his 40s, the hospital suggested to those who had almost recovered that they should live and work in the community by themselves. Mr Aoki wanted to get married as well as to live in his own home, so he tried to persuade his mother to let him out, but she disagreed and said that he was unable to get a wife. So he gave up. Later he was discharged and began to work in a printing company in Higashimurayama City. But without his mother's permission, he was unable to live in his home, which had already been succeeded to by his elder brother. He lived in the 1DK apartment his brother rented him near the Hagiyama Station. He recalled the hardships when he lived by himself:

Can you imagine how difficult it was for a man to start an independent life at the age of about 50? I had to learn every bit of housework from the very beginning: to go shopping, to cook and to do the laundry. I felt envious when I saw my neighbours sitting around the table eating Japanese hotpot (*oden*). I told my father during a family visit that I wanted to go back home and I wanted to eat family dishes. He promised to talk to my mother but it turned out to be in vain. After that I lived in my small apartment alone for nearly 16 years. And I worked for the company continuously for nine years as a proofreader. I resigned ahead of the compulsory retirement age because the company moved to a district too far away for me to commute.

Since Mr Aoki understood that it was impossible for him to live in his own home, he thought that his last refuge might be a home for the elderly. His doctor advised him to apply for a *yōgo* home. Mr Aoki told what the doctor had said to his caseworker, who later contacted the Welfare Department in Higashimurayama City where he resided. The officials gave him several addresses of *keihi* homes in the city and his brother also brought him some pamphlets about *yōgo* homes. Mr Arai, the one who had told him not to waste time in the mental hospital, was then living in Kotobuki, so Mr Aoki went to ask him about the conditions of the home. Since it sounded like a nice place, he applied for admission to Akashia a few days later.

At that time he was living on the Welfare Pension and a remittance from his brother, so he had no financial problems living alone. In addition, he still had a desire to live a social life and enjoy freedom. That was why he turned down the offer when the official called to tell him that he was admitted. Several years later, his brother and a staff member from the hospital who came to visit him suggested again that he start the application procedure. He followed their suggestion and moved to live in Akashia at the age of 66.

Kotobuki was not unfamiliar to Mr Aoki, because he had commuted to the day care centre for several years before he entered Akashia. Since he had long lived in a mental hospital, he was used to group life. Consequently, it was quite easy for him to adapt to the new environment. His mild character and his willingness to offer to do errands for others helped him to get along well with other residents. He continued subscribing to the Asahi and Yomiuri newspapers and gave them to the matrons after he finished reading them. He also kept on writing essays and painting watercolours, and showed them both to the matrons and other residents. By doing so he intended to enhance the mutual familiarity between him and others, because a friend told him that a resident should develop a relationship with the surrounding environments by his/her own efforts in the home. He was quite satisfied with his cultural life in Kotobuki.

> Being a member of the *haiku* club here, I compose about 60 *haiku* each month. I bring a notebook with me when I go on overnight trips so that I can write down some impromptu sentences. I have contributed my *haiku* to the Asahi Haiku Column and the city newspaper. I have also published a small book that is a collection of my essays. It is a really delightful thing to see my own work in print. The matrons said that I was a type of naturalistic writer. I have kept on studying and reading as well. Since I came here I have read about 200 books and improved my study method. I am happy that I can have a cultural life in the home.

Mr Aoki thought it was very convenient with many shops, banks and the post office near the home. He liked to keep in touch with his middle-school classmates, as well as inmates and staff in the hospital by letters, so it was good to have the post office nearby. The other good points of the home, according to him, included the openness towards people who had psychological disorders and the freedom to spend money. He said:

> A number of residents with illnesses similar to mine and other kinds of disabilities are living with the ordinary elderly here. And I am managing my money on my own. So as a whole, I am satisfied with my life here. My studies are progressing smoothly. I still have the dream of becoming a scholar. Compared to other patients, I think I am successful in leading a social life. I am living a life according to my own will.

The only unsatisfactory thing about living in Akashia was that the limitations on time. A resident has to get up at six o'clock in the morning and go to bed at nine in the evening. As all room lights were turned off at 9:00 p.m., Mr Aoki stayed in the reading room to study till 9:15 p.m. and go to sleep around 9:30. He used to get up at 10 a.m. and study till 10:30 p.m. when he was in his own apartment. So it was too early for him to get up and to go to bed.

One other thing he was concerned about was that he was unable to stay overnight with his family. In the mental hospital, a patient would get a reward if he/she stayed outside for three consecutive days. However there was no such regulation in Kotobuki. He looked forward to going back home to meet his family, especially during holidays such as the Japanese New Year, but he was unable to. 'I think that the most probable reason is that my mother and my brother don't want me back. Maybe they feel that it is unpleasant to have me, a former mental patient, near them. You know, my mother is such an exacting person that my brother couldn't get married until he was 60'; his eyes darkened.

> My brother asked me not to come back home without informing him. He said 'Mother is too quarrelsome to get along well with my wife. It will become more troublesome if you come.' I know that my mother has treated me differently since I was a child. I feel she has never loved me. She didn't inform me when my father died or when my brother got married. I learned from the newspaper that my father died in a traffic accident. Since my family didn't tell me I was unable to attend his funeral. I have told my mother many times on the phone that I wanted to stay overnight at home, but it seems that she never told my brother about this. Without my brother's permission I can't go back home.
>
> I feel mortified at the unfairness with which my family has treated me. However I will endure it. I am very happy every time my brother comes to see me. I also felt delighted when my parents came to visit me in the hospital. You know, love from my family is important to me. Till last year my brother came to give me pocket money every month and I used to send home a letter of thanks each month. But he was diagnosed with cancer in the stomach and has been in the hospital for a year. I worry about him. If he dies, what will happen to his wife and their little

child who is only a middle school student? My mother is bedridden now. She is 90 years old. I have kept on writing her letters and calling her on Mother's Day ever since I was institutionalised. She is always my mother! I hope I can meet her again while she is still alive.

Despite some discontent with his family, Mr Aoki was quite satisfied with his achievements and the quality of life in Akashia. He thought of himself as a mental patient who had returned to society successfully. Sometimes he would think about death and feel dreadful. But in thinking that human beings would remain in existence even if he were dead, he felt at ease. His wish was to keep fit as long as possible and keep on studying. 'My life's desire is to become a scholar. I will continue working to realise my dream', he said.

Tsumako Yamaguchi

'My life is one that burns with enthusiasm.'

After setting a cup of Pocari Sweat and a cup of green tea on the drinks tray, I brought it to Mrs Yamaguchi's room on the third floor on the north-ernmost side of Aoba. Those who lived on the north side of the floor were residents with a relatively high level of independence. So except for changing diapers or supplying water to those who needed assistance, the matrons rarely came to see them.

The first time I came to Mrs Yamaguchi's room, I was captivated by the many books on her bedside nightstand, some of which were written by the famous Christian Kanzō Uchimura and the psychoanalyst Hayao Kawai. 'She must be a person related to academia. What kind of life story is concealed behind the small body of this old granny?' I became curious about the old woman who was busy folding tissue papers on her bed. After that I often stood by her bed and talked to her for several minutes whenever I came to her room. At first, she was quite restrained. But when she learned that I came from China to study the welfare conditions of the elderly in Japan, her eyes lit up:

It's the first time I've talked to a Chinese person since I came back from China more than 50 years ago. You are doing the same thing I did in my younger days. You make me recall my past when I burned with enthu-siasm to teach Japanese in foreign countries.

I found out that she was an ardent student of human beings. She had taught Japanese in Manchuria, Mongolia and Korea during the war and after the war she had devoted herself to the world of Japanese welfare enterprises together with her husband.

Mrs Yamaguchi was born in 1906, the youngest child in a farm family in Hiroshima. Maybe it was because of the influence of her parents, who had studied in a temple school (*terakoya*),[9] that Mrs Yamaguchi liked to study when she was very young.

> I have almost forgotten my childhood. The only thing I remember is that there was a school near my home. From my home, I could hear the melody of physical exercise and music classes, and the voices of reading and playing of the children. This made me feel as if my home was in the school. When I was a little child, I looked forward to studying in a school.

She tried to hold on to the memories of her remote past.

The strong desire to study in a university drove her to Tokyo after she graduated from middle school. Boarding at her uncle's home, Mrs Yamaguchi studied at the Department of Japanese Literature in Nihon University while at the same time earning her tuition by working as a private tutor. Although Nihon University is a coeducational university, few female students could be found on the campus. Mrs Yamaguchi was the only female student who majored in classical literature in her class. Among the subjects she learned, she liked *haiku* and English best. Since her dream was to receive the highest education and become an independent professional woman, she objected to the words of her English teacher who said 'A woman is happier at home rather than studying in a university.' To realise her ideal, she worked hard and graduated with excellent grades. After that, she became a teacher, teaching English and Japanese at a girls' school.

Around the age of 28, a good friend introduced her to a man who was interested in social welfare. Their common enthusiasm for their jobs drew them together and soon they got married on the premise that she could continue working. At that time, the Japanese government was promoting economic and cultural policies under the 'Great East Asia Co-prosperity Sphere' scheme in East Asian countries. One of the cultural promotion programmes sponsored by the Ministry of Foreign Affairs was to dispatch teachers to the mainland to spread the Japanese language. The couple went to work in Manchuria after their marriage. Mrs Yamaguchi worked as a curriculum coordinator in a 'good-neighbour women's school' (*zenrin joshi gakkō*) in Hōten in Manchuria when her husband was dispatched there as a section chief in the welfare department of the South Manchuria Railway Company. Later she went to Mongolia to teach Japanese in the 'School for Building-up Mongolia' (*kōmō gakkō*), which was established by the Mongolian government with funds from the Foreign Affairs Ministry and the Japanese Women's Union in Mongolia.

> All students were the children of the kings and feudal lords from the 47 *ki*.[10] I was responsible for teaching Japanese in the primary school

section. The classes were taught in Baos, a kind of round-shaped house common in Mongolia. Waiting for me to turn up, the students always gathered in the Bao far earlier than I did. And they always had endless questions to ask me. I was so moved by their enthusiasm for learning that I made strenuous efforts to teach them. I loved my students very much. I also loved the beautiful grasslands and carriages as well as the genuine character of the people. I was really happy during the five years I taught there.

After finishing the term in Mongolia, she went to teach at a girls' school in Korea for a while. One of her students there later came to study in Kyoto and became a teacher in a women's college in Nara. She said her teaching career in foreign countries had left with her numerous beautiful memories.

My best time in my 30s was spent in teaching Japanese in foreign countries. I think I was really burning at that time. Working always took precedence over my family life. My husband and I had lived separately for many years when we were on the mainland: I teaching Japanese in Mongolia and other places, and he working and teaching in various places in Manchuria and Beijing. Both of us were so absorbed in our jobs that we did not even have the time to think about having a baby. However I felt fulfilled during that period of my life. I think he was satisfied too.

Mrs Yamaguchi fixed her eyes on a photo on the nightstand with admiration. It was her deceased husband, a nice gentleman with an affectionate smile. 'He was ten years older than me. So he was more a brother than a husband to me', she said, 'Influenced by him, I became a Christian too.'

As soon as the war ended, they went back to Yamagata Prefecture, her husband's hometown. A good friend of his, also a senior official who had run a relief institution funded by a church, asked Mr Yamaguchi to take over the institution before he went to study social work in the United States. This started their careers in social work. Mr Yamaguchi had been in charge of welfare affairs before he went to China. After he became the warden of the institution, he began to establish a facility to house children who had lost their parents in the war and children who for some reasons could not be cared for by their parents. Mrs Yamaguchi assisted him in his job and became the nurse director and later the principal of the nursing institution for children (*jidō yōgo shisetsu*).[11] Some of the children there later studied at the College of Social Work in Tokyo and took up leadership positions in the field of social welfare.

Mrs Yamaguchi also helped her husband to expand his welfare enterprise by establishing a *yōgo* home and a *tokuyō* home for the elderly. Her husband was a member of the advisory committee that created the Law for the Welfare of the Children and the Law for the Welfare of the Elderly. They also made efforts to cultivate grassroots volunteering among high school students and local citizens. During the operation of the institution, she found herself so ignorant in developmental childhood psychology that she went to study in the College of Social Work for a year.

Mrs Yamaguchi thought it important for people working in nursing institutions for children to learn something about clinical psychology, because the staff must deal with a lot of counselling related to the development of the children. 'Can you see those pictures over there?' she pointed to a pile of pictures on the chair beside the portable toilet:

These 143 pictures were drawn by a child who came to live in the institution due to maltreatment and abandonment by his parents. I collected them over a two-year period and studied the personality formation of the child by analysing the changes in the paintings. I presented the results at the children's well-being study meeting of the Ninth International Conference for Social Welfare and the paper was highly evaluated by many specialists. It was a major achievement in my life.

She continued to talk about her achievements in the area of practical social work:

My husband and I established a research institute for the welfare of children in 1966, the year he retired. We mainly treated autistic children at our institute. After I retired at the age of 60, I went to study speech therapy at the Yokohama Junior College for three years while at the same time working as a lecturer in the Child Guidance Clinic (*jidō sōdan-jo*). Having obtained the certificate, I went back to work for our own research institute, using speech therapy and game therapy in treatment. In 1989, my husband died of cancer and I had to close the institute and move to live with my daughter in Tokyo.

Mrs Yamaguchi lived with her daughter, son-in-law and grandson in a 2DK apartment for a couple of years, and she later rented a small house nearby to live on her own. Since she knew that her daughter worried about her but was unable to take care of her on account of the business she was running, she applied to a *yōgo* home. She had lived in Sazanka for several years before she was transferred to Aoba a year ago.

I fell and badly injured my hip when I was in the washroom. I broke my hipbones and the contusions spread a sunset of colours over my buttocks and thigh. I was sent to the hospital but the doctor said it was too dangerous to operate on me, as I was over 90. So I have had to suffer the bitter pains and live a life confined to my wheelchair and bed ever since.

With this, she strenuously lifted her body from the bed, wanting to transfer to the wheelchair at the bedside. Slowly moving her body and lowering her feet to the ground, Mrs Yamaguchi took a breath for a few minutes while preparing for the bitter struggle of standing up.

The most distressing thing in her life now was the stinging pain she has to endure each time she changed her position. It usually took her half an hour or so to get into the wheelchair from the bed and vice versa. With an unmovable body, the things she could do were limited. Although she wanted to put the pictures in order and send them back to the library she borrowed them from, she could not do that. She also wanted to write letters and keep a diary. Sometimes she tried to write something but had to stop very soon because of the pain of maintaining a fixed position and the trembling of her hand. And her poor eyesight did not allow her to read long. So most of the day she was lost in meditation (*meisō*): recalling her younger days, her dreams and endeavours in the past. She said, 'I have no regret for I have burned with enthusiasm all my life and I have carried out what I was pursuing in my life. I devoted myself to my career.'

But when thinking about her family life, she always felt sorry for her daughter.

> I was so busy working and lived apart from my husband so much that I could not afford to think about having a baby in my 30s. I delivered my only daughter by Caesarean section at the age of 41. I wanted to look after her by myself, but the heavy responsibility of running three institutions forced me to put my career before my daughter. Many unfortunate children needed my care and love. As a result, I was unable to manage both family and career. Some years later, I cried when I heard my daughter say: 'I respect my father but I could not respect you as my biological mother.' I regret that I had not been able to give enough care to my daughter who longed for my love. I still remember what she said. This is the biggest failure in my life.

There were some ill feelings between them when her daughter was a teenager. But now they were getting along quite well. Her daughter married her high school classmate, who was very nice to Mrs Yamaguchi. The couple and her grandson came to visit her regularly and bring her food and pocket money. They also sent her cards and presents on special days such as her birthday, Mother's Day and New Year's Day. 'Nothing is better than their coming to see me. With my daughter in my heart, I don't feel lonely', she said. Although her health was deteriorating and she had no friends to talk to in Aoba, she was satisfied with her institutional life.

> The staff members take good care of us. And I am trying my best to maintain my autonomy. I attend my favourite *haiku* club twice a month. The warden is a very understanding and nice person. We sometimes

discuss the problems and current trends in the field of social welfare. I feel satisfied with living here. And I had the honour of representing all the residents in Kotobuki in giving an address of thanks at the celebration meeting on the Respect-for-the-Aged Day last year.

Her wish was to live a psychologically independent life as long as possible and to try her best to keep fit till God came to welcome her. She had asked the warden to hold her funeral service in Aoba, and her daughter would bring her ashes back to Yamagata Prefecture to bury them together with her husband. She said that she had prepared herself well for death. She felt at ease with God and her faith was with her.

Satisfaction, accomplishment and failure

Freed, an American clinical social worker, states that life review or reminiscing about the past can provide old people with a chance to look back over the paths they have walked, and to evaluate the achievements and failures they have made in their lives (Freed 1993: 16). Savishinsky pointed out that when institutionalised elderly spoke about their lives and sense of self, they centred on 'themes' such as 'accomplishment, rewards, and punishments' (1991: 106).

Reminiscing about the past also helps the residents in Kotobuki value their lives. In remembering their histories and recounting their current lives, the residents concentrated on the issues of accomplishment, reward, failure and punishment when they tried to identify their past and current ego. The five residents in this chapter, Mrs Matsumoto, Mr Gotō, Mrs Sugiyama, Mr Aoki and Mrs Yamaguchi present five distinct life experiences. They each used their own language to express what they thought about their career, their war experiences, their marriages and family life, their achievement and failure, their coping strategies for institutionalisation and life satisfaction. All of them knew where they were and why they were there, regardless of whether they liked it or not. Mrs Matsumoto and Mr Aoki became acclimatised to their situation, Mr Gotō was resigned, Mrs Sugiyama enjoyed it, and Mrs Yamaguchi was grateful.

Overall, they showed satisfaction with living in Kotobuki for its security and services. Asked about 'the best period of their lives', except for a sixth of my informants (those who had experienced extreme hardship or mishaps in their earlier years), all replied that the present was the happiest. Most informants regarded their 30s and 40s as the most productive time of their life, for women usually a period when they were the caretakers of their children and for men a golden age in their careers.

Among the people I interviewed, Mrs Matsumoto felt the most fulfilled in the period when she raised her six children and ran the home business at the same time, even though it was quite tough. A person with strong religious faith, she attributed the hardship she endured, her unhappy marriage and the mishaps her children were trapped in, such as her son's frequent remarriages and her daughter's divorce, to karmic bonds. She believed that the sexual sin committed by her great grandfather, who had divorced three times, was manifested in all the punishments suffered by her and her children. Thus she sought salvation in Ōyamanezu no Mikoto and her personified shaman Tomomaru-hime. She thought her healthy body and security in living in Sazanka was brought by her devotion to her religion.

Mr Gotō, in the eyes of some of the residents and staff members, was a failure fed on welfare. But he had his own evaluation of his life. His accounts of the past and the present were a blend of hubris and regret. He regarded his 30s and early 40s as his golden age, when he was able to make big money, buy property, marry a younger wife and was surrounded by many fawning friends and relatives. He boasted of his ability to make money and his flexibility in quickly adapting to his surroundings. But his eyes turned dark as he spoke of his connection with his family and his status of being institutionalised. Greatly remorseful for his greed, enchantment with gambling, irrational investment in stocks and neglect of his family in his earlier years, he religiously put his physical disability as well as his destiny of ending up in an institution down to the sins he had committed. Such a spiritual enlightenment made him ready to be punished and to tolerate loneliness.

Mrs Sugiyama was content with her life. Though early experiences during the war did not bring her happy memories, her power in her family, her children, career and material comforts offset the anguish of losing her home. She chose to live in Akashia on her own. Whereas entering a home usually cost others their freedom, it had brought Mrs Sugiyama opportunity. A private room ensured her privacy and freedom. Her extrovert character and wide interests made it easy for her to make friends in the community and find new roles instead of losing them. Rather than confine herself to the small world of the institution, she endeavoured to widen her horizon by involving herself in community activities. This not only generated a network but also brought her the beautiful memories of a romance in her twilight years.

Mr Aoki, a recovered mental patient, related his past and present life mainly through comparing with his experience in a mental hospital with his current life. He evaluated his life focusing on two issues: his life-long studies and the interaction with his family. His unfulfilled dream of becoming a scholar had made him keep on studying and successes from his self-learning, such as having published his *haiku* and essays in newspapers and magazines as well as getting compliments from peers and matrons gave him a sense of achievement. His biggest dissatisfaction was the impossibility of living with his family, and the discrimination shown towards him by his mother. He understood that his long hospitalisation in the mental hospital was caused by his weak will power, but more importantly, the following factor – 'the continuing social prejudice toward the mentally ill may have led to virtual abandonment of the patient by his or her family' (Lebra and Lebra 1986: 343). Unable to obtain his family's love and acceptance that he had always longed for, he felt both anguish and despair. Except for this discontent, he was proud of having been able to build up his will power and return to society successfully. He regarded Akashia as his last refuge.

Mrs Yamaguchi regarded her life-long career as the most satisfying endeavour in her life. She considered the influence of her husband on her life remarkable. Though poor memory often caused her to repeat what she had said a moment ago, she could speak clearly of her university education, the schools and associations she worked for in Manchuria and Mongolia, the title of her paper presented at an international conference, and the opening date of the Yamaguchi Library that volunteers established as a memorial to the achievements of her husband and herself in the field of social work. A period when she had burned with dreams and enthusiasm as a professional thus became the most memorable for a woman who was now living mainly in an inner world of her own. However, a sense of regret for having been unable to be a good mother sometimes marred her feeling of career success.

QOL and its factors

In analysing the life stories told by nursing home residents, Gubrium (1993) found that residents' perception of their institutional experiences and their assessment of their quality of life and care could not be separated from their life-long experience in or outside the institution. Reasons for institutionalisation, their images of domestic life, religious beliefs, and sense of independence and dignity could shape residents' views of their institutionalisation. This was the case for the residents in Kotobuki.

The five persons came to Kotobuki in different trajectories: Mrs Matsumoto because of intra-familial tension; Mr Gotō out of homelessness, illness and indigence; Mrs Sugiyama for poor housing conditions; Mr Aoki because of mental illness and the absence of family caretakers; and Mrs Yamaguchi for her severe physical impairments. As shown in the narratives of these five residents, different reasons for entry, differences in personal character, life history, attitudes toward elderly care and institutionalisation, have inevitably generated a kaleidoscopic view of institutional life, different degrees of life satisfaction and different coping strategies for living a group life.

From the narration of the five residents, we can ascertain that material comfort and security, services and activity programmes provided by the homes are primary factors to be connected to life satisfaction and the quality of life of the residents. Mr Gotō's physical disability, the complaints of Mrs Yamaguchi and other residents of Aoba about their ailments, as well as most informants' intention to maintain good health indicate that health is crucial in later life. Mrs Sugiyama's decision to enter Akashia of her own volition has meant she is more satisfied than those who were forced to come to the home. Apart from these, the stories also suggest some major issues that influence QOL of the institutionalised elderly: religion, interpersonal relationships, autonomy and the issue of death. Here I would like to enumerate these factors by incorporating other residents' views and their behaviours.

Attitudes towards elderly care and institutionalisation

In Kotobuki, a number of residents, who had suffered from distress related to family friction, hardship and loneliness, found that living in the home gave them the opportunity to construct new meanings in their lives. However, as I have mentioned, living with their eldest son, surrounded by their respectful grandchildren and receiving attentive care from their daughter-in-law was the ideal for ageing parents. Residents, especially those who were born in the Meiji and Taisho periods (who were aged 75 years and above at the time I conducted my fieldwork) and brought up in the *ie* households, still hold on to this ideal. Institutionalisation was explained, for instance, as follows: 'Her sons live very near but they never come to visit her', 'If she could have got along well with her daughter-in-law, she would not have come here', 'If my son was still alive, I would not have been here' and so on. In other words, institutionalisation was seen as a failure to achieve this ideal, and as abandonment by one's own children. And the name of 'a home for the elderly' (*rōjin hōmu*) was often identified with the pre-war 'old-age home' (*yōrō-in*), a kind of public relief institution for single or childless elderly, or sometimes even with the legend of *Obasuteyama* by the residents. In short, these old people's attitudes towards institutionalisation were negative.

Residents seldom felt that a home for the elderly was a 'real home'. For instance, Mrs Matsumoto's image of a home for the elderly some 25 years ago was similar to that of a prison. She entered Sazanka with a feeling of having killed herself and with the humiliation of being abandoned, because she had thought that she deserved to live with her eldest son and receive care from the young couple. Entering a home was the last resort for her at the time. Even though she had stayed in Sazanka for a long time and had adapted well to the home life with the help of her religious beliefs, she showed envy when she heard that Chinese elderly were still living in big families with their children and grandchildren. She often commented that the Japanese younger generation was losing virtues such as loyalty, filial piety and perseverance, and that they had become more selfish. She felt her generation to be the victims of the old and new institutions. When she was young, she was taught to follow her father and husband; when she got married, she had to serve her husband and children; and when she became old, she found herself no longer able to depend on her only son. Accordingly she had to take responsibility for her own later life.

Many elderly who came to live in Kotobuki were in a similar situation to that of Mrs Matsumoto, and they shared her ideas and feelings. One day, the oldest male resident on the third floor was seen to be weeping in the reading room. He had hoped to go to and soak in a hot spring with his son before he died. He called his son several times to ask when he would come, but he was always told 'I am too busy to pick you up.' The old man felt sad, and he lamented that children nowadays were no longer '*oya kōkō*' (dutiful to parents) as his generation had been.

Even Mr Gotō, a representative of those who had long deserted their family responsibilities, was nostalgic about the good points of the old *ie* system, such as warmth of family relationships, respect for elderly parents and the obligation to take care of their old relatives, the sick or the handicapped. Though grateful to the government that had enabled him to live a decent life, he still felt it was the last resort to be living in a home, because institutional life only reminded him of isolation, hopelessness, senility and impending death. He thought his deep sadness and loneliness of ending up in a home was caused by his neglect of family duties. But at the same time he also had a feeling of abandonment by his family because his daughter had never tried to find him.

However, the later cohort, who had been born in the Showa period, had adapted to Western values such as democracy and freedom in the post-war educational system, and were largely influenced by modern material life and mass media. Therefore they had a stronger consciousness of basic rights and a different view of institutionalisation. In particular, the development of social services and social concern for the elderly since the 1980s had changed the residents' view of their status. In Kotobuki, many residents in their 60s and early 70s believed that the general image of institutions had become more positive and the standard of life in homes had improved a great deal.

Mrs Matsumoto, for instance, had stopped thinking it shameful to live in Sazanka and began to regard the home as a paradise for its comfort, security and services. The many inquiries about how to apply for entry into a home from her hospitalised room-mates from the local community made her think that institutionalisation had become a recognised social phenomenon. Also she felt lucky to have been able to live in Sazanka when she heard that more than 200 persons were waiting for entry to the home. Mr Gotō found it surprising that there was a boom in elderly people who had children choosing to live in institutions.

Mrs Sugiyama was never embarrassed to tell her outside friends that she was living in a home. Like many other residents in Akashia who did not feel ashamed of being institutionalised, she thought she had the right to receive some welfare services to counteract potential financial problems in old age. Because she had paid taxes when she was working and she entered the home on contract, it was reasonable to buy some welfare services at low prices. And the cessation of constructing new *keihi* homes allowed her to feel fortunate that she was able to live in warmth, security and autonomy cheaply. For Mr Aoki, the freedom to use money, the open environment of the home as well as his acceptance by other residents made him think that Akashia was better than a mental hospital. In the case of Mrs Yamaguchi, her former work experience in welfare institutions had prepared her well for adapting to life in the home.

Interpersonal relationships

Interpersonal relations[12] in Kotobuki include resident–resident relationships, resident–staff relationships and resident–family/other outside visitor relationships. Among these, the most significant one is the resident–resident relationship. Many of my informants held the opinion that 'except for the human relationships, this is a paradise'. From this we may see that interpersonal relationships comprise the most difficult issue facing every resident, especially those who live in Sazanka, because they have to share their room with someone else.

The stories told by the five residents in this chapter show us different ways of handling this difficult issue. Mrs Matsumoto, who thought that friendship was important in leading a happy life in the home, tried to make as many friends as she could. As her philosophy of human relationships was to keep harmony with everybody, she was wary of speaking ill of others in conversations with others. She spoke to everyone, even those she did not like; she kept herself away from potential conflicts by withdrawing from club activities, and she exchanged presents with other residents in order to fulfil obligations (*giri*) in interpersonal relations. She could also tolerate those who spoke ill of her because she knew from her religion that human beings are imperfect. With such an attitude, her interaction with her peers went quite smoothly. The same was true for her relationships with staff members, although she had some negative comments about a certain matron. After she came to Sazanka, she had kept in contact with her daughters by phone and through overnight stays, and she had received pocket money from her son. Thus her relationship with her family was good, too. Her capacity to maintain good interpersonal relationships ensured her a sense of life satisfaction.

Mr Gotō's interpersonal relationships were predominantly restricted to the home because he had no connection with outside friends or family. Thinking it unnecessary to make friends in the home, except for his roommate who was his only close friend or partner in Sazanka, he kept a distance from both his peers and the staff members.

Just as Shield (1988: 138–55) observed in Franklin Nursing Home, restraining oneself from interpersonal interaction is common among the residents in Kotobuki. Few neighbours were observed to visit each other. Even when a person had something to say to another resident, he/she would not enter the room but would stand by the door to have a brief talk. In most cases, residents keep to themselves in their rooms, lying in bed or eating in bed or watching TV. Some stay in the dayroom all day, smoking, dozing and watching TV, mostly speechless. Many said that although their relationships with room-mates and other peers were smooth, they had few close friends in the home. And few residents had any regrets about the shallowness of their neighbourhood interactions. One possible reason why residents withdrew from associating with each other is the inclination towards disengagement (Cumming and Henry 1961).[13]

The social exchange and reciprocity theory[14] may also be able to explain why many residents maintain a superficial relationship with others, and why some of the elderly are reserved in their interpersonal interaction. This could be exemplified in what Mr Gotō had said:

A room-mate may be a help in an emergency. So except for interactions with my room-mate, my relations with other people here are basically *tatemae*.[15] Even if I need help, I'd rather turn to the matrons than to my peers because there is no need to owe *giri* to them. I haven't the resources to repay. You see, after I buy my favourite cigarettes, I have little money left.

He wanted to keep a casual relationship with other residents in order to avoid heavy obligations that he perceived himself as being unable to reciprocate.

It seems that female residents are more aware of social obligations and have more interactions than males do. Some old-timers in Kotobuki were found to give food to their former room-mates or friends in the hallway or in rooms. Mrs Hosokawa, a very popular old woman in Sazanka, saw Mrs Kishimoto, a very wealthy widow who always gave out confectionery to both other residents and matrons, as her friend, but not a very close one.

She is one of the persons I keep association with (*otsukiai no tomodachi*). She brings me food nearly every day. She is rich. She has her own welfare pension, her husband's survivor's pension and a lot of stocks. Even though she pays more than 140,000 yen a month, she still has a lot left, so she can do that. But I cannot.

As she only had a meagre National Pension allowance that was not enough for her to pay for her cigarettes, she mainly depended on her daughter's remittance. She felt pressed when receiving gifts from Mrs Kishimoto, because she had to buy something better to repay her. She thought a poor old woman like her was unable to keep close friendships with many persons. She said:

Even if the person who gives the present may not really expect my repayment, I feel obliged to reciprocate. And even though I really don't want it, I can't ask her not to give it to me. I am repaying once every three times Mrs Kishimoto gives me something. I can't afford more than that.

The examples of Mr Gotō and Mrs Hosokawa tell us that limited financial resources in old age are a big handicap in development and maintenance of friendship. It shows that, despite the frequency of interactions between the residents (who meet each other every day on their floor, in corridors, the dining hall, recreational clubs), their relationship remains at a level that Reiko Atsumi (1989) defines as a '*tsukiai* relationship', whereby a feeling of obligation or social necessity is present and intimacy is difficult to achieve because of the casual and superficial nature of the relationship. There are also other reasons for the lack of interaction, such as the lack of compatible socio-economic backgrounds, similar interests and basic attitudes towards life that could be shared by each other, communication difficulties caused by physical and psychological disabilities, competent residents' 'distancing' or avoidance of the senile (Gubrium 1975: 108–13), and residents' wish to avoid conflicts.

For Mrs Sugiyama, her involvement in activities exclusively with friends in the local community, her diminished network inside the home because of the death of her familiar friends and her unwillingness to join in gossip with others had kept her either only interacting with friends from outside or keeping to herself alone in her room. In the case of Mrs Yamaguchi, her lack of interaction with other residents resulted from her physical impairment, the communicational incapability of her room-mates, and her inclination to meditation. Apart from necessary contacts with staff members, such as receiving care services and attending club activities, neither of them had much communication with the staff. Thus their satisfaction in interpersonal relations was generated mainly from contacts with outside friends and their families.

Though mainly concentrating on his studies and not often involving himself in interaction with others, Mr Aoki used the same strategies to deal with relationships with other residents and the staff members by offering favours to both. He was content with his status in the home because both his peers and the staff treated him the same as the ordinary residents. He had regular contacts with his family, middle-school classmates and his inmate friends in the mental hospital, but his relationship with his family still left much to be desired. He felt a bit frustrated because of his inability to improve this, even though he was very concerned about his family.

Religion

In Japan, a large number of people are flocking to various non-medical healers, especially among the new religions. Those who have psychiatric problems or somatic problems as well as those who want to avoid danger, problems and illnesses seem especially inclined to magico-religious cures. Through teaching the followers that they should blame themselves for failing to choose the right way and by holding lectures and discussions of personal experience as well as ritual activities, conversion to one of these new religions apparently produces a beneficial change for the followers by facilitating greater self-insight, social awareness, and moral responsibility (Sasaki 1986: 355–67).

Mrs Matsumoto was a good example, showing that religion had helped her to cope well with her life. She believed in the many miraculous cures other followers of her religion had written about in the sectarian books: 'Thanks to faith, I am cured of gastric cancer ... sterility ... depression; my son has turned from a delinquent into a disciplined boy; my business has started going along the right lines again' etc., because she thought of herself as an example of someone visited by miracles.

Regarding her institutional life, Mrs Matsumoto talked in a religious way. At the beginning, the experience of institutionalisation was a torment for her. However, Tomomaru-hime helped her gradually adjust to the home environment and the complicated human relationships. According to her, the goddess had not only brought her to a place free of familial tensions, enabled her to enjoy leisure activities, and given her a sense of security through regular health checks, but also had protected her from accidents and illnesses. Mrs Matsumoto believed in the power of her *kamisama* in healing and felt secure with the goddess in her heart. Her strong religious faith in her goddess ensured quite high satisfaction with institutional life and an absence of fear of death.

Such faith in religious healing is not uncommon among elderly residents in Kotobuki. Many residents are followers of Sōka Gakkai, an important new religion in contemporary Japan. They have altars in their rooms. Their devotions to their religion include doing their daily tasks by serving water and food before the altars, chanting a sutra and reflecting on their conduct, and participating in religious activities organised by the church. Others believe in Christ. And the most common faith is devotion to one's own family ancestors. Many of my informants said that they would obtain a psychological tranquillity after finishing their daily services, no matter whether it concerned a *kamisama*, a *Kannon* or the family ancestors. It is evident that religious belief is a very important factor that influences how elderly residents evaluate their life in institutions.

Autonomy

In Kotobuki, the life of the residents was governed by a clockwork schedule of getting up, meals, PT and OT training, club and recreational activities, bathing, going to bed, and the work shifts of the staff members. Individual needs, whether it was for a special type of food, the timing of a treatment or a change of room-mate, had to be accommodated to the routine of the home in order to maintain a well-ordered institutional life. So the issue of autonomy appears to be another point that affects people's perception of home life.

Except for a few residents in Sazanka and most residents in Aoba whose personal preferences were controlled under the institutional regime because of senility and physical disability, other residents could create a schedule of their own. They built it around some meaningful activities: for example, for Mrs Matsumoto, a monthly church pilgrimage, recreational participation, knitting and chatting; for Mr Gotō, the passive pursuit of sitting and watching in the dayroom; for Mrs Sugiyama, hobbies and various inside and outside recreational events; for Mr Aoki, study; and reminiscence and reading for Mrs Yamaguchi.

Some residents challenged the irksomeness of institutional life by assuming their own responsibilities in the home in addition to their entrusted duties, such as dining hall duty, lavatory duty, rubbish duty, newspaper delivery and so on. Mrs Kawamoto had looked after the flower garden and Mr Shinozaki had tended to the garden plants in the courtyard ever since they entered Sazanka. By taking care of the flowers and plants, they gained a sense of 'domesticity' (Savishinsky 1991: 113) – as if they were continuing doing housekeeping tasks in their own home.

Mrs Matsumoto volunteered to clean the teapots after each meal; Mrs Sugiyama swept the stairs and the dining hall in Akashia; Mrs Noji took charge of preparing the damp towels and the sets of seasoning before each meal; and in Aoba Mrs Sugiwara helped to clear away the leftovers and put the dishes in order on the meal cart. These tasks let them think that they were continuing their roles as housewives. Mr Aoki and Mr Akimoto, also a resident in Akashia, took the responsibility of carrying the sacks of sorted rubbish to the garbage pit in order to do something good for others. Mrs Aoki helped Alzheimer's victims, confused residents and persons in wheelchairs in order to feel useful and contented with herself. Even Mr Gotō, who sometimes felt it burdensome to carry the clothes bucket for cleaning down to the laundry room on days he did not feel well, would faithfully fulfil his duties because others were waiting for their clean clothes to wear. In Kotobuki, these self-appointed as well as attributed roles as housekeepers, assistants and volunteers enabled the residents to feel useful and productive and to indirectly reciprocate the home for its services.

Many informants said that their present wishes were to keep fit as long as possible, or not to become senile, and to die quickly without much pain. Witnessing the tremendous changes in her former room-mate, who had gone from being a sane person to a wanderer who needed to be watched all the time, Mrs Matsumoto was sympathetic and said 'It's dreadful to become a senile, to think of the fact that one cannot recognise oneself.' In order to avoid the same fate, she prayed for protection from her *kamisama* every day. And she attended clubs such as table tennis, card playing, Japanese chess and *Go* to keep her body fit and brain active. So did Mrs Sugiyama. She said she would rather die than become senile or bedridden, because she did not want to be a burden to others. Her purpose in playing gateball, table tennis and so forth was to keep fit as long as possible.

Mr Gotō thought it silly to behave like a child when he heard his neighbours, two demented women, sing some nursery songs while clapping their hands. He said that he was not likely to become a senile like Mrs Yanagi who was made fun of by the matrons. He was sad that his memory was declining, but he felt somehow relieved because he was still able to think about something. Both he and Mr Aoki regarded health as the most important issue in their present lives.

Though Mrs Yamaguchi occasionally complained that her body did not follow her brain and that her poor memory failed her a lot, she restrained herself from asking additional favours from the staff members, and she strenuously fought for her autonomy by transferring herself from bed to wheelchair and vice versa in order to wheel herself to the dining hall, the rehabilitation room or the bathroom downstairs.

To these residents, senility means one has to enter a 'relationship of increasingly unilateral dependency' on staff members (Traphagan 1998: 95). To counter this, they wished to die suddenly or to 'exit gracefully from this world', and to extract themselves from the web of their relationships with 'a satisfying sense of not having succumbed to the vicissitudes of helplessness and hopelessness' (Young and Ikeuchi 1997: 236). In short, their fear of senility and hope of dying quickly without suffering chronic illnesses indicate that they want to be in control of themselves and not to be dependent on others. This explains why these residents were active participants in the daily life of the home.

With respect to dependency on indulgence (*amae*), most informants, including those who got along quite well with the matrons and whose personality made it easy for them to get favours from staff members, remarked that although the matrons were very kind and were providing good services for them, they could not 'presume on their goodwill' because there were no blood ties between them and the staff. 'No matter what, they are not my family members' was the common explanation for why the residents refrained from expressing their demands to the staff. They claimed that they should manage their lives by themselves. This evidence contradicts previous studies that suggest that Japanese elderly can *amaeru* to and depend totally on their caretakers (Caudill 1961, 1962; Doi 1962, 1971, 1992; Kiefer 1987, 1990). It seems to me that dependency on indulgence or *amae* of an adult can only occur among family members or affectionate friends.

Dealing with impending death

Just like Mr Gotō, who had said that Sazanka might be the place where he would die, many residents regarded Kotobuki as their last home. It was an terminus for them, coming in alive with luggage and going out dead in a coffin. Ordinarily, it is a taboo to talk about death in public. However in Kotobuki, especially in Aoba, death is not a hidden issue because often we would hear somebody let out an 'I hope God will welcome me soon' or 'It is no good to live too long, I hope to die soon.' All residents have to confront their fate of death: their peers are dying around them; they have attended numerous farewell gatherings for dead residents; and they have to prepare for their own death.

Showing the residents how they would be treated after their death, Kotobuki performs the farewell ritual whenever a resident is dead in order to console the living and make peace with the deceased. This was also observed in the Aotani home described by Bethel (1992b: 128–9). At the farewell ceremony of Mr Tachibana, a homeless recipient of Livelihood Protection who was found dead in his room two days after he was picked up from a police station (he had wandered away for several days), he was put in a coffin dressed in a pure white kimono before the Buddhist altar in the home mortuary. Since Mr Tachibana had no relatives, the home held the whole responsibility for performing the funeral service, with the warden and the head matron representing his family.

After an announcement was made over the loudspeaker, residents who wanted to pay their last respects to Mr Tachibana's departing spirit and who were interested in how the deceased was handled all came downstairs. They lined up to offer incense in front of the coffin and whispered softly to reassure the soul not to be afraid on his journey to the other world. After they finished their prayer, residents gathered before the mortuary, and a sombre mood prevailed. They did not move away until they had paid their last respects by dropping white chrysanthemum flowers on the corpse. Mrs Sugiyama said, 'He is lucky, he went so quickly. I hope I can go like him.' Many others nodded in agreement. Mr Gotō watched the whole process with a sombre look, knowing that he would be treated the same way when he died. He later asked me to take a picture of him because he wanted to prepare a photo for his funeral, unlike Mr Tachibana who was sent to the crematorium without a picture.

Conducting Buddhist memorial services for the dead in the home is another way for Kotobuki to relieve the anxiety about death for the residents. On all major Buddhist holidays, such as the spring and autumn equinox and the *Obon* (Festival for the Dead), a Buddhist priest from a local temple, where the ashes of deceased residents without families are temporarily kept in custody before they are transferred to the public grave, comes to chant sutras and hold proper memorial services. This practice ensures that all deceased residents are awarded the proper Buddhist rituals, so that they can live peacefully and achieve their posthumous status in the other world.

A death at Kotobuki reminds the rest of the residents of their own death. The day after Mr Tachibana's funeral, Mrs Ōkubo said that recently she had been constantly thinking about death. She wanted to put aside more money by buying fewer refreshments, because she worried that her savings would not be enough to pay for a funeral in which a Buddhist priest would come to recite a sutra. 'I am thinking of committing suicide but I haven't the courage. I am unable to do so for it will cause trouble to the home. I hope my husband will hurry up to fetch me.'

Other residents, mostly women, also said that they were waiting for either their parents or their deceased spouse or children to take them to the next world. They told their dead relatives about this when they carried out their daily ancestor memorial service[16] before their small family altars or memorial tablets in their rooms. By serving small sacrificial meals to their ancestors, paying their daily respects and praying for protection, they gained a sense of security that they would have a peaceful death and rejoin their family in the next world. However, few male residents were observed to conduct the same ancestor ritual as females did. This, in Smith's explanation (1974: 119), is because the male or the head of a household is expected to assume the responsibility for formal memorial services, while the purely domestic activity of offering food and drink on a daily basis is conceived as a woman's duty.

Mr Gotō said that he was not afraid of death because he did not believe in the existence of a posthumous world. Yet, on the other hand, he cared much about his funeral ritual. He was saving money for his funeral little by little from his small amount of monthly pocket money. Understanding that he would become a *muen-botoke*, he was sure that his funeral would be held by the home and that the ashes would be interred in the public grave that the Tokyo Metropolis built for all the elderly without a family. This gave him a sense of reassurance because at least he would not be alone: he could meet many former residents of Kotobuki there.

Those who have both children and family graves do not worry much about their funeral because they believe that their family will handle their funeral and memorial services properly. For instance, both Mrs Matsumoto and Mrs Sugiyama said that they would join their family grave after they died and that their children had promised to take the responsibility of performing their funeral. In the case of Mrs Yamaguchi, although she was a Christian, she had prepared for her death by getting the promise of the warden to hold her funeral according to the way funerals were usually conducted in Aoba and to have her ashes buried together with her husband by her daughter.

But women who are alone, childless, unsure of their children's loyalty or who do not want to burden their children, usually their daughters, may prepare for their death by purchasing 'eternal care' (*eitai kuyō*)[17] in advance. Mrs Mita had spent a lot of money buying 'eternal care' both for her deceased parents and her husband. She, alone, would join in the grave of Kotobuki. 'I belong here because I am indebted to Sazanka', she said, 'by doing so, I can die free of worry.'

After relieving their anxiety about their posthumous rituals by preparing them in advance, the residents still face the problem of how to die. Nearly every informant said that they wanted to die quickly or die without severe illnesses. Mrs Matsumoto wanted to die in peace; Mr Gotō wished to die in his sleep; Mrs Sugiyama hoped she would not be bedridden and that she would die *pokkuri*;[18] Mr Aoki said that he would like to avoid chronic illness; and Mrs Yamaguchi wanted to leave it to God.

In order to achieve their wishes, Mrs Matsumoto took recourse to her goddess, while Mrs Sugiyama and many other female residents prayed to their ancestors. They also kept on participating in various clubs to exercise their bodies in order to keep fit. Mr Gotō and Mr Aoki paid attention to other issues, such as nutrition, sleep and medication, in order to lead a healthy life, while Mrs Yamaguchi was following the regime she had been given by the staff members.

Boredom, illness, loneliness and the lack of care from one's family may intensify a resident's wish to die. However, the courage to face one's impending death and ability to prepare for one's death both psychologically and strategically ensure that the residents have a sense of self-control and free them from worries. The examples of the five residents described, as well as others mentioned, show that whether or not one can deal with one's own death properly will greatly affect the psychological satisfaction of life in the home.

Notes

1 In the pre-war *ie* household, the head of the family, usually the father or the eldest son who inherited the household, was responsible for arranging marriages for its members. A daughter was expected to marry the person her parents had arranged for her even though she might love someone else. An *o-miai* is a meeting with a prospective spouse.

2 Though the New Constitution and the New Civil Codes after the Second World War eliminated the legal basis for the *ie* and a new family system was established based on new imported traits, such as equal inheritance by all children, equal rights for women and free choice of spouse, etc., the traditional *ie* ideology has remained embedded in Japanese social life. Primogeniture and the oldest son's responsibility for caring for old parents remain as social norms and practice in actual family life. Daughters who do not succeed to a household are not expected to take the responsibility for parents' care.

3 According to Mrs Matsumoto, Tomomaru-hime is the direct envoy dispatched from Ōyamanezu no Mikoto, a female goddess who helps those suffering from illness and agonies in the secular world. She is a reborn human being. The religious group, named Shinji Kyōkai, believes in Ōyamanezu no Mikoto and it is a new Shinto group with its head office in Yokohama.

4 In Japanese, *happō bijin* is a critical expression. Here Mrs Matsumoto meant that as a number of female residents, especially those without close friends in the home, felt jealous of her wide circle of friends, they used this word to criticise her in secret.

5 The family register under the Law of Family Register (1947) is an official document that certifies a Japanese individual's relationships by blood and marriage. It is also a means for the national government to keep track of its people for the purpose of ruling over the country. The family register is compiled by treating a household as a unit. In principle, recording of the creation, alteration and extinction of an individual's relationship with the household is made on his/her notification. As the household is treated as a whole unit, even if a couple's marriage ends with a mutual agreement divorce, its record remains on the household's family register. So it is possible to locate a family member by examining his/her family register if his/her relatives really want to find him/her.

6 According to Smith (1974: 41), *muen-botoke* refers to wandering spirits or buddhas without attachment or affiliation. *Gaki* (hungry ghosts) are a kind of *muen-botoke*. The souls of those who are not worshipped by their descendants are also *muen-botoke*.

7 1DK is an apartment that has one bedroom and a dining room kitchen. 3DK means an apartment with three rooms and a dining room kitchen.

8 Throughout the 1970s, influenced by the ideas of anti-psychiatry and therapeutic community, psychiatrists began to open up the wards and try social living therapy and community psychiatry to treat mental patients (Harding *et al.* 1984: 11–14).

9 A kind of private elementary school in the Edo period.
10 An administrative unit in Mongolia which is equivalent to a province.
11 A kind of welfare institution for children younger than 18 who have no guardians, or who are ill-treated by their parents or other guardians. It is regulated by the Law for the Welfare of Children (1947) (Sakurai and Imura 1991: 82).
12 My findings about interpersonal relationships of the residents in Kotobuki, especially in Sazanka and Akashia, were quite different from those of Bethel (1992a), who emphasises the active social interactions among the residents in Aotani Home. The differences, I think, arise from the following reasons. First, our approaches to observation are different. Bethel focuses on how the residents are able to create a familiar community by manipulating their resources, including human relationships, despite the social stigma of institutionalisation. However, my purpose is to point out the difficulties in making friends among elderly in Kotobuki and the possible reasons for avoidance of social interactions among the residents.

Second, room structures in Aotani and Kotobuki are different. In Aotani, four residents live in a room. So friendships can be more easily formed or interpersonal relationships more easily manipulated than in Kotobuki where a healthy elderly person shares a room with one other person, or lives in a private room. In the latter situation, choices to make friends are limited. A third possible reason is that socialisation patterns of the residents may be different in an elderly home in a rural community and in a suburb of Tokyo. Normally the interpersonal relationships of the former are considered warmer. Fourth, in Kotobuki there is a regulation that forbids male residents from visiting their female peers, so interactions among the elderly are restricted.

Finally, our understandings of 'friendship' in Japan are different. Bethel mentions that the elderly residents in Aotani make friends by visiting each other and gift-giving. She does not point out that there is a distinction between real friends and '*otsukiai*' friends. I think that the friendships she describes remains at the '*otsukiai*' level defined by Reiko Atsumi (1989), because they obviously involve social obligation. What I suggest in my analysis is that there are different kinds of friendship in Japan. In Kotobuki, friendship only remains on *otsukiai* level and real friendship out of affection is rare. This point deserves further exploration in the future.
13 According to Cumming and Henry (1961), when one enters later life, one's disengagement occurs at three levels: physical, psychological and social. With declining health, diminishing vigour and reduced capacity for economic self-sufficiency, an elderly person tends to turn his/her concerns to the inner world of his own feelings and thoughts, and it is natural for him gradually to withdraw from social activity. Disengagement leads to better health and psychological well-being because of the conservation of energy.
14 The exchange and reciprocity theory deals with how individuals provide and accept social support. Exchange means giving and receiving. Reciprocity, according to Alvin Gouldner's (1960) definition, refers to equal or comparable exchanges of tangible aid, emotional affection, advice or information between individuals or groups. Gary Lee (1985) uses the reciprocity notion to explore supportive interactions and their consequences for the well-being of older persons. He argues that the American elderly tend to hesitate to accept help if they feel unable to reciprocate. Unbalanced exchange relations would cause dependence and could have detrimental emotional consequences.

In Japan, reciprocity suggests the terms of *on* and *giri* which are relational concepts combining a benevolence or favour granted by A to B and the resulting debt B owes to A. The balance in the relationship between A and B is not restored until the completion of the repayment of obligation from B. Sentiments of indebtedness, observing duty and repaying social debts have been thought to be a characteristic in Japanese social interactions (Akiyama *et al.* 1990; Befu 1977, 1986; Benedict 1946; Doi 1971; Lebra 1976; Steven 1997).

15 *Tatemae* means a public position or one's social self, as opposed to one's private, real intention, or *honne*. When one is in *tatemae* relationships with others, the concept of *enryo*, restraint or holding back, guides one's behaviour. So it is a 'negative yardstick in measuring the intimacy of human relationships' (Doi 1973: 38).

16 The most common ritual for ancestor worship is carried out on a daily basis. Most old female residents greeted their family ancestors and offered flowers, water and food to them before their altars or tablets every morning and night, either before breakfast or before the evening meal.

17 A kind of memorial service for the dead. After receiving a large sum of money donated by a parishioner, the priest of the temple to which the parishioner' family grave belongs will hold masses regularly forever for the repose of the souls of the parishioner and his ancestors after his death.

18 *Pokkuri* is the sudden snap of an object when it breaks. Particularly, it means the abrupt and unexpected death of a physically healthy person.

4   The staff

The staff is another important component of the population in institutions for the elderly. They can be seen everywhere in the homes, nursing the elderly, cleaning the floors, preparing meals, planning a programme, drawing up a draft to get subsidies from the government or doing the laundry. Not only do their daily jobs fit into the home's daily routine, but also they themselves have become the routine.

As Mrs Matsumoto, a resident in Sazanka, said, residents are the central characters performing their last scenes of life on the stage of the home. The staff members are supportive players in these scenes and are there to satisfy various needs of the former, be they physical, medical, nutritional or social in nature. On one hand, they make their living from the elderly; on the other hand, they are also the means for the elderly to survive. As both supporters and audience, the staff members have a great deal to say about not only their work but also the people they serve.

As a parallel to the narrative of the residents, the first part of this chapter presents descriptions by four staff members from different departments about their experiences of institutional work, about their responsibilities, rewards and frustrations, about their view of institutional life and their plans for their own future. Here I deliberately leave out the nurses' voice and place more emphasis on the viewpoints of the matrons. The staff members I chosen are all mature and experienced. They had worked in different kinds of institutions, and thus have more to say about institutional life and the differences between different institutions for the elderly than the younger ones.

The second part of the chapter describes the corporate culture of the staff members. Data collected from interviews and questionnaires of the staff reveal some major themes with respect to institutional work: reasons for working in a welfare institution; sources of satisfaction and dissatisfaction; the effects of gender and institutional organisation on their work; and their methods for coping with stress and difficulties. Staff members' attitudes towards institutionalisation and social welfare, their prospects for their own later life, and their reflections on the quality of life of the residents will also be discussed. This chapter actually illuminates another dimension of institutional life: how the employees view the residents' quality of life and their own.

Narratives of four staff members

Mr Masao Itō: Director of the Nursing Department

'Institutional work is both challenging and easy.'

Mr Itō, Director of the Nursing Department when I conducted fieldwork in 1999, had worked in Kotobuki nearly as long as the home had been in existence. He was responsible for the overall supervision of sections that provide direct care for the residents and served as the communication channel between the administrators and employees. Besides, he was the field training coordinator for trainee students and volunteers from welfare and health care educational institutions and from community social service sectors. With the qualification of 'care manager' under the LTCI scheme, he had been engaged in making care plans for the residents in Kotobuki for the first two years after the programme was enacted. He was promoted to warden of Aoba in 2001.

As a Buddhist of the Jōdo Sect (*jōdo-shu*), Mr Itō grew up in his grandmother's temple. During his boyhood, he had come across a great number of people who came for refuge or salvation from illness and psychological distress. Influenced by his grandmother, who was always willing to help people wholeheartedly, he hoped that he would be a help to others too. When he grew older, he concluded from observing the career of his father as a salary-man that the role of the individual in the hierarchical organisation of a company was virtually invisible. So he began to think of a welfare career, where one could not only help people in need but also obtain great work satisfaction. He chose to study in the social welfare department in Taisho University, a Buddhist university. After graduation, he was employed by Airin-kai as a welfare supervisor in Aoba in 1978, a year after the home started its business.

A new university graduate with neither field training experience to rely on nor senior staff to tutor him, Mr Itō learned to master the responsibilities and skills of a welfare supervisor by himself. His main job was to coordinate both with outside institutions and among different departments inside the home. When he received calls from welfare offices about the admission of an old citizen in that city or ward, he arranged a face-to-face interview with the applicant and his/her family, if available, with a matron, a nurse and a dietician also in attendance.

After the admission of an elderly person, Mr Itō kept contact with his/her welfare office through regular reports about the adjustment process and other conditions such as hospitalisation, medication, stability of physical and mental state, and demise of the elderly. He reported these conditions to the families of the elderly as well, if there was any. He had to contact suitable hospitals, the Buddhist temple and the undertaker if the elderly needed to be hospitalised or died. He also took charge of the administration of the money or property entrusted to him by the residents or their families. He organised various cultural and recreational clubs, and planned the monthly and annual events such as birthday parties, overnight trips, the Bon Festival, etc. for the elderly as well.

Another big part of his job was to coordinate with staff members in different departments. In order to provide good care and services for the residents, staff members who supported the elderly directly in the sections of nursing, health care, rehabilitation and meal provision must work hand in hand. So Mr Itō devised a series of recording forms for each department and organised a 'contact and coordination meeting' that included members from different departments. In addition, there were individual case conferences in which staff from different sections could exchange opinions regarding care plans for individual elderly persons. Apart from all these responsibilities, Mr Itō also helped bathe the elderly, change diapers and helped out in the rotation schedule because of the shortage of care staff in the early years. Also, he fixed the facilities and served as a driver.

After having worked in Aoba for 14 years, Mr Itō became the director of the Sakura Day Service Centre when it was established. He was responsible for coordinating with the city welfare office and the Social Welfare Council regarding clients' applications for services. He went to interview elderly individuals in their homes, coordinated with other staff members, and provided day care services for the elderly clients. In 1995 he transferred to Sazanka to supervise the nursing department. During his years' of service in Kotobuki, he had contributed greatly to the systemic organisation of the homes by developing a series of manuals for each institution.

Mr Itō did not find it easy to do a job that involved dealing with both the elderly and the staff members. Because of the differences in characters, interests, ADL ability, mental condition and personal demands of the residents, he had to treat them differently and consider carefully when developing a programme. As the home is a 'place of living' for the residents, he needed not only to create a genuine family atmosphere with minimum regulations so that the elderly could live happily, but also an open environment so that employees could work easily and provide high quality care and services efficiently.

According to him, Kotobuki had some basic rules such as no smoking in the rooms, no quarrels, and no borrowing and lending money between each other, in order to prevent fires and to avoid conflicts. Residents of different sexes in Sazanka were not encouraged to visit each other because of concerns about accidental injuries caused by troubles in love affairs.[1] Some years before there had been an incident of murder, in which an envious old man killed his rival and a 'sulphuric acid' accident which victimised a female resident. If the residents can follow the daily routines and abide by these basic rules, the home leaves it in their own hands to regulate their life. Even those who drank heavily and caused problems were not blamed. So Mr Itō was sometimes criticised by some matrons for 'being too lenient'.

Regarding self-control and self-determination of the residents, Mr Itō said that because of the severe physical and mental impairments, the life of most residents in Aoba was determined by the scheduled routines of meals, diaper changes, baths, rehabilitation and medication. However, in Sazanka and Akashia where most residents were still very fit, as the residents did not need to spend time going shopping, cooking, cleaning the dishes and boiling water for a bath, they had a great deal of spare time. He admitted that it was comfortable for residents just to sit or lie in bed watching TV, and receive services from staff members, but he thought they should maintain autonomy. He said:

> We think it best not to deprive them of all the roles in their former life, especially the role of women as the housekeeper. So we ask them to do some daily tasks such as cleaning their own rooms, helping to serve the meals, keeping the washing room tidy and so on. Many of them stick to their roles and regard their duties as their purpose in life. Male residents are also encouraged to carry out such tasks, but they were obviously not as good as their female peers.
>
> Another thing we expect is that the residents can find new roles in the home through participating in the various clubs we organise for them. While young, these elderly had to work hard to make a living and take care of their families. There was no room for them to pursue their hobbies. Now they have a handful of spare time, so it's time for them to enjoy themselves. We have 15 clubs, many annual events, handicraft shows, inter-institutional hobby competitions as well as small excursions and trips.

According to Mr Itō, at present fewer than half of the members of the 15 clubs were participating in the activities and many 'old' club members were resigning, either because of their declining energy or because of troubles in interpersonal relations. So it was a challenge for the home to develop some programmes to attract the elderly and keep them active. Recently they had created a 'rapport group' (*fureai gurūpu*)[2] for those with physical disabilities as well as those with light or medium dementia.

Mr Itō felt that a crucial factor in determining the quality of life of the residents was the quality of the employees and the efficiency of teamwork. At the time when welfare institutions for elderly were rare, only middle-aged housewives chose to work in Kotobuki, mostly in order to make ends meet. No specific skills were needed, and many worked as an extension of their family life. However, the variety of physical disabilities and the complications of geriatric illnesses of the recent residents have required staff members to have more professional knowledge about ageing, geriatric illnesses and nursing care technology. As a result, in recent years, the home has been trying to employ more young graduates from professional schools as well as housewives who have home-help qualifications. Mr Itō thought that qualifications were a criterion in determining the quality of an employee, but a loving heart as well as a spirit of dedication and cooperation was as important as qualifications.

About teamwork, since different people, different occupations and different generations believe in different values, Mr Itō did not think it easy to build an efficient team within the homes. In Aoba, there were different views between those who spoke from a medical perspective and those who spoke from a sense of daily life regarding an individual's care plan. In Sazanka and Akashia, on the other hand, the work styles of the old and young matrons were different. Middle-aged matrons, with experience in both their own life and work, were more understanding towards the elderly while the young either lacked confidence in their jobs or tended to force their own ideas on the residents.

In order to enhance smooth communication between the senior staff and the young employees, Mr Itō encouraged young staff to express their opinions freely and asked the experienced matrons to make manuals for new employees. 'Following such basic ways of operating', he said, 'the young will be able to learn how to carry out their duties and thus ensure the homes are on the right track.' He thought that this system was doing well.

When talking about problems in the homes, Mr Itō mentioned several. In Sazanka, as two residents share a room, room-mates are a big concern. Much of the time residents manage to compromise with each other. However, there are always some pairs who cannot get along well. He said:

> Basically a newcomer is unable to choose his/her room-mate because he/she comes to fill up a vacancy. He/she has to fit with the person already there. If the two cannot get along, we try to exchange room-mates. We try to put together people who have similar interests, backgrounds and compatible temperaments, but chances are limited. Those who cannot tune in with others will never be able to get along well with their room-mates whichever room they go to. So some people have to live with someone they do not like, or even detest. This is the fate involved in double rooms.

> Among the male residents, many newcomers are homeless persons. Since they have become used to a free life, they find it painful to live a life with regulations. Some become depressed because of the stress, and some run away and became vagrants again. Among the female residents, a number of those newly admitted have mental disorders such as schizophrenia. It would make our job and position easier if we did not accept people with mental disorders. But it would be unfair to these persons, because they have waited for entrance for so long, mostly over five years! So we have accepted some in recent years both in Sazanka and Akashia. However, together with their entrance, we also get the problem of how to take care of them, and how to deal with conflicts between these patients and ordinary residents. Most of our staff

members lack both knowledge and experience in dealing with mental patients. We have organised a study meeting under the orientation of a psychiatric doctor on how to treat people with psychological disorders. We need to do more.

One more difficulty, Mr Itō said, lay in the problems caused by the 'same treatment'[3] in Sazanka and Akashia. Many of the residents in Sazanka were paying more than those in Akashia, but they were unable to live in a private room. The elderly in Akashia, on the other hand, tended to be more self-assertive and less cooperative than those in Sazanka, as they thought that they had come to the home on their own money rather than on welfare. Living in private rooms, they had a tendency to isolate themselves from others and had fewer chances to learn how to get along with others, thus they were more likely to adapt badly to the home environment, get mental disorders and quarrel with each other because of the lack of tolerance. And they tended to look down upon the elderly in Sazanka, whom they thought of as 'on welfare'. Some Akashia residents thought the residents in Sazanka were dirty, refused to talk to them or even forbade them to enter a certain place in the public bathtub. 'But they have forgotten some facts', Mr Itō said, 'it is because of the support[4] from many matrons in Sazanka that they can live a comfortable life in Akashia.'

Having recounted his job responsibilities and the difficulties in dealing with both the residents and the staff members, Mr Itō turned to how he thought about institutionalisation. Since institutional care could ensure the elderly a safe, healthy and decent later life and relieve the family from heavy care burden, he thought institutions are good choices for those who needed them.

Mr Itō said that at the time when he began to work in Kotobuki, people's image of institutions for the elderly was *yōrō-in*, or a kind of *Obasuteyama*. With the establishment of the Law for the Welfare of the Elderly, the name of '*yōrō-in*' was changed to '*rōjin hōmu*'. After that, people's attitude towards the institutions began to change gradually. 'At present, the elderly residents are still obsessed by the sense of being indebted to the government, but with the increasing awareness of basic rights, maybe in a few years institutionalisation will no longer be a social stigma for the elderly', Mr Itō said:

> I myself think it is OK to enter a home when I am old. If my parents become bedridden or senile and my family is unable to take care of them at home, I would consider sending them to a hospital or a nursing home. For myself, if I am severely impaired, I do not want treatment to prolong my life.

Looking back over his career, Mr Itō felt satisfied that he had been able to accompany many residents until the end of their lives. He thought it important to help the elderly residents draw a full stop to their lives, no matter what kind of life they had led. Regarding 'ensuring the old people the utmost life satisfaction in the last stop of their life' as his motto, he and his colleagues had made efforts to create a comfortable environment for the residents to live in Kotobuki. He also tried to build a harmonious and efficient teamwork to provide good services for the residents. He liked his job and would like to keep on working in Kotobuki and improving the work conditions for the staff and quality of care for the residents.

Ms Reiko Shinozaki: head matron in Sazanka

'A Home is Never a Real Home'

Ms Shinozaki came from a coastal town in southern Japan. Her father died when she was a primary school student. As the second oldest daughter with two brothers and a sister older than her, she helped to take care of the household chores and the other five younger siblings. The hardship endured in her early days nurtured in her a spirit of independence. After her high school graduation, she came to Tokyo, the capital that had attracted thousands of young people of her age, in search of dreams and opportunities. Having worked in a department store for several years, she got married, and soon had her only daughter. She stayed at home when her daughter was very small, only doing some part-time jobs such as a cashier in a supermarket. Her marriage ended in divorce. In order to support herself and her daughter, she began to work in a life insurance company in her late 30s to earn good money. However, instability in income and high expenditure for transportation and other expenses related to sales could not give her a sense of economic security. So at the age of 38 she turned to work in a *tokuyō* home, where the average salary of the staff members was at the same level as that of public servants.

Having worked as a matron for eight years, Ms Shinozaki was forced to change her job again because of the collapse of the home. She started her career as a matron in Kotobuki in 1993. She was an ordinary matron on the second floor of Sazanka and Akashia for the first two years. Being an experienced worker and having already obtained the certificate of Care and Welfare Work in her former workplace, she was promoted to head matron in 1995. With respect to her job, Ms Shinozaki said:

> When I was a matron in the previous *tokuyō* home, what I needed to do was to take care of diaper changing, bathing, feeding, water supply, etc. Most of the time I was doing the physical labour without thinking too much. If you treat the elderly with a smile, a soft voice and a skilled hand, everything goes smoothly. However, it is different here in Sazanka and Akashia. I had thought of the residents here as just ordinary grannies and grandpas. But I was too simplistic. The work is both

profound and difficult. The elderly are more experienced in life than I am, they are always on the move, some look younger and healthier than we matrons do, and their brains work fast. It is hard to deal with these people with independent minds.

When she was a matron, Ms Shinozaki was only in charge of ten persons on the floor. Following the other matrons, she learned her job responsibilities at her own pace. When she was nominated as the head matron, she worried a great deal for she did not think she was prepared for a responsible job: to look after all the elderly on the third and fourth floors as well as the work of other matrons! Observing the ways her colleagues worked, discussing with other staff members and thinking hard for herself, she gradually managed to master her job.

She thought that gaining insight into every resident was the starting point for doing a good job in Sazanka and Akashia. She said that only when a matron had an insight into the characters of all residents would she be able to talk to them in suitable ways and handle their conflicts properly. Since all the residents in Sazanka lived in double rooms and tended to restrain their demands, and the elderly in Akashia tended to confine themselves to their own rooms, it was difficult to find out whether all residents were getting along with others, what kinds of support they needed, and whether or not they were satisfied with their life. 'In order to have a clear view of each resident, you must always greet them with great concern, observe their expressions when they walk in the hallway or pass by the station, and pay attention to subtle changes in them', Ms Shinozaki emphasised.

It seemed to Ms Shinozaki that dealing with discord among the residents was a difficult thing in her job.

When one becomes older, one tends to be obstinate and less accommodating. One sticks to the idea that only his/her way is right. So when the behaviour of one's room-mate is different from one's own, one becomes critical. Then tension arises. Others are self-centred. They do everything only for their own convenience, ignoring that of their room-mates. Thus discontent comes out. And some like to speak ill of others behind their backs. Like in the old saying, 'The mouth is the root of evil', quarrels break out. Whenever there is trouble, we talk to the two troublemakers first, asking them to be patient with each other. If this does not work, we change rooms for them. But we are unable to meet their demands all the time. First, it takes time to make a 'perfect' match; second, any room-mate change means potential new problems because we cannot change the fact that two persons must share a room. So if an elderly person still wants to change room-mates after we have changed for her several times, we will ask her to tell us who she wants to live with and with whom she is confident she can get along well. Otherwise, she will never be able to understand her own situation that she is disliked by others. Through such 'education', we try to remind some residents of their weaknesses and encourage them to maintain a harmonious relationship with others, because someday they might need care or help from others.

For those who got along quite well, Ms Shinozaki always expressed her appreciation to the person who accepted a newcomer with a 'thank you very much'. 'We should be grateful to these elderly. Because of their consideration we have been saved from a great many problems.' She thought it was the humane part of their job to show the staff's gratitude to the residents.

Ms Shinozaki thought that bullying of the mentally handicapped was the biggest issue annoying her and other colleagues. According to her, quite a number of mental patients were living in Sazanka and Akashia. Many recovered patients such as Mr Aoki could manage their life quite well. However, due to people's prejudice towards mental patients, some patients, especially those who had been diagnosed with paranoia, had difficulties in living peacefully. Ms Shinozaki mentioned Miss Nishikawa, who was a typical example of someone who was isolated by other residents in Akashia (see Chapter 6). Recently, there had been a big confrontation where Miss Nishikawa was violently assaulted by Mrs Takagi and other residents who had intended to oust the former. Ms Shinozaki was on the spot to solve the problem. She made the following comments about the abusers.

I can't understand why these persons couldn't treat the weak more kindly. Why do they want to exclude people more unfortunate than themselves? By making others miserable, can they feel happy? To look at the affair as an outsider, I think a lot about the way of one's life. The family life of these elderly people was unhappy before they came here: despite the fact that they have children, they were sent around from their sons to their daughters. So they do not have the room to be kind to others. In addition, the home is a strange world to them. Living in an unfamiliar place may be very stressful. In order to get rid of this stress, someone will take up leadership and stir up some of her congenial friends to attack the person she doesn't like. I think these elderly wretched. They have descended to the same level as a mentally disabled person.

Describing the difficulties in her job, Ms Shinozaki said that although she was familiar with the content of her duties, she felt tired psychologically because part of her stress also came from the interaction with her colleagues. She said:

When one reaches one's 40s, one's individuality or personality comes out. So a middle-aged matron tends to have her own way of dealing with the happenings in daily life and is more likely to be aware of other matrons' way of working. And she tends to be inflexible in thinking and her ways might also be unacceptable to others. In addition her colleagues will not take her part. So it is difficult for a woman to change jobs in her 40s, especially in a welfare field that needs flexibility, patience and team spirit to handle human relationships. Since the history of Kotobuki is quite long, there are some customary practices in the home. If new matrons do not follow these traditions and do things their own way, they might be criticised for lack of team spirit.

Ms Shinozaki thought it important to keep the good traditions of the home, but since society, norms and technology were changing rapidly, it was also necessary to listen to the opinions of the young staff members. She admitted that the young staff had brought vigour to the home, but she felt that the work in Sazanka and Akashia was more suitable to middle-aged women. She said:

> Elderly people feel it easier to get along with older matrons than with the younger. For them our age is similar to their daughters, there is a kind of closeness between our generation and the elderly residents. However, many newly employed matrons are only in their late teens or early 20s. For the elderly, these young matrons are equal to their grandchildren or even great-grandchildren. How can a grandparent ask protection from their grandchildren? Older matrons, on the other hand, have good analytic abilities gained from their experience. They can get to the bottom of an affair, grasp the characters of the elderly quite easily, understand the feelings of the old people and handle emergencies with composure.

As the head matron, Ms Shinozaki assume quite heavy responsibilities. In addition to taking care of the residents, she was also responsible for looking after the new staff members. She taught them how to keep a diary, take notes for Resident's Case Records, remember daily routines and handle emergencies, etc. She said, 'Maybe I am ageing myself. I feel tired when I go back home. On holidays I do nothing but arrange flowers. The beautiful flowers always appease my mind.'

When turning to talk about the life of the residents, she commented that if it were just about the material aspects of institutional life, the elderly in welfare institutions were leading a more comfortable life than those who lived alone in their homes on moderate pensions. But she continued to emphasise that a good material life did not always mean happiness. She said:

> I thought those who have lived on the street fortunate to be able to live here. Yet, who knows the real feelings of these persons? Look at the residents in Sazanka and Akashia, aren't most of them unfortunate people? Some are left in our care without any visits from their families; some wanted to live in their own homes but were unable to do so; the unmar-

ried ones have been solitary all their life; and for others, their families refused to claim their ashes even when they died. To some extent, this cannot be helped, since this is the life they have chosen for themselves. Since they are tied to their past, they will bear the loneliness until they die. I pity them. Especially those who didn't marry must be very lonely. If they had children, they would not necessarily end their life in this world alone, because they would still live with their alter ego. I think many elderly here will pass away in misery. This is their fate.

Despite her pessimistic view of the fate of the elderly, Ms Shinozaki felt rewarded in her work. For her, both her and her daughter's life depended on her job. 'But more importantly, if I hadn't worked in a welfare institution for the elderly, I might have been unable to know of so many ways of living in the world', she said, 'through the interactions with these seniors in our life, I learned a great deal, not only wisdom but also views of life.' She thought she had benefited a great deal from her job: first, she had become more mature; and, second, she was able to think about her own later life. She hoped that her job had been helpful to the elderly. And it was her biggest reward if the elderly had lived or would have a peaceful life in the homes in the last stage of their life.

With regard to her own later life, Ms Shinozaki said straightforwardly that she was unwilling to live in a *yōgo* home such as Sazanka because of the lack of privacy and limitation of freedom. She would like to live with her daughter if possible. She realised fully that the family was the real home for an institutionalised elderly when she was working in the *tokuyō* home. No matter how hard she tried to feed, change diapers and dress the elderly, she could not win the radiant smiles they gave to their families when they came to visit them. She would be very happy if her daughter took care of her when she became physically disabled. But she was unwilling to become a burden. If her daughter got married, had her own life, and was unable to look after her, she would manage her life by herself through utilising in-home services. 'I would like to die in my own home', she said.

Ms Shinozaki worked in Kotobuki in order to make a living. The hardships she had endured in her life and tragic fates of many residents that she had witnessed made her a bit pessimistic about life. She regarded life in institutions as wretched, so she wished strongly to avoid institutionalisation in her late life. As she was sympathetic towards the elderly residents, she was dedicated to her job, hoping her service would make the residents happy. Besides her daughter, the everyday interaction with the residents had become 'something' she was living for.

Mrs Yumiko Suzuki: matron in Aoba

'I am serving the "Buddha" (*Hotoke-san*) and innocent children.'

Like Ms Shinozaki, Mrs Suzuki had started her second career in her 30s. When her second son became a third grade student in primary school, she went to work as a clerk in a bank and then as an accounting clerk in an international trading company. As she was not good at the abacus, she did not think that she could do well in a job that required meticulous calculation. So she resigned and decided to look for more physically oriented work. A colleague who quit together with her and later became one of her best friends suggested that they go and learn some techniques for job-finding in a public vocational retraining school. The two studied at the school for half a year, learned the skill of taking care of disabled and elderly persons, and got the first-class home-helper certificate. With this certificate, Mrs Suzuki could choose to work in either an institution for the elderly, a day care centre or an institution for handicapped persons.

Since Mrs Suzuki's husband was the eldest son of the family, her mother-in-law was living with them. And there was a promise between her family and her husband's siblings that Mrs Suzuki would be responsible for taking care of their mother if she became bedridden. So in order to get some preliminary knowledge and skill in caring for an old person, she came to work in Kotobuki in 1983. For the first three years, she was a matron on the fourth floor of Sazanka, then she was transferred to Aoba. 'You know, I am well suited to do physical work. I like to work here much better than in Sazanka. Even if I get tired from my work, I feel refreshed after soaking in the bath tub for half an hour.' She made fun of herself for being too stupid to deal with the complicated human relations and troubles in Sazanka. She said:

> In *Sazanka*, most residents are healthy and they can put their affairs in order by themselves. The female residents, especially, tend to think of their rooms as their castle, and they do not like to have a stranger intrude into their territory. I felt a sense of alienation when I knocked on a door to ask a feeble old woman whether she needed me to clean her room and got the reply 'No, thanks. I can do it myself.' It is uncomfortable for a matron to enter the territory of a resident who has both free will and physical energy (though only little). The case is different in Aoba. Except for a small number of old people who can manage some affairs of their own, the majority are either bedridden or senile and thus need total care. We can easily enter their rooms and carry out our daily tasks. Taking care of toilet, meals and bathing are the three biggest duties of us matrons in a *tokuyō* home. So if we have enough strength and have mastered the basic skills of nursing care, we are able to achieve our responsibilities without many problems In this aspect, I think working in a *tokuyō* home is easier than in a *yōgo* home.

However, matrons in Aoba had different difficulties from those in Sazanka. First of all, there was the problem of communicating with the residents. Most residents in Aoba had difficulties in communication because of their physical impairments or mental illnesses. It was good for those who could still say something because at least they could say which part of their bodies felt pain and what they needed. However, for Alzheimer's patients, deaf-mute elderly, and those who were both bedridden and had speech disorders, care staff could only grasp their needs through careful observation and search out methods to communicate with these persons. Besides, the staff had to observe every aspect of the conditions of an elderly person, including emotion, excretion, indigestion and temperature, and write down every subtle change so as to keep good communication among others with regard to the administration of care to the residents. So recording was important not only in intradepartmental communication but also in interdepartmental contacts.

Second, staff members worked in a team, so they needed to be cooperative and respect the opinions of other staff such as nurses, PT staff and the dietician regarding the care plans of the elderly. Most of the time Mrs Suzuki felt the teamwork functioned well, but sometimes she also felt frustrated because of disagreements with other staff members in different occupations.

How to communicate with the residents? According to Mrs Suzuki, '*sukinshippu*' (skinship), that is, close contact between the nurturer and the nurtured through non-verbal behaviour such as changing diapers, helping with toilet, feeding and bathing, could enhance the communication between the staff and the residents. She said:

> Though at the very beginning, the elderly were embarrassed to have their personal needs tended to by strangers, when they got used to the hands touching their bodies, got familiar with our voices and faces, and felt the comfort after our care, they usually responded with a 'thank you' or a pleasant smile, even those who seem to be emotionless look calmer. I feel happy when the residents appreciate my warm hands in diaper changing.

A second tool, language, is as important as *sukinshippu* in communication. Mrs Suzuki said that basically they followed the home's regime to speak politely to the residents. However, to some elderly, especially senile elderly and those who had lived a long family life, they also used familiar language as well as jokes. 'We use language selectively according to situations and persons', Mrs Suzuki said.

> Have you ever heard the old saying 'old people become like children again with age'? Have you ever noticed the facial expression of some demented elderly such as Mrs Miura? Don't they look like a *Hotoke* (Buddha) and laugh like a lovely innocent child? So we use children's language and familiar language to speak to such persons. For example, we call Mrs Miura '*Se-cchan*', Mrs Minezawa '*Koyo-san*', Mrs Nishimura '*Okā-san*', Mrs Tanabe '*Obā-chan*' and so on.

In Japanese, *Chan* is a term of endearment usually used for a child. It can be used for an adult to express fondness (*aikyō*). And family members and friends usually use one's last name. According to Mrs Suzuki, to a resident who had gotten used to being called '*okā-san*' (mother), or '*obā-chan*' (grandma) in their family, a formal 'xx *san*' would sound unfamiliar to her. She said that Mrs Nishimura did not respond to the matrons no matter how hard they tried to feed her when she first came to Aoba. Later a matron tried to call her '*okā-san*', and she miraculously opened her eyes. After that they all called her '*okā-san*'. Mrs Suzuki continued to explain,

> Mrs Nishimura seems to only remember her role as a mother. She thinks of the stuffed doll of Mickey Mouse as her son, and she gives her breast to the doll and holds it in her arms when she sleeps. Since she can sleep well with the doll, we always put Mickey in her arms and ask her to 'Embrace your black son to sleep.' Though there is criticism of the phenomenon of infantilisation in nursing homes, I think sometimes there are good effects of treating some elderly in that way.

In addition to friendly language, Mrs Suzuki said that they also paid attention to tone of speech and sometimes used jokes. They could make fun of Mrs Ōshima by asking who she would marry next time and when she would deliver a child and so on because she liked such topics, but they could never say that to Mrs Kondō who was raised in the house of a prince of the blood (*miyake*).

Besides the issue of communication, Mrs Suzuki mentioned two other difficulties in working with the elderly. According to policy, providing services for the residents was intended to maintain their existing functions and to maximise their independence or ADL ability. So basically the elderly who still had the ability to sit up, wheel their wheelchairs, eat and carry things by themselves, were encouraged to do so. However, the home must be run efficiently conforming to a timetable. For instance, the meal cart must be taken downstairs at a fixed time, so matrons tended to feed slow eaters in order to catch up. And some residents would rather presume on the staff than do something like fetching a cup of tea on their own. They thought it comfortable to have things done by others. Thus if a matron neglected the demand of a resident in order to let that person have some exercise, she might be resented by that person and witness his/her turning to her colleagues for help. On the other hand, if she satisfied the residents by doing everything they asked, then the subsistence functions of the elderly would not have a chance to be practised. This was a dilemma.

The other issue was self-determination. 'This is an eternal problem in a *tokuyō* home', Mrs Suzuki said.

> Take Mr Hirano, if he follows the advice of his doctor, he should refrain from eating sugar as he has a number of illnesses such as diabetes,

hyper-tension and stroke. But every day he drinks about seven cans of coffee and smokes a pack of cigarettes he buys from the vending machine. We cannot criticise him for over-drinking or over-smoking because he would reply with an 'It's none of your business because this is my own body.' We must respect the right of self-determination of the residents.

Mrs Suzuki regarded Aoba as a good place for women to work throughout their life. Ranging from the late teenage years to the late 50s, various age groups with different backgrounds were working in the same place, so staff could listen to different opinions and learn from each other. There was neither any obvious senior-junior relationships nor bullying. Working conditions made it easy for women to continue working, since, for example, maternity leave, childcare leave as well as leave for caring for old family members were fully established. In order to improve the quality of the staff members as well as the quality of the care, in-service training such as staff exchange training programmes between the home and the Higashimurayama Nursing Home, study meetings about the LTCI and so on were frequently held.

For Mrs Suzuki, her only dissatisfaction with her job was that she was too busy with the nursing tasks to have time to tend to the personal needs of the residents. And she also felt a bit annoyed when she disagreed with staff members in other departments, usually the nurses, about the care of some residents. She said:

> Since we matrons care for the residents every day, we certainly know the conditions of the elderly best and we have our own ways to deal with them. The nurses, however, tend to treat the elderly from their professional perspective. It isn't wrong to do so. But I have reservations about using methods for treating patients in a hospital in dealing with our residents. This is a 'place for living', where I personally think a sense of daily living is essential.

Mrs Suzuki used the case of Mrs Nakamura to exemplify her occasional disagreement with nurses' decision in a certain individual's care plan. Mrs Nakamura was a 92-year-old lady who had had her left arm amputated. Since she fell from her bed a week ago, she had lain in her bed without taking in much food. The nurses thought it was bad for her to stay in her bed all day long because she was not hurt. They said 'She shouldn't break her life rhythm, she should get up.' So after the care conference, they came to wheel her down to the nurses' station and told the matrons not to give the old lady the ice bag any more because she did not have a fever. The poor old lady was made to sit in the wheelchair for two full days and was seen always crying 'Send me back' and 'Give me the ice bag.' Regarding this, Mrs Suzuki said:

Since she had her arm amputated, Mrs Nakamura has been accustomed to lying in her bed and having an ice bag to put on her forehead, no matter whether she has a fever or not. Suddenly she was robbed of her ice and forced to stay in her wheelchair for so long. It's unreasonable to expect an old granny more than 90 years old to withstand such sudden changes. She told us 'The last place I want to go is the nurses' station'. She is so angry at being taken down that she refuses to ingest anything except water. If this continues, she will be worn out. We would never treat an old relative so harshly, would we? It's miserable. For Mrs Nakamura, the ice is a stabiliser. She feels insecure when her psychological tranquilliser is suddenly taken away. I think this sudden change in her life will worsen her condition. We should do things at a slower tempo.

Turning to talk about how she thinks of the elderly and their life in a *tokuyō* home, Mrs Suzuki said that, compared with the elderly who had the same disabilities and were cared for by their families in their own homes, the elderly in Aoba were leading a much better life. She said:

They are carefully nursed by us; they can participate in various all-year-round traditional events and enjoy dishes for celebrations, some of which are no longer held in ordinary families; nutritionally and healthily balanced menus are made by a professional dietician and cooked by dietary workers; and there are well-equipped facilities such as air-conditioning, special machine bathtubs and a variety of care equipment. On the other hand, bedridden and senile elderly people living in their own homes may not receive good care because their daughter-in-laws are working outside. Or even when they have family members to take care of them, the caretakers tend to be their old spouses or old relatives who can't manage the position changes of the body or diaper changes. Some senile elderly are restrained by their families in wheelchairs and others are locked in a small room. It is usually their families who hurt the elderly the most when they can't bear the heavy burden of care and express their disgust to their old relatives. Here there is no such emotional tension between the caregivers and the elderly, because we are professional caretakers hired to nurse these people.

Mrs Suzuki was generally satisfied with her job. With the skill and knowledge she had gained from her work, she was able to take care of her bedridden mother before she died and her skills would also be very helpful to her mother-in-law in the near future. And she had been consulted by a lot of friends who were considering putting their demented or bedridden parents in a *tokuyō* home and who were annoyed by the problems of care such as what to do with a bedsore, and how to apply for a short stay. Mrs Suzuki felt happy that she was useful to both her family members and her friends. Within Aoba, she felt most rewarded when a very sick resident had achieved recovery under her care, and when she was appreciated for the services she provided. As a veteran matron in Aoba, Mrs Suzuki liked her job. The physical nature of her job, though it gave her back-ache, suited her character as well as her career expectation. Since she thought a *tokuyō* home a place where disabled elderly could live in peace, she, too, would like to enter a nursing home if she became bedridden or senile. And she planned to become a volunteer to deliver meals to those old people living alone in the community after she retired.

Mrs Yoshi Yoshiwara: dietician

'I feel fulfilled as a professional.'

When Miss Watanabe, a trainee student, and I knocked on the sliding door of her small office, Mrs Yoshiwara, the dietician of Aoba, was sitting in front of her computer typing the menus for the next day. Every time trainee students come for field training in Aoba, she gives a talk on what a dietician and the dietary department do in a *tokuyō* home. She decided to do this seven or eight years ago when she read a report of a trainee student who had commented on the leftovers in the home. It was the only report mentioning meals that Mrs Yoshiwara had ever read, because issues of how to transfer patients, feed them, or help them with toilet and bath were the ones that interested the students the most. She thought it necessary to have the students understand the work of the dietary department because, for her, meals were the starting point of care.

Showing us the materials and photos she had prepared for the talk, Mrs Yoshiwara began to describe her duties.

Meals are the most vital factor for the survival of the elderly. However, because of the variety of illnesses, 40 years' difference in age range, and the complicated physical conditions of the residents, it is difficult for us to make meals that can satisfy everybody. In order to make good dishes to satisfy the residents, it is important for us to know their tastes.

In order to grasp the residents' tastes, Mrs Yoshiwara wrote down each individual's favourite food and his/her ingestive functions whenever she attended an interview. For those who could express themselves clearly, she and her colleagues regularly asked what they thought about the meals, usually at their birthday parties. Based on this information and suggestions as well as requirements from the doctors, nurses and the matrons, they prepared a variety of meals. She said:

For the staples, we have ordinary meals, rice porridge, fluid meals (NG tube) and paste; for the side dishes, we have ones that are not cut up, ones that are cut into larger pieces, ones that are cut into very small pieces and ones that are paste. For those who dislike the dishes we prepare because of the unbalanced diet formed from their long habits, we provide substitutes they can eat. About the standard amount of nutrition, we have an average criterion, that is, 1,380 calories and 58 grammes of protein per person each day. And since the small quantity of nutrients are insufficient for the elderly, we add some salted rice-bran paste for pickling and rice shoots which are rich in vitamins to their diet. In addition to the staple, side dishes, pickles and soup, we provide seasonal fruits, yoghurt, milk or milky coffee with each meal in order to maintain a balanced diet for the residents.

Since most residents are confined within the home, in order to help them develop a sense of the seasons, the home programmes a variety of traditional events around the year and we make corresponding dishes at such festivals to cheer up the elderly. For instance, there is soup with rice cakes (*zōni*) and festive food (*osechi-ryōri*) for the New Year, unrolled *sushi* (*chirashi-zushi*) at the Girls' Festival, lunch boxes in the cherry-blossom season, rice seasoned with soy sauce and boiled with meat or seafood and other savoury vegetables (*takikomi-gohan*) on Mother's Day, three-coloured fine noodles (*sanshoku sōmen*) at the Festival of the Weaver, vegetarian dishes at the Bon Festival, red rice on Respect-for-the-Aged Day, and special dishes for Christmas, etc. Besides these we also have a 'desired meal',[5] birthday party and a 'selective meal'[6] each month. Meals are basically provided in Japanese traditional styles.

Aged 58 in 1999, Mrs Yoshiwara had been working as a dietician in Kotobuki for eleven and a half years. Born the youngest daughter in a rural family in Fukushima Prefecture, she had yearned for city life in Tokyo since she was a high school student. So instead of entering a school to learn dressmaking and knitting or becoming a bride like most young women did at that time, she chose to start her new life in Tokyo. Using the money her parents prepared for her dowry as tuition, she studied nutritional science at a college for two years, and became a qualified managerial dietician after having worked in a hospital for two years.

After she got married and pregnant, she quit her job and stayed at home taking care of her son for four years. In the year when her son went to kindergarten, a dietician from her former workplace invited her to resume her job because they were short-handed. Considering the necessity of taking care of both household chores and her son, she only worked part-time at the hospital until her son went to primary school. With the help of her neighbours as well as her parents, who looked after her son after school and during the vacations, she was able to continue her career in the hospital for another 19 years.

Disgusted with the complicated human relationships in the dietary department, she resigned her job and became an in-home dietician (*zaitaku eiyōshi*)[7] at the local health centre. There she lectured in the 'Adult Disease Prevention Class' and gave 'nutrition lessons for infants', and went to families with physically disabled persons to teach how to make balanced meals. Through contacts with the aged persons who came to listen to her lectures and the visits to disabled persons in the community, she learned a lot about the living conditions of the elderly and wanted to contribute her professional knowledge to the elderly who needed advice on diet. At the same time, however, she felt that something was lacking because her role at the health centre was only that of a helper. She wanted to settle down in a fixed job and maintain a more constant relationship with a certain population.

Right at that time, an old friend of hers, who was a dietician in Aoba, informed her that there was a vacancy in the dietary section in Sazanka because of the retirement of a staff member. Only ten minutes' walk away from her home, she thought the distance was quite convenient for her to both work longer and tend to her family. So she applied for the job and was employed. After having worked in Sazanka for a year, she rotated to work as a managerial dietician in Aoba.

Mrs Yoshiwara spoke of the difficulty in making diets for medical treatment in the home. According to her, in a hospital, as everybody entered because of illness, the diet for a certain patient was clearly decided by his/her illness. When she first came to Aoba, what bewildered her most was that she could not make the same diet for medical treatment as she had done in the hospital. Though the residents were neither ill nor healthy, nearly everyone had some kind of illness. She said:

> In a hospital, hospitalisation is only a temporary situation for a patient, because one has the hope to return to one's own home through medication and diet treatment. However, the case is different here. There is no hope for the residents to return to their homes, for this is their home. I can't make the same diet here as in a hospital. Nor can I make ordinary family meals, because there are a lot of actual 'patients' who have illnesses such as cardiac insufficiency and kidney failure. I have tried to make diet treatment in the home once in a while, but I was unsuccessful.

She mentioned one failure in her work experience. There was once an old lady in Aoba who needed dialysis because of kidney failure and serious diabetes, but she refused to be hospitalised. So the doctor in Kotobuki clinic asked Mrs Yoshiwara to use diet treatment for her. She tried hard to make the meals for a week, but they were left untouched because all the dishes were salt-free. Eventually, the pitiful old woman was sent to the hospital and died there. This made Mrs Yoshiwara feel very sorry because she had been unable to prepare a suitable diet for the old woman. She thought it meaningless to have diet treatment for the elderly over 80 years of age. She began to think if she could make something that a resident could eat, and if he/she regarded it as delicious, it was unnecessary to prepare a medically perfect diet in the home. After that she asked the dietary workers to cook the same dishes for all the residents. 'If the elderly having the above illnesses can take in one third of their meals, it's enough, for it's better than having nothing', she said.

Since she was in full charge of the dietary department and had the responsibility of managing the diet of a group, Mrs Yoshiwara had to pay attention to issues such as food poisoning and to the jobs other dietary workers did. In order to run the department smoothly, she paired the six dietary workers into three groups, the early shift responsible for cooking breakfast and lunch, one for clearing away the dishes, disinfecting utensils and washing the cooking pots, and the day shift for cooking the dinner and preparing the breakfast for next day. And she asked all the staff to work cooperatively because only by working in a good atmosphere could the staff maintain good relationships and continue their career.

Since the home was a place where female staff dominated, inevitably there was gossip and backbiting, but Mrs Yoshiwara did not care much about it. First of all, there is no perfect person in the world. 'Everyone is a human being with many feelings, so it is natural for staff members to vent their anger, frustration and stress somewhere', she said. But she thought staff members should control their emotions in the workplace because the mood of the staff would affect the quality of the care of the residents. About cooperation with other departments, Mrs Yoshiwara thought it was going quite smoothly. She could get advice about the taste of the dishes from the matrons after they had the 'test dinners'. And she could discuss with nurses and matrons when deciding the diet pattern of a resident in the care conference.

Mrs Yoshiwara said that the most rewarding thing in her job was to look at the beaming faces of the residents when they had their meals. Another satisfaction came from her connection with the organisations outside the home. She explained:

> Some eleven years ago when I was helping with the classes on nutrition held by the health centre, the elderly, mostly old men living alone in the community, asked the city Social Welfare Council to find a professional dietician to teach them how to cook. As I was connected with the council as well as the health centre, I was asked to do that. I opened a cooking class twice a month at the Central Community Centre. I took the old men shopping and taught them how to buy materials for cooking. I taught them how to use a frying pan and a kitchen knife, how to cut the vegetables into various patterns, how to cook and how to make menus, etc. At present I have two such classes in the community, each having 20 or so 'students'.

Another organisation Mrs Yoshiwara had connected with was the Institute Liaison Group of Higashimurayama City in the city Social Welfare Council. It is an organisation consisting of ten institutions in the city, established in order to promote communication between the institutions and the citizens in the local community. Dieticians of the ten facilities were asked to open a class to teach the elderly living alone in the community about nutrition and how to cook. The dieticians take turns to teach the class once a month. Mrs Yoshiwara went to teach once or twice each year and she had continued this duty for seven years.

Inside Kotobuki, she taught the 'Nursing Care Class for the Family' for the Sakura Day Service Centre. It is a class held for the families of the elderly clients of the day care centre, mainly teaching the skills of how to take care of an elderly in one's own home. Mrs Yoshiwara was responsible for talking about nutrition and diet for the elderly. She commented on the satisfaction she had achieved from her involvement in these activities.

> Through such activities, I feel that I play a part in the local community. Especially when I am greeted by 'Many thanks for your kind help' or 'Thanks to your lectures, I have learned to cook by myself' in the street, I feel very fulfilled.

Mrs Yoshiwara was also a member of the Institution Meal Supply Association of Metropolitan Tokyo, a professional society for dieticians in facilities such as hospitals and institutions for the elderly, children and disabled persons. She belonged to the subgroup consisting of dieticians from Kiyose City, Higashikurume City and Higashimurayama City. She had the chance to present papers at the two seminars held by the association as well as the annual conference organised by their subgroup. As the vice-president of their subgroup, Mrs Yoshiwara had participated in organising various activities to enhance dieticians' role in the community. For instance, they had established a nutrition-consulting corner at the Tama Yamato Health Centre to give diet advice to local citizens, and they held an exhibition every year. In 1999, the exhibition was entitled 'Diet for Preventing People Becoming Bedridden'. As cerebral infarction and fracture of the bones were the two main causes of becoming bedridden, Mrs Yoshiwara and her friends were considering preventive methods from the angle of dietary customs of the elderly, to prevent people becoming bedridden. For example, they sorted out the kinds of diet that could make it easy for the elderly to absorb calcium as well as those that could alleviate hypertension and heart attacks. She commented on her professional activities as follows:

> I think it is good for us professional dieticians to have such a society to exchange information and to learn from each other. Compared with other professionals such as nurses, we dieticians are a much smaller population. We have our problems that other specialists cannot understand, so we

need a place to talk to each other about such problems. The association as well as our subgroup is not only a place for study but also a place to get rid of our stress.

Mrs Yoshiwara thought her job gave her a sense of achievement, not only within the home but also in the wider community. But she was a bit discontented with the facilities of the home. Since Aoba was an old home, and different from many new institutions in which the kitchen and the dining halls are adjacent, the dining halls were placed far away from the kitchen, which made it impossible to provide a type of counter service of the meals, or self-service. She wished that each floor had a mini-kitchen and a dining hall that could keep the dishes and soups warm.

Mrs Yoshiwara also wished that the old residents could die in the home. She said, 'It's an ideal for us to satisfy the residents with delicious food in the last period of their life and let them die a natural death.' At present, except for those who passed away suddenly, most terminated their lives in hospitals because in a *tokuyō* home, there was no first-aid equipment and medicine to handle emergency cases. Residents were sent to hospitals for treatment when their health condition worsened. Mrs Yoshiwara commented:

I think it too harsh for the elderly close to 90 or 100 years old to be plugged up to a variety of medical equipment in the hospital before they die. If conditions permit, and if we have terminal nursing care, I think it better to have them die naturally here. But as it is an issue related to the human rights of a person, dying in an institution may be difficult.

When turning to talk about whether she thought that the elderly were living a satisfied life in the home, she said it depended on the person.

Those who entered the home by their own decision and those who couldn't maintain their daily lives any more by themselves, might feel comfortable living here. But I am not sure whether they are satisfied psychologically. I think the material life of the residents is quite good.

She then took meal provisions as an example to support her claim. She said:

There is a world of difference between a welfare institution and a hospital regarding meal provision. In a private hospital, the budget for meals is covered by the total income of the hospital, so it is necessary to consider the price of materials first, then make the menus and dishes. However, in a welfare institution, up until now, there has been a large fixed budget for food supply every year. What we need to do is to finish up this budget. As a result we never consider the price of materials and usually buy the same materials as a hospital in the local market at higher prices. Our budget for purchasing raw materials for one elderly per meal is 880 yen (about $7.6 in 1999) a day, a bit lower than the 960 yen ($8.3) of last year. However compared with that of a private hospital, it is at least 300 yen ($2.7) higher. In addition, we have a lot of festival meals that an ordinary hospital cannot afford.

Mrs Yoshiwara said she would prefer to live in a *tokuyō* home if she became bedridden or demented. She said when she looked at the senile elderly in Aoba, she thought that the lives of the children of these elderly persons would have been ruined if they were cared for in their own homes. She would not like to become a burden to her son and his family, so she would choose to enter a *tokuyō* home or a hospital when she needed constant care some day. She said:

> This might be different from the elderly residing in Aoba, most of whom are survivors of the war and who have an ideal of living in a big family. I received higher education after the war, witnessed the prosperity of the Japanese economy and have lived a peaceful life, so the psychological structure of people of my age is different from the residents living here. To some extent we are ready to take responsibility for our own old age. In addition, I know what a home is like after so many years' work, and I don't think it is a horrible place but a quite nice one for those who need it. Aoba is an old home, it has many limitations in personal space, facilities and choices in self-determination. But these conditions will be improved after the LTCI is enacted, so I think I can live in a better home that has private rooms, loose regulations and more freedom when I am old.

With regard to her plans after her retirement, Mrs Yoshiwara smiled, her eyes gleamed with her dream.

> I have several good friends who share the same dream as mine. They are all dieticians. We want to open a restaurant to make lunch boxes for the elderly living alone in the community, of course using our own recipes. If this cannot be realised, I would like to become a volunteer to deliver meals to the elderly who are unable to cook for themselves.

In this way, she wanted to be useful to other people living in her community as long as she was healthy.

Corporate culture of Kotobuki

Career paths

As at the Elmwood Grove nursing home where few professionals had originally considered careers in a geriatric institution (Savishinsky 1991: 172), among the staff in Kotobuki, only a handful had originally planned to work with the elderly. Mr Itō had wanted to work with people, but he had not specified which population he wanted to serve. He entered the field because there was a vacancy in Aoba just when he graduated from the university. Among the other welfare supervisors in Kotobuki, except for one or two newly employed who were graduate students specialised in elderly welfare, others either had experience of working in homes for children or were promoted from dietician or matron.

Most nurses had originally worked in an emergency hospital or ordinary hospitals. They preferred the home to a hospital because the job in an institution was not so fettered to the busy routines in a hospital, and it allowed them to develop long-term relationships with the residents rather than the temporary ones in the hospital. The dieticians had also been employed in hospitals. For example, Mrs Yoshiwara had long worked in a hospital and helped teach a number of nutrition classes in the community before she came to work in Aoba.

Direct care staff - the matrons, and the dietary workers - came from the local area holding high school diplomas. Apart from the single young employees from welfare vocational schools, the majority of the middle-aged female staff entered the homes after they finished the tasks of childrearing. Some employees in their 50s, for example Mrs Suzuki, wanted to learn knowledge and skills of caring for an elderly person in advance of having to do so for her own family members. Ms Shinozaki, however, was more practical because her status as a divorced woman had forced her to choose an occupation that could ensure a stable income to support herself and her daughter. Her case was not unique at the home. A number of matrons chose to work in Kotobuki because of their status as single mothers as a result of divorce or the death of their spouses.

To a considerable degree, the work that such caregivers did at the homes did not require specific qualifications, because it was 'an extension of the traditional female domestic skills they had already practiced in their own houses, namely, cleaning, cooking, caring, laundering, and nurturing' (Savishinsky 1991: 178). This was reflected in the words of one matron who said that her job was 'one of maternal instincts', and of another one who ironically called herself 'a cleaning woman'. The nature of institutional work, the cultural ideal of woman's role as 'a nurturer' (Long 1996: 159), and the minimal job prerequisites combine to explain why many former housewives chose to work in Kotobuki.

Another reason why both middle-aged women and young persons entered the care workforce was that salary and welfare provisions in a welfare institution were quite stable. Staff members in a private non-profit institution such as Kotobuki were underpaid before the 1970s. However, during the period when Minobe Ryokichi was Governor of Tokyo Metropolis, the 'policy for equalisation of the public and private institutions' (*kōshi kakusa zesei seido*) was enacted to abolish the salary differences between public institutions and private homes in order to improve well-being of the employees in the private sectors. Since then, the employees in private institutions in Tokyo have been paid an average salary similar to the amount a public servant gets. Under the current welfare system, a private welfare institution receives its operational budget from the national government, local government and municipalities that have entrusted it with the care of their elderly citizens. As such, compared with many private companies, which were beset with restructuring and bankruptcy during the economic recession, the labour costs of a welfare institution were guaranteed. Two new welfare supervisors I interviewed remarked that their salaries were higher than those of their classmates who were working in private companies, and therefore expressed great satisfaction about their incomes. Three of the six young male care workers (most in their early 20s) also showed satisfaction with their monthly net income of about 190,000 yen (about $1,650 in 1999), which was a bit higher than that of their peers with similar education but working in a private company. This coincides with Ruth Campbell's research into the reasons for lower staff turnover and higher motivation of Japanese care workers in elderly institutions compared to America, in which she listed the competitive wage of care staff as an advantage. She notes that as early as in 1983, a care worker just starting a job in an average welfare institution in Tokyo already earned as much as US$ 522 per month and received annual bonus totalling five months' salary (Campbell 1998: 186).

When one is employed as a full-time employee and has passed the three-months probation period, he/she enters the permanent employment system of the home, and will receive welfare pension and other benefits at the compulsory retirement age of 60. This explains why many matrons have remained in their jobs for more than 20 years. The seniority wage system is a reason why middle-aged women are willing to become full-time employees in welfare institutions. In Kotobuki's current salary structure, a middle-aged women entering the home at the same time as a young school graduate would be paid higher than the latter because payment is favourably related to age. Most middle-aged matrons I interviewed were quite content with their salaries.

Young male care workers were generally satisfied with their salary, though considering their workload, the amount might not appear to be so high. Being single, they did not need to support their families. Consequently, they found their salaries sufficient for the time being and were quite satisfied with their present jobs. However, once they got married and had children, especially when the wives could not work because of childrearing, financial difficulties would arise. At present, promotion opportunities for young care workers were minimal. As men were supposed to undertake the responsibility to support their families and to achieve success in their lives, they thought that their jobs were only suitable when young. If there were no ways to advance to the position of a welfare supervisor or a care manager, they would consider changing careers or switch to a public nursing home for the elderly or other geriatric health care facilities, where average salaries are higher.

Among the young female staff members, single care workers in their early 20s said that they did not know whether they would need to quit if they got married or had babies, but at least at present they wanted to continue. Most of those in their late 20s who had already got married or been pregnant expressed their willingness to continue working after childbirth. During my stay in Kotobuki, four female workers returned to their workplace after one year's maternal leave. A number of care workers in their early 30s who already had children felt themselves lucky to be able to have a full-time job in the era of a 'job shortage for women'. This indicates that young female workers' willingness to persist in their career is relatively strong. But as shown from the answers to my questionnaires, most of these care workers are high school graduates or vocational school graduates, I could not exclude the possibility that these women preferred an institutional career because they could not find better paid full-time jobs in areas other than health care.

Foner (1995: 169-70) gives credit to the unionisation of Crescent Home for the relatively high wages and benefits of the nurse aides and the lower turnover rate among them when compared with those in other nursing homes nationwide. Kotobuki is also unionised. According to Mr Itō, their union (*rōdō kumiai*) has done a great deal to improve work environment and protect the welfare and benefits of its workers. Since I did not look deeply into this issue, I am unsure whether the union has a great role to play in ensuring workers' high level of work satisfaction as well as their low turnover rate. Both Ōkuma (1992: 180) and Yamanoi (1991: 110-11) mentioned that the care labour force in American nursing homes depended on immigrant nurse aides and that low wages of these care workers were the main reasons for their frequent change of jobs. In Japanese welfare institutions, in contrast, the official 'measure system',[8] the lifelong employment system, the seniority wage system as well as a harmonious work environment have ensured a stable salary for the employees along with their relatively high motivation to continue their career.

Satisfaction and dissatisfaction

Satisfaction in one's job is an important aspect of institutional work life. Growing up together with Kotobuki, Mr Itō had a strong sense of belonging. His religious faith or spirit of mercy instilled in his childhood made him choose a lifelong job in the welfare field. His wish was to minimise the managerial aspect of the home and maximise a family atmosphere, to have the residents feel at home and live a peaceful later life. He treated the residents fairly, regardless of their past, never scolding a resident even when he/she had done wrong. As a result, he was appreciated by most residents for his tenderness and for the programmes he planned for them. He felt fulfilled that he had been able to help at least 200 persons complete their lives and have them sleep peacefully in their graves. And he enjoyed the way the residents rewarded him: with a smile, a wave of the hand and a warm greeting. This made him feel that he was not an administrator but a friend of the residents, a feeling that Gordon, the assistant director in Elmwood Grove, achieved in his interactions with certain elderly residents (Savishinsky 1991: 180).

With respect to his managerial work, Mr Itō thought it inevitable to have some discord in teamwork. He tried his best to create an open atmosphere where it was easy for everyone to express their opinions. As a whole, he was proud that the management system in Kotobuki was a democratic one when compared with many paternalistic institutions in the welfare field. He thought that the work atmosphere of the home was better than in comparable institutions in terms of cooperation and absence of conflicts among workers. Now as the warden of Aoba, Mr Itō felt pleased that the home had a good reputation in the local community. Despite its obsolete facilities, many clients still preferred Aoba's long-term care and short-stay services to those of others. This was because of its dedicated and highly qualified care workers. In order to recruit good staff, he drafted appealing advertisements to circulate in welfare professional schools and other vocational training centres. He also went to these centres to introduce Aoba to the students. He was proud that, through his effort in constructing networks, the home had a strong workforce of care workers. And he felt that he had made some contribution to enhancing communication between the home and the outside world, and nurturing the young welfare manpower, because a lot of volunteers came to help in the home, while a great number of trainee students in universities and vocational schools had chosen Kotobuki as their field-training place.

However, two managerial issues disturbed Mr Itō. One was the successive budgetary cutbacks in recent years; the other was the buildings of Kotobuki. With the deterioration of the national finances and policy emphasis on expansion of in-home services, subsidies from both the central government and Metropolitan government were cut year by year (Shimizu et al. 1994: 103-5). Since the enactment of the LTCI programme, because the old official 'measure system' by which Aoba was regulated went out of use, the home no longer receives public subsidies known as 'measure fees' (*shochi-hi*). But in order to prevent drastic financial problems brought about by the new programme, Aoba is still granted some public subsidies during the initial years. In 2000, it obtained a total amount of 56,000,000 yen of (about $459,000 in 2000) in public subsidy. This amount was reduced to 19,000,000 yen (about $154,470) in 2002, and further reduced to 8,000,000 yen (about $68,376) in 2003. From 2004 onward, with no public subsidy, operation of the home will rely entirely on income generated by the LTIC. As a result, subsidies for meal provision as well as for recreation and festivals have been cut totally. With total budget shrinkage, maintaining the management level of the home as well as the quality of life and care of the residents has become a big challenge.

Witnessing the many troubles that arose between room-mates in Sazanka, Mr Itō felt sorry that the home could not ensure the privacy of each resident due to space limitation. He also concerned about the outdated facilities of Aoba. A home established more than 20 years ago, its facilities such as kitchen, dining halls, living space, furniture and so on have become obsolete. Without good 'hardware', the home is at a disadvantage in attracting clients in the competitive health care market. He worried that a number of its current residents would be tempted to move by the new geriatric health care facility under construction a few blocks away, if the administration did not take steps to improve the condition of the building. In order to keep up the reputation of Aoba and win clients, Mr Itō hoped to accumulate enough funds to rebuild Aoba within the next five years. Thus he was busy developing plans and projects together with directors of each department and the board of directors, and drafting convincing reports to obtain funds from the Metropolitan government. In Japan, where community chests (*kyōdō bokin*) and the system of funding charities by individuals, companies and NGOs are less developed than in Britain and other industrial countries (Ōhashi 1999: 144-54). It is quite difficult to raise funds from private enterprises and individuals.

Among the direct care staff, there were some who saw their job as just a pay cheque. But most felt rewarded by other aspects of institutional work. The nurses enjoyed the relative ease of work in a home, and mentioned the physical tiredness and stretched nerves they got from working in a hospital. Though their salaries were lower than those of hospital nurses, they were satisfied with their roles as consultants, listening to the afflictions of the residents and giving medical advice that the matrons could not provide. They felt fulfilled when the elderly recovered after medication or hospitalisation at their suggestion. Like Louise, the nurse at Elmwood Grove, they felt satisfied to be able to 'care for patients for the long term' (Savishinsky 1991: 159) so that they were able to know the residents as people. What they felt discontented about was that there were no facilities for them to administer first aid in emergencies or for ordinary treatment, such as giving intravenous drip injections, in the home.

Rehabilitation staff, whose job responsibility was restoration and maintenance of the physical functions of the residents, were delighted to see every improvement in the residents such as standing up from a wheelchair, maintaining a standing position longer, and using a spoon to feed him/herself. They also had their frustrations: the residents were surrounded by age-mates with comparable frailty and had difficulties finding the motivation to exercise hard because they lacked the presence of healthier peers to model what hard work might have yielded. And staff felt sad when a function regained lapsed again because of the interruptions in training.

Most matrons in Kotobuki were satisfied with the good work environment as well as the smooth staff relationships: both young staff and senior employees could express their opinions regarding the care of certain residents; all staff members could learn from each other; there were in-service training programmes for care workers; work conditions allowed women to continue working; and there was no bullying. This is quite different from Crescent Nursing Home where a supervisory nursing hierarchy existed between nurses and nursing aides, and where nurse aides, overseen and administered by nurses, having little autonomy but enduring much stress, tended to be hostile to nurses (Foner 1994: 78-90).

Senior matrons in Sazanka were happy to be trusted and relied upon by the residents. 'The job helps us build up our human nature, and our feelings have become enriched since we came here', they said. Institutional work made them think about their own later life. Ms Shinozaki was thinking of an ideal image of herself as an old person when referring to the residents in the home. Her emotional satisfaction lay in her relations with particular residents. Her own personal tragedy aroused an internal sympathy towards Miss Nishikawa, a powerless mental patient and miserable victim of bullying. She paid special attention to Miss Nishikawa and took her part when she had troubles with other residents. In return, Miss Nishikawa always sought refuge with Ms Shinozaki. Mrs Suzuki, on the other hand, was pleased to hear the compliments from the residents for her warm hands. She was glad that the health condition of Mrs Nakamura became stable again after the section chief of the nursing department adopted suggestions put forward by her and her colleagues.

What disturbed the matrons the most? In Aoba, it was the occasional disagreement with nurses regarding the care plan of certain residents mentioned in Mrs Suzuki's account. She felt sorry that she was unable to care for the personal needs of individuals because of the tight schedule of care tasks. In Sazanka and Akashia, some young matrons were unsatisfied with the senior-junior relations: their ways of working were not appreciated by the seniors who tended to emphasise the traditional ways, while their autonomy in caring for the elderly under their administration was sometimes usurped by their supervisors. Meanwhile the senior matrons worried that if the home employed more young matrons, the elderly residents would be less satisfied as the young staff were less dependable and more likely to impose their ideas on the elderly without considering their feelings very much.

Furthermore, although the home regime said that all the residents must be treated disinterestedly, both the nurses and the matrons thought that their opinions for solving the conflicts between mental patients and normal residents were sometimes neglected. In the case of the conflict between Miss Nishikawa and Mrs Takagi (see Chapter 6), both the nurses and the matrons thought that since both parties must be responsible for the affair, it would be a fair solution to have both change their rooms. However, the administrators resolved the conflict by only transferring Miss Nishikawa to another floor. The nurses and matrons attributed this to the will of the administrators to save face for the home. Because Mrs Takagi was a normal person, she could say anything she wanted to persons in the community. If she spoke ill of the home, the reputation of Kotobuki would be damaged. So Mrs Takagi could remain on the floor and her intention to expel a mental patient she disliked could be realised. This measure displeased the direct care staff, who thought that QOL of mentally disabled residents would not be improved if their environment, especially the attitudes of other residents, did not change for the better.

Like the nurses, the professional dietician in Aoba, Mrs Yoshiwara, was happy to have a permanent job in which she could establish long-term relationships with the population she served. She felt satisfied to see the contented faces of the residents when they had their meals. She thought that the dietary section was cooperating well with the nurses and the matrons. Another source of her satisfaction came from her involvement in the community. Gratitude expressed by the people who had benefited from her lectures on nutrition and diet gave her a sense of fulfilment, and the role she played in the dietician society made her feel proud to be a professional. What worried her most was the budget cut for meal provision under the LTCI system. This would directly affect residents' quality of life as well as the job security of her colleagues.

Overall, my staff informants expressed high levels of satisfaction with their jobs. Despite the stress of their physical labour, most of them said that a job involving personal relationships was worth doing, and that if they only focused on their work with the elderly residents they felt fulfilled. The job not only let them feel that they were useful to others but also helped them grow through looking at the kinds of lives the elderly persons had lived and through interactions with these clients.

To the staff members, financial reward was of course important, but it seemed to me that they were more likely to relate their reward to emotional satisfaction and personal achievements. Did they express their high job satisfaction from *honne* (real intention) or were they just mouthing platitudes (*tatemae*)? Mr Itō's accounts about how he wanted to make a good home for both the residents and the staff may sound too ideal. He may have included a lot of *tatemae*. However, I think, as an administrator of the home, he has his particular standpoint. It's normal for him to show an outside researcher the general principles of operating a home and the good aspects of Kotobuki. With regard to the employees, I think most mature staff members were reporting their authentic feelings towards their work with the residents, but for those who were alienated by the residents the conditions may be different. Mrs Oda, a matron in Akashia, asked the warden to transfer her from her floor to the laundry room. As she was accused by a resident of having broken into her room during her absence and a number of residents refused to talk to her, Mrs Oda found it difficult to work on the floor. She was more frustrated than fulfilled in her job.

Regarding staff relationships, it was more complicated. Informants' claims that they had good teamwork may be just *tatemae*. I heard privately a number of criticisms and complaints about the bureaucratic system, senior supervisors and interdepartmental cooperation. For instance, direct care workers expressed scorn that a couple of wardens in Kotobuki were *amaku-dari* (parachuting in)[9] from government institutions and that they knew nothing about the conditions of the residents or the work of the staff. Younger staff members complained that the administrators only adopted the opinions of the senior members.

Gender

In Kotobuki, the female majority was present at all levels, especially among the direct caregivers. The reason is not surprising. Minimal educational requirements, and emphasis on such traditionally female domestic tasks as cleaning and nurturing made the lower-skill jobs in housekeeping, cooking, cleaning and nursing the domain of women (Foner 1994: 152; Long 1996: 158; Savishinsky 1991: 187). About two-thirds of the current care staff were former housewives in the local community. To begin with, employees came to work in the homes without any formal training while the more recently employed normally had qualifications as home-helpers or care and welfare workers. Like the care workers in Elmwood Grove (Savishinsky 1991), those who had little geriatric care training learned the practical skills of nursing care as well as the strategies for dealing with human relationships after they entered the field.

By contrast, the male employees were found in jobs such as administrators, accountants and welfare supervisors. Except for welfare supervisors and a few administrators such as Mr Itō, top administrators are authoritative figures for both residents and employees. They, together with some male office employees, are less significant in lives of the residents' and employees.

In recent years, with the recession of economy and the development of geriatric facilities, male care workers began to appear in nursing homes. The six male workers in Aoba were all graduates from professional welfare schools with care and welfare worker qualifications. They were nursing the elderly residents exactly as their female colleagues did. Two of them had handicapped classmates in their high schools. Their desire to help disadvantaged persons drove them into the welfare field. One said that, through the influence of his mother who was a kindergarten teacher, he became fond of taking care of others. Most said that their friends were puzzled why they had chosen a career belonging to the province of women. They admitted that they were not accustomed to the care jobs at the very beginning, but the training they received had nurtured them as professional care workers.

Many senior matrons thought it praiseworthy that young men took part in the nursing care work, which was known as one of the 3 Ks.[10] Young matrons also thought it good to have a balance between workers of both sexes because it was easier to do jobs such as transferring, bathing, etc. with the help of male colleagues. And it would make the male residents feel more comfortable to receive care from staff of the same sex (*dōsei kaigo*). Some matrons and trainee students who were former teachers of nurseries or kindergartens said there were male colleagues in their former workplaces. This indicates that Japanese males, though only a minority, have entered nurturing occupations that are traditionally regarded as female domains such as childcare and elderly care. With more young male workers participating in the care workforce, it seems that the attitude towards the traditional division of responsibility between sexes as well as the occupational preference of the young Japanese are undergoing a transition.

Coping with stress

As Mrs Yoshiwara said, no job is free of stress. In Aoba stress came from physical labour, while in Sazanka and Akashia it came from dealing with human relationships. Mr Itō said that as he enjoyed doing his job, he did not feel much stress; but he needed to be careful in how he talked to his subordinates and the matrons so as to avoid misunderstandings. He would go driving, fishing or buying bags[11] in shops to get away from the disturbances in his workplace.

Ms Shinozaki felt stressed when dealing with the complicated relationships with both the residents and her colleagues. Since she came to Sazanka in her 40s, she found it difficult to fit herself into the existing work atmosphere and to work in her own way. Even though she was the head matron, she sometimes found it difficult to convince her co-workers whose work histories in Sazanka were longer than hers. As she preferred a transparent style of communication, she chose to put her ideas before her colleagues for mutual discussion. The lack of a psychiatrist in the home had also put a lot of pressure on her in dealing with mental patients and their conflicts with other residents. In order to grasp the conditions of the residents, she observed carefully every aspect of their daily life. She also asked other matrons to write down the details of any problems in the Matrons' Diary so that the administrators could refer to them for good solutions. Enjoying the beauty of the flowers through flower arrangement during her holidays was her way of coping with stress.

Mrs Suzuki said she was suited to doing jobs requiring physical strength. Though she was frustrated when matrons' opinions were not adopted at the care conference once in a while, she would feel pleased when their ways of treating the elderly were considered. As the team on her floor operated smoothly, she did not have much stress from human relationships with the others. However she felt tired after returning home from her shift. The ways she chose to relax were soaking in her bathtub, reading a funny book, chatting with friends on the phone and eating.

For Mrs Yoshiwara, apart from the occasional uneasiness resulting from communication with her subordinates, her feeling of stress was minimal, because she was optimistic and cared little about gossip. She would go jogging when she felt stressed.

In Kotobuki, the senior matrons who had worked in a *tokuyō* home all said that it was easier to work in Aoba than in Sazanka and Akashia because physical fatigue was more tolerable than psychological stress. They suggested young workers switch to Aoba if there was a chance for intra-home job transfer. On the other hand, older matrons in Aoba said that jobs requiring physical labour also have constraints, as they were feeling gradu-ally unable physically to keep up with the pace of work.

Savishinsky (1991) observed in his study that there was no place in Elmwood Grove where staff members could search for support and relieve stress. In Kotobuki it was the same. In all three homes, there were no formal channels for staff to vent their anger or frustration accumulated in their jobs. Many said that they had no close friends in the workplace from whom they could get comfort and support, and that they would like to maintain casual relationships with their co-workers. Some said if they really wanted to consult someone for advice or to complain about something, they would like to talk to a person external to their own department. Thus most staff found their ways of getting rid of stress outside the workplace. Some sought it in art hobbies such as arranging flowers or playing the *koto*; some by drinking and singing *karaoke* with friends, or soaking in a bathtub, or just sleeping; others planned excursions with their families or friends.

Attitudes towards institutionalisation

Views of institutional life and institutionalisation

Every day staff members were working with the residents and talking about the elderly. Their views of institutional life and institutionalisation were slightly different depending on their age group and the type of home they talked about. For the residents in Sazanka, almost all my staff informants regarded them as 'people who could not live in their own homes for some kind of reasons' and the 'reasons' were usually referred to as social handi-caps such as being childless, celibacy, widowhood, neglect by children, homelessness and so on. So the residents were commonly regarded as persons on welfare, that is, 'the weak of society' according to Mr Itō, or 'miserable persons' according to Ms Shinozaki. Both thought that these elderly were forced into being institutionalised rather than having made the decision of their own free will. As all residents had to share rooms and had little choice in whom they were paired with, the staff were sympathetic with their lack of privacy but commended them for being more considerate and less troublesome than those in Akashia. Because the residents felt indebted to the home and the staff members for the services they received, they seldom made requests. Thus the employees thought that their relationship with most residents was good and their jobs were easily done.

On the other hand, the residents of Akashia were referred to as 'people with low income' who entered the home on contract. They tended to think that they had the rights to receive services because they were paying fees. Ms Shinozaki said 'in Akashia, many are self-centred persons never feeling grateful'. The nurses agreed with her and added 'although they might have come to the home because of their bad relationships with their families, we do not think them pitiful'.

The residents of Aoba were 'old people with severe physical and mental impairments who could not be cared for at home'. Their extreme frailty and dependency, however, was acceptable to most of the workers in Aoba. 'It's unreasonable for a family member to care for such seriously bedridden and demented elderly people at home', Mrs Suzuki said, which was representative of the opinions of other employees about the residents.

Mr Itō and Ms Shinozaki thought that institutionalisation was both a blessing and a curse to the residents. For those who suffered from intra-familial tensions, who were isolated in the community, and who could not manage their lives at home, living in a home might be happier; but for those who were put into the home by their families and who had hoped to be cared for by their children, entering a home might mean humiliation, because the image of a home as an *Obasuteyama* or a *yōrō-in* still existed. Most staff members in Sazanka shared this idea. Regarding their own view of institutionalisation, Mr Itō said that in big cities such as Tokyo the image of a home as a *yōrō-in* had become blunted with the development of welfare policy and services for the elderly. Institutions for the elderly had evolved from relief facilities into welfare institutions, where people's basic rights were respected. He himself had no resistance towards entering a home. But he would prefer one with private rooms and minimum regulations.

Having witnessed conflicts among residents and the limitations of the home, Ms Shinozaki said that a home was the last place she would like to live in. Her own home was the most ideal place to spend her later life because it ensured her freedom, privacy, autonomy as well as the love of her family. In Aoba, both Mrs Suzuki and Mrs Yoshiwara thought that entering a *tokuyō* home was an inevitable outcome of population ageing. Living in an institution would be beneficial for both the elderly and their families. The elderly could receive good care and live their life in a humane setting; the families would be relieved from the stress of caregiving. Under the LTCI scheme, it became a client's right to choose an institution rather than be assigned to a home by the welfare office. They preferred to enter a *tokuyō* home if they became bedridden or senile.

Actually, regarding their willingness to live in a home, there were two types of attitude. One was 'resistance' which was represented by employees such as Ms Shinozaki, who preferred either living with their children or managing their lives by themselves. Mrs Suzuki and Mrs Yoshiwara were the representatives of those holding the other attitude, that of 'approval'. Most staff members thought a *tokuyō* home was an acceptable choice, especially when one became impaired. This indicates that physical impairments justify institutional care. The number of informants who expressed their willingness to live in a *yōgo* home was small, while a majority said if they had to live in an institution, they preferred a *yuryō* home (home for the elderly charging a fee) or a care house where they could not only receive care but also have their private rooms

Fairness in welfare institutions

A common topic among the employees was fairness in welfare institutions or welfare systems. Staff members were living in two places, their workplace and their family. In the workplace, their subjects were the elderly residents, and outside Kotobuki, the elderly they had connections with were mainly their own old parents, relatives and other elderly in the community. So comparisons were always made between the residents in the homes and the elderly who lived outside. Focusing on the material life of the institution-alised elderly, the workers thought that the residents were living a far better life than those living a marginal life in the community. They mentioned such expensive dishes as unrolled *sushi*, *sashimi* (sliced raw fish) and fried shrimp, and various planned programmes such as trips to a hot spring resort and festivals that each institutionalised elderly person could enjoy, which was an obvious advantage compared with those elderly who were living on their small pensions in their own homes.

They also compared the life of the Livelihood Protection recipients with those elderly who had worked hard and paid taxes all their lives but received no welfare benefits. According to them, the majority of these recipients were people who had not worked hard while young. In spite of their getting married and having children, they had thrown away their families in order to escape from debt, and led a vagrant life, gambling, drinking and doing everything they wanted to. When they became older and were unable to support themselves, they depended on welfare.

> Those who are lazy and haven't carried out any social responsibility can live an easy life on welfare. However, those who have worked hard and been responsible for their own lives have to manage their lives without any assistance from the welfare. That is unfair. They, the recipients of Livelihood Protection, are also given pocket money. But they spend every penny on alcohol. We expect, at least, that they should pay for their own funeral services. We also hope that they buy daily living arti-cles such as toilet paper, soap and towel from their pocket money. They should learn to take responsibility.

The above opinion was embraced by the majority of staff members such as matrons and nurses in Sazanka and Akashia. In their view, Japanese welfare policy was not equal for all people. On one hand, it helped the needy. On the other hand, it fostered human 'parasites'. The institutionalised elderly were provided with too much, while the elderly living in their own homes were given too little. They hoped that the government would spend more money developing in-home services. Some matrons in Aoba, such as Mrs Suzuki, thought that since the elderly residents were provided with everything in the home, they had no need to spend their own money except for the monthly fee. As a result, they could save a lot of money from their income. Though the government was taking care of the elderly, when they died, the great amount of property left by the residents always went to their relatives who never came to visit them. As such, they suggested establishing a 'donation policy' (*kifukin seido*) to contribute some of the money left over by the deceased residents to the home or to the elderly living a marginal life in the communities.

The same unfairness also exists between Sazanka and Akashia. Although residents in both institutions were paying fees according to their income, what they received did not correspond to their payment. For instance, many residents in Sazanka were paying more than those in Akashia. Some even paid as much as 140,000 yen ($1,170 in 1999) a month, an amount far more than the highest fee of 98,000 yen ($852) in Akashia. But they still had to share a room with another person, which meant a loss of privacy and more potential conflicts; while the residents in Akashia could pay less but enjoy freedom and privacy. Most staff thought it necessary to revise the fee charging standards of the homes to make them fairer. For them, ensuring private rooms in both kinds of institutions was essential.

QOL and its factors

With respect to QOL of the residents, integrating viewpoints of all staff members, we will find that food and other material provisions, activity programmes, events and festivals, care services provided by staff members, and support from elderly residents' families are regarded as factors that related to residents' quality of life.

Food and other material provisions

Most staff members regarded food provision as an important aspect of institutional care. They were proud that Kotobuki had a good reputation for providing good food to the residents among welfare institutions in the Tokyo area. Although it could not compete with some new institutions equipped with facilities that could provide counter-style self-service, the quality of its meal provision was not only commended by the residents but also evaluated well by an official judging committee that examined food provisions in institutions.

The diversity, nutrition and health aspects, and traditional style of food provision in the home are universally praised by staff members. In addition to daily meals, there were everyday refreshments, weekly tea drinking,[12] monthly meals for 'birthday party', 'selective meals' and 'desired meals', seasonal barbecues, annual eating in an outside restaurant and various festival meals around the year. According to staff members, many of the seasonal and festival foods were no longer served in ordinary Japanese families, and some were so expensive that elderly persons living alone on their small pensions could not afford them.

There were professional dieticians calculating the nutrients and calories, and preparing nutritional and healthily balanced food for the residents. The budget for food provision was guaranteed so that the home could buy good materials to make dishes. As meals were provided free of charge on a daily basis, the residents could save not only money but also the trouble of going shopping, selecting menus and cooking by themselves.

Besides meal provisions, staff also mentioned other material provisions as strong points of institutional life. They listed the free supply of articles for daily living such as tissues, towels, soap, razors and coupons for purchasing clothes, and they commended the cleanness of 'home life'. For instance, rooms were cleaned every day and sheets were changed every week.

Itō (1975) mentioned in his paper on a Japanese nursing home in America that services for Japanese American elderly were totally provided within 'a Japanese environment' according to the language, dietary, physical and social needs of the clients. In Kotobuki, without any doubt, all residents were living in a total Japanese environment. The traditional food styles catered to the dietary habits of the residents, while bath services were provided every day, to match residents' habits of daily living.

Quality of care

Staff members thought the services they provided could directly influence residents' quality of life. Nearly every staff member I interviewed or who filled in my questionnaire said that workers in welfare institutions should have qualities such as thoughtfulness, a loving heart, keen judgement and cooperation. These are prerequisites for good quality of care.

Typified in the remarks by Ms Shinozaki, that is, 'in Sazaka and Akashia, we care for the soul (*kokoro*), while in Aoba, it is the body that is tended to', the characteristics of personal care in Kotobuki were different in different institutions. In Sazanka and Akashia, services are provided to help the residents lead an autonomous and enjoyable life. Care is directed towards residents' emotional or psychological aspects of well-being. Staff members needed to be more involved with the residents in order to know them, win their trust and address their troubles. Whether or not a staff member is favoured by the residents depends largely on her personality, authority, coping strategy and fairness towards the residents. Many older matrons, who had worked in the homes for a long time, were pleased that they were trusted and relied on by the residents. They said that the average quality of their care was good.

Similar to Campbell's study (1998) that characterises Japanese institutional care as putting high priority on keeping the elderly neat and clean and encouraging dependency of the patients, care in Aoba emphasises the bodily comfort or the basic physical needs of the elderly. Staff members thought that the quality of their services, namely, feeding, dressing, toileting, bathing and monitoring health conditions, was the most important factor that connected with residents' quality of life. They faithfully carried out these tasks, feeding the elderly with great concern, carefully cleaning, powdering, applying lotion and turning the bodies of the elderly at the six times' a day diaper-changes, tenderly rubbing the bodies of the elderly and having them soak in the bathtub at a comfortable temperature, to ensure residents' physical comfort and the stability of their health condition. Through such skinship contact between the elderly and the care worker, a reliable relationship between the two was expected to grow. As the debilitated elderly were regarded as hopeless children, their dependency on caretakers was acceptable. Residents were permitted to lie on their beds all the time and they were protected from falling when unattended. This kind of care can be characterised as 'custodial care' (McLean and Perkinson 1995: 144-5) that emphasises pragmatic routine care of the body (Long 1996: 161).

Recreational programmes and events

The staff members listed the variety of activity programmes, annual events and festivals offered by the home as things the residents could enjoy but were unavailable to most elderly persons living by themselves. In Sazanka and Akashia, there were 15 cultural recreational clubs where residents could enjoy their hobbies such as flower arrangement, calligraphy, folk songs and dances, *haiku*, handicraft, etc. There were gateball, table tennis and Japanese chess competitions with other institutions, as well as handicraft exhibitions. These activity programmes could enrich elderly residents' leisure time and broaden their social network. Besides these, the home also held monthly birthday parties, seasonal events and annual festivals for the residents. The cherry blossom viewing, Bon Festival and grave visiting were the most favoured programmes, attracting enthusiastic participation by the residents. Many elderly persons also enjoyed the day trips and overnight trips.

In Aoba, programmes were fewer than those in Sazanka and Akashia due to mental and physical impairments of the residents and shortage of helping hands.

Family

Staff members admitted that family was a big psychological support for institutionalised residents. Ms Shinozaki knew this from residents' radiant faces when their families came to visit. Mrs Suzuki took Mrs Shimizu, a resident in Aoba, as an example of one who 'lives entirely on the support of and for the sake of their families'. Mrs Shimizu was forced to enter the home because her only daughter went to live in America after her marriage. After she came to the home, she kept on talking about her daughter and her granddaughter to both staff and other residents. In July 1999, a month before her daughter returned to attend the 31st anniversary of her father's death, Mrs Shimizu began to tell everyone that her daughter was coming.

She was always knitting, saying that the hat she was making was for her granddaughter and the muffler for her daughter.

Mr Baba, a schizophrenia patient in Sazanka, found his tower of strength in his brother and his sister-in-law. He had depended on his brother after his parents died. He seldom spent his pension for mentally disabled people, but handed it over to his brother because he worried about his brother's finances. It was his only pleasure in life when he went out to drink tea with his brother and sister-in-law every month. He worried that he would break down if his brother died before he did.

Recounting these examples, staff members said that there was no way for those who had broken off their relationships with their families to have family visits or have their relatives come to visit, but for those who had families, they hoped their family members would come more frequently to visit.

Others

The staff informants also raised some moral concerns about institutional life. On the one hand, Mrs Suzuki felt it inappropriate to use childish terms to speak to the residents who were her seniors in life and have them play with dolls, because she should respect them even when their personality was missing. On the other hand, she thought infantilisation was sometimes an effective way in dealing with demented elderly. When speaking about senility, staff could never resolve the conundrum of its attack on human dignity: why an elderly person would revert to being a child again.

That both residents and staff members have to confront death has been noted in studies of other nursing homes such as Murray Manor (Gubrium 1975: 203-11), Franklin (Shield 1988: 69-71) and Elmwood Grove (Savinshinsky 1991: 161, 181-3). In Kotobuki, especially Aoba, death was also an inevitable topic among the staff. Looking at some elderly who were fed on NG tubes to sustain life and who were dying from cancer, staff members often discussed whether or not a resident should have the right to die a dignified death if they did not want to use any treatment to prolong their lives, or be entitled to be informed about their health condition and prepare for death. As workers who had been with the residents for a pretty long time, they wished that they could see off the elderly to paradise in the home. However, restricted by the present medical treatment in Japan, they could not let the older residents die in the home. They wished that the current elderly health care system would consider 'terminal care' in nursing homes and that someday the home would be able to become a real last place for death in peace.

Notes

1 Basically, the home keeps a neutral stance towards residents' love affairs. Due to the building structure and other problems that may be involved in old residents' love affairs, it neither encourages the elderly to engage in love affairs nor meddles

when residents are keeping company with each other. If they really want to get married, the home will hold a ceremony before all the residents and try to find a spare room for them to live together. In the history of Kotobuki, one couple got married in public, but their marriage remained a common-law one, while one female resident moved out to get married. It is said that if the residents engaged in an affair want sex, they do it in outside hotels.

2 *Fureai* comes from the verb '*fureau*'. Literally it means 'to touch each other by hand', 'to come in contact with' or 'to sympathize with others'. In the social welfare area, the word has the meaning that healthy and normal people make communion with people with some kind of disabilities. In Kotobuki, the *fureai gurūpu* is formed to help the elderly with disabilities take part in some activities, keep contact with others and enhance relationships between the staff and the residents. Nowadays, *fureai* is commonly used for keeping company with others, forming rapport relationships and so on.

3 The same treatment means that, although finances, entrance routes and fee charge methods of Sazanka and Akashia are independent, as the residents of the two homes live in the same building, they share floor space and care staff, and receive the same services.

4 According to the official requirement of establishing a *keihi* home, four matrons are employed to take care of 50 residents. Mr Itō meant that as quite a number of residents in Akashia had serious physical or mental disabilities, it was hard for four matrons to look after the 50 elderly in Akashia. It was because the matrons in Sazanka worked in team with the care staff in Akashia that the residents in the latter home were able to receive such good care.

5 Once a month, a meal, either lunch or dinner, is ordered from outside restaurants according to residents' desires. This is called 'desired meal'.

6 Once a month, either at lunchtime or dinner, the home prepares three sets of dishes for the residents. Each elderly person can choose one he/she favours from the three. This is called a 'selective meal'.

7 An in-home dietician is a dietician hired part time by the local health centre to provide advice on domestic cooking and nutrition for local citizens.

8 Under the current welfare system, institutional care for the elderly is regulated by the official 'measure system' (*sochi seido*). The admission of residents, operation and funding of a home, even a private one, are regulated by public administration.

9 Former government officials moving to a responsible position in a private company.

10 3Ks: *kitanai:* dirty; *kiken* : dangerous; and *kitsui:* harsh.

11 His hobby is collecting various kinds of bags. Strolling about through the town and searching for shops selling bags can help disperse his stress.

12 Every Sunday, a tea drinking party is held in the recreational hall on the fifth floor. Tea, beer and sake are provided at low prices, and *adzuki*-bean soup with rice cake (*o-shiruko*), fried chicken wings, eggs, dumplings and other hors d' oeuvres are sold.

5   The visitors

For the elderly residents, living in an environment that consists exclusively of elderly people and staff members, and receiving social services without thinking too much has gradually changed them into 'institutional human beings.'[1] Their daily life tends to become stereotyped: everything is managed around routines with little stimulation and few excitements. Difficulties in making friends who have real sympathy with each other have made the residents maintain only casual relationships with others. Under such circumstances, who are their sources of emotional support? Who brings the occasional excitement and joy to their prosaic life? For some people it is their beloved families; for some, it is their old friends; and for others it may be the volunteers and trainee students who have no direct interests in common with the home. Coming to the home on different trajectories, visitors are the third group whose existence can directly or indirectly influence the lives of the elderly people.

For the visitors, their interaction with the residents means different things to different individuals. There are those who want to share their intellectual knowledge or specific skills with the elderly persons. For certain individuals, the home is a place where they can find meaning for their existence in service to others. For others it is a relevant experience for a future career in social services for the elderly. And for the families of the residents, it is a chance to give the joy of family reunion to their old folks. As a force detached from home administration and a factor that influences the lives of the elderly, the visitors also have something to say about what they have seen and felt about the elderly and their institutional life. And they have their own evaluation of their activities in the home.

In the first section of this chapter, I shall present a volunteer's narration of his volunteering experience in the home and his opinions about institutional life. Also included are some other voices about how families, students and other visitors come to the home and how they evaluate lives in institutions. Then, I go on to look at how visitors to Kotobuki see their involvement with the residents. Is their investment of time and energy an act of reciprocity, genuine altruism or a self-rewarding act? What are their rewards and costs? My own feelings of being a volunteer are mingled with those of the trainee students. Finally, the chapter discusses visitors' attitudes towards institutionalisation.

Volunteers

Volunteering is the most common form of altruism. It is thought to be a kind of 'symmetry' that balances the 'generosity of some with the neediness of others'. And the 'offerings of time and attention may be recompensed with gratitude, or they can be seen as rewarding in their own right' (Savishinsky 1991: 223).

How is volunteering viewed in Japanese society? According to Kensaku Ōhashi, it was not until the 1970s that the Japanese people began to become familiar with the word of 'volunteer'. Before that the notions of 'service' (*hōshi*) and 'charity' (*jizen*) were commonly used in the welfare field as well as among citizens when referring to altruistic actions towards marginal persons in society. In the 1970s, with the expansion of grassroots movements, some voluntary groups were organised to work for people living in welfare institutions and handicapped persons in community (Ōhashi 1999). From the 1980s, regarding in-home services as an answer to the increasing problems of caring for the elderly in their homes and neighbourhoods, middle-aged housewives began to develop small mutual assistance groups on membership basis to provide home-help services in return for a small gratuity.

After the Great Hanshin Earthquake (1994), not only adolescents, housewives and retired old men, but also philanthropic participation of both public sector and business enterprises and their employees have been encouraged to take part in volunteer activities. In the area of elderly care in particular, the Central Social Welfare Advisory Committee, an advisory council to the Ministry of Health and Welfare, hoped that more people would take part in volunteer welfare services and become manpower for social service providers to assist them in addressing the escalating and diversifying welfare needs of the community (Adachi 2000). A quiet boom of volunteerism has occurred nationwide.

With a sense of political activism, the word 'volunteering' has been redefined as an activity which offers benefits such as reinforcing one's 'self realisation' through making a rapport with others. And there are four important features of volunteer activity: that it involves active participation through one's own choice; that it allows volunteers the happiness of self-expression; that it is free of charge; and that it involves solidarity or cooperation. So volunteer activity is both an action that emphasises mutual help and conduct that confirms one's own existence (Ōhashi, 1999: 107–9).

In Kotobuki, in order to have the elderly residents live a life worth living and to feel happiness in their life, the home organised many recreational clubs for the residents. These clubs included those for the refinement of tastes and artistic sensibilities such as recitation of Chinese poems (*shigin*), *haiku*, calligraphy, flower arrangement, folk songs and folk dances, and those for entertainment and health such as *karaoke*, Japanese chess and *go*, table tennis and gateball. People who had professional knowledge and talent in the above areas were invited as volunteer teachers to supervise the activities of the clubs. Basically, these persons were registered volunteers of the Tokyo Metropolis or Higashimurayama City. They were introduced by the Tokyo Metropolitan welfare office or the city Social Welfare Council to the home. They came to the home twice a month to supervise club activities. Some of them had continued their volunteering career for more than 15 years. Except for transport costs and a small honorarium, they worked without pay. Mr Tanizaki and his wife were two such volunteers in Sazanka.

Mr Atsushi Tanizaki

'Making fun out of our lives together.'

Mr Tanizaki was born in a village in Nagano prefecture in 1935. After graduation from high school, he became a civil servant in the National Revenue Office. From 1954 till his retirement in 1992, Mr Tanizaki was in charge of levying revenue, collecting evidence on tax evasion, and serving as a judge of the Office's complaints appeal court. After retirement, he has run his own office as a licensed tax accountant while volunteering at Sazanka as the coach of the table tennis club.

Mr Tanizaki began to play table tennis when he was a primary school student. He often played with his friends on a small wooden table in the village shrine of the local deity. Since playing on a real table at the age of 13, he had kept his favourite bat with him. Apart from the periods when he had to help with childrearing or was occupied with work, he had kept on playing table tennis as his favourite sport. He had won many trophies in the contests held in his workplace.

There was a table tennis club in the neighbourhood where Mr Tanizaki lives. As a member, he often went there to play with his friends. In 1989, three elderly residents in Kotobuki appeared in the club, asking whether someone in the club could teach them to play table tennis in the home. Mr Tanizaki said if it was on Sundays, he and his wife could give it a try. The couple fulfilled their promise the following Sunday. Afterwards, a matron in charge of club activities and the three elderly people visited his home, asking him to continue coaching them. This led to his long history of volunteering in Kotobuki. As he was still working at that time, he could only coach once a month on Sundays. After he retired, however, he began to play with the elderly twice a month on weekdays.

Considering it difficult for the elderly players to exercise for matches, Mr Tanizaki decided to train them to play for enjoyment instead of competition. In the mornings of the second and fourth Tuesday each month, he and his wife came to the recreational hall on the fifth floor at nine o'clock. In the ensuing two hours' exercise, the elderly members took turns to play with Mr Tanizaki and his wife, 5 minutes per round per person. Mr Tanizaki and his wife would decide whether to strike the balls quickly or slowly according to specific abilities of the individual learners. If two poor hands played together, both of them would feel dull as it turned out to be a ball-picking exercise. What Mr Tanizaki and his wife did was to keep the ball going on as long as possible. It was the elderly persons' delight that they could hit the ball many times continuously. Mr Tanizaki talked about his coaching style:

> Originally the club begins at nine thirty in the morning. However, the elderly asked us to play a little bit longer. So we come at about nine o'clock to have more time to exercise. After two hours' exercise, we have tea together, talk about each other's recent well-being, and ask the elderly whether they have any requests to improve our club activity. Mr Akimoto and I often play the tunes of many familiar old songs on our harmonicas while others sing the songs together. Though the elderly seldom make demands or discuss their personal affairs deeply with us, as time goes on, we feel close with each other and are able to talk about something both sides are interested in. The table tennis club has become a place where we can enjoy ourselves. Sometimes I did not feel well because of a cold or other small illnesses. When I thought that the elderly were waiting for us, however, I would brace myself to come.

More than ten years has flown by since Mr Tanizaki and his wife began volunteering in Kotobuki. During that period, members of the club changed a lot. Some passed away, some resigned because of bad health, and some were new entrants. Among the five members who kept on with exercise from the very beginning, three were the elderly persons who first went to visit Mr Tanizaki and ask him to be their coach. The number of club members had increased from 12 at the beginning to 26 at present, and the number of tables had also increased from one to three.

Active participation of the elderly made the Tanizaki couple feel that their volunteer work was worth doing. They were glad that their activity had made the elderly happy. At the same time, they were surprised by the energy the elderly persons demonstrated despite their old age. Through the interaction with the elderly residents, Mr Tanizaki and his wife were able to imagine their own later life. They often encouraged each other by saying 'the people much older than us in Kotobuki can live an active life, we should be more vigorous'. Feeling rewarded by such volunteering work, they began to serve in institutions for the mentally retarded persons and for the handicapped as well. Mrs Tanizaki became a welfare cooperator (*fukushi kyōryoku-in*) of the city Social Welfare Council. She often invited her husband to participate in various voluntary activities their group organised, for example, helping with preparing the rapport concerts (*fureai consāto*) for institutionalised elderly persons and the handicapped.[2] 'I feel as if I am a full-time volunteer. I am spending much more time on volunteer activities than on my own business.' Mr Tanizaki smiled a delightful smile.

As we are registered volunteers of the city Social Welfare Council, we became involved in its voluntary activities. My wife and I often go to help with the bazaars opened in our community. She also keeps her eye on the elderly persons living in our block and informs the welfare commissioner if any of them falls ill. Through the interactions with other people in our community, we gain a better understanding about the people and the society surrounding us. We find all this very rewarding. We built a spacious house for the purpose of having our only son and his family live with us. However, it is impossible for him to come back because of his job and his own family life. So we are considering refurbishing the first floor into a mini day home for the elderly persons living nearby. They can come in the morning, have lunch at our house and go back to their own home in the afternoon. We want to do something for the people living in our neighbourhood.

Mr Tanizaki said that it was a regrettable thing that the more civilised a society was, the weaker interpersonal relationships became. Japan was a country where old persons had been respected and the family's responsibility for caring for its members had been emphasised. However, with the influence of the post-war democratic education, people tend to exclusively emphasise their rights but forget about their obligations. In addition, the mass media have played an important role in reinforcing such trends. Because there were so many TV programmes making fools of the parents and disparaging older people, younger persons became even more egoistic. With the weakening sense of obligation of the younger generation and the nuclearisation of the family, the family's ability to care for old parents had declined. In order to make up for the inability of families to care for the elderly, the government devised the LTCI programme under which care services could be purchased.

'I feel a bit sad', Mr Tanizaki said, 'that our old people are becoming commodities in an economic system of exchange. Can't we consider any other care system, paying more attention to the warmth of human bonds?' He indicated that he was the type of person who was nostalgic for the past. He thought it necessary to reconstruct a community where people living in the neighbourhood could support each other and the elderly could lead a secure life in their own home. He and his wife would try their best to serve their community and build rapport relationships with people in it.

When talking about how he thought about the elderly in institutions, Mr Tanizaki said that if one followed the traditional norm of elderly care, these elderly were abandoned grannies. Mr Tanizaki stated:

A long time ago, all elderly parents were cared for by their children or grandchildren in their own homes. Institutions were relief facilities for unfortunate older persons and institutionalisation was regarded as a social stigma. However, things have changed a lot. A lot of elderly become institutionalised even though they have children. As this is an era when society shoulders the responsibility of taking care of its old people, I think it is necessary to further facilitate such institutions and to ensure the elderly a free and comfortable life.

Mr Tanizaki said that some ten years ago Kotobuki was an isolated society for local residents. There was a resistance movement among the local citizens when the home was established. There was not much communication between the elderly residents in the home and local citizens. He himself had never known a single resident of Kotobuki before he volunteered in the home. However, with the socialisation movement of welfare institutions from the late 1980s, the home had done a lot to make itself open to local residents. For instance, it had organised seasonal bazaars and held festivals such as *Obon* to involve local citizens. Now the home had become a recognised social organisation in the local community. When walking his dog in the nearby park, Mr Tanizaki was often greeted by the elderly residents who played gateball. He himself felt it natural to say hello to the elderly of Kotobuki when he came across them in the street. 'This is a good trend', he said.

> But there is still something that reminds you the elderly are living an unnatural life and that the home is an isolated world. For instance, in our table tennis club, the staff member told us that an elderly member was on leave when we couldn't see them. Only when we asked why this person still didn't appear after some time were we informed that he/she was dead. At that time, I thought that, although the home was quite splendid, it was far away from the real concept of 'welfare'. Although we are outsiders, we have become comrades with the elderly because we have spent time together and enjoyed our lives together. My wife and I want to ask about a resident's health if he/she is hospitalised. As many of the residents do not have relatives, if we go to visit them, they would be cheered up. And we want to pay our last respects to a friend if he/she passes away. It is a regrettable thing that there is still no channel through which the home administration listens to the voice of us outsiders.

Another thing Mr Tanizaki thought undesirable about institutional life was that self-determination of the residents was limited. Some of the club members told him that, although they had expressed their personal wishes to the matrons, they could not get a satisfactory response from them. The staff members tended to ask the residents to hold back their demands and to follow the regulations in order to ensure smooth management. So, even though the residents wanted to be independent, the result tended to be that the elderly residents became more dependent in the home regime. It was the organisation itself that restrained the freedom of the residents. This was the limitation of institutional life, Mr Tanizaki thought.

Regarding whether he would put his own parents in a *tokuyō* home if they became bedridden or senile, Mr Tanizaki said he would prefer to take care of them at home.

> My generation, and that of my parents still think that children should take care of their own parents. I don't want to have our parents leave this world with the regret that they have been abandoned. My wife and I will make full use of in-home services to look after our parents at home. With respect to ourselves, you might think that we would like to make easy use of public services; but considering the heavy labour that care tasks require from the standpoint of our children, we are unwilling to have our children go through such hardships but would rather rely on public services. We will choose to live in a nursing home when we become unable to move.

In short, Mr Tanizaki thought that, apart for some social disadvantages that forced the elderly residents to come to live in the home, basically they were the same as the ordinary old people in community. Most members in the club were nice people who were cooperative, considerate and grateful. They respected him and his wife, and referred to them honourably as their 'teacher' (*sensei*). As his interaction with the elderly was limited to club activities, he was unable to become close friends with the elderly, someone they could go to for counselling when they had problems. Yet he was happy to listen to their worries and the dissatisfactions they occasionally revealed in their conversations. He thought he had benefited a great deal from his volunteer activity. It had not only provided a chance to enrich his own later life but also broadened his horizon regarding the local community.

He thought that, with the dramatic socio-demographic changes in recent decades, homes for the elderly had become not only acceptable but unavoidable resources for caring for elderly persons. However, due to the traditional explanation of Japanese welfare as 'favours given by the government', the idea that institutions were asylums lingered on, and outsiders to the home were unable to become advocates for the residents. Only if the policy-makers came down to the same level as ordinary people and the meaning of 'welfare' as 'services for weak or marginal people' disappeared, could Japan bring into being a 'welfare society'.

Family

Family, according to the staff members in Kotobuki, is the spiritual home for the elderly residents. For elderly with good relationship with their families, this may be true. Just as Sodei (1999) observed that family visits are rare in a private retirement home where her mother lived, apart from a couple of exceptional families who visited their old parents every day, and some who came to the home regularly, most families rarely visit their elderly relatives once they have sent them to institutions, especially in the case of Sazanka. This is partly because elderly facilities are located too far away from the centre of the cities for the family to visit. In other cases, before the elderly came to the home, there were already severe quarrels and conflicts between family members and the elderly person. Their relationship deteriorated so much that the latter was sent away. Elderly residents who came to the home for this reason are normally unwilling to mention their families in order to avoid recalling their bitter experiences. Institutionalisation of the elderly, however, may sometimes offer a chance for the family relationship to be restored, and for responsibility to be shared among the siblings.

How do the families of residents in Kotobuki think about their institutionalised older relatives? Do they have any regrets about having put their old parents in an institution? How do they think about institutional care for the elderly? Mr Minezawa and Mrs Ogawa gave us their short comments.

One rainy Sunday morning, Mr Minezawa and his wife came to Aoba to see his mother, Mrs Minezawa, the 76-year-old demented elderly woman who was seen urinate outside her room in Chapter 2. Since Mrs Minezawa came to live in Aoba two years ago, her son and her daughter-in-law have continued visiting her once a month. Each time the couple came, they went to the matrons' room first to express their appreciation for staff members' care for their mother. Then they distributed some candies and cakes to the room-mates of Mrs Minezawa, thanking them for having watched over their mother. The elderly residents, for their part, spoke to Mrs Minezawa who was smiling an innocent smile like a child, 'Koyo-san, you have such a sweet son and such a wonderful daughter-in-law, you are really a lucky woman.' This time, Mr Minezawa brought with him some photos taken during a day trip to the NHK studio two weeks before.

Mrs Minezawa had lived with her eldest son and his family in Chūō-ku. She became senile six years ago. To begin with, she was not in her dotage and sometimes she acted like a normal person. But she forgot the things she had just done. Gradually she began to say that her things were missing, and she blamed her daughter-in-law for having stolen her wallet. This occasional senile delusion (*madara-boke*) lasted almost two years. Then she began to forget to turn off the gas and water, and wandered away from home. Mrs Minezawa's 'things stolen delusion' was always aimed at her daughter-in-law, so that it inevitably led to skirmishes between the two women in the same household. And her wandering caused inconvenience for the neighbours. Despite the hardships in caring for a demented old parent at home, Mr Minezawa and his wife managed to take care of their mother for two years. Due to the heavy care burden, the health of his wife collapsed. As Mr Minezawa himself was running a convenience store, he could not take leave all the time to look after his mother. He had no choice but to go to the ward welfare office for consultation. The official in the office suggested that he put his mother in a *yōgo* home. One month later after the applicating for entrance, Mrs Minezawa moved to live in Sazanka in Higashimurayama City.

To begin with, because of the sudden change of environment, the senility of Mrs Minezawa got worse. She wandered about the home, stayed awake at night, messed up the room and became incontinent. Her activities became troublesome for her room-mate and other residents. As it was difficult to live with normal elderly in Sazanka, Mrs Minezawa was transferred to Aoba six months later. With many other residents sharing the same condition as hers, she was no longer 'abnormal'. Gradually her situation became stable, except for some strange behaviour such as putting away her shoes and pillow in the closet, pretending to sew something in her blanket in the evening, and occasionally passing water outside her room. She never forgot to say 'Thank you' after receiving help from a matron, and she always smiled like a child. Although her memory deteriorated, she could remember her son's name.

Showing photos to his mother, Mr Minezawa asked her whether she remembered the place and persons in the pictures. Mrs Minezawa responded with a smile again. Her son began to explain something to her. It seemed there was an invisible channel that made communication possible between the son and the mother.

With respect to his mother's institutionalisation, Mr Minezawa said it was difficult for him and his wife to make the decision to put their mother in an institution. He said:

> It was hard for us to make the decision. We thought we would take care of our mother by ourselves. You see, it was my mother alone who had worked hard to bring me up after my father passed away when I was four. I wanted her to have a happy later life with us. Both my wife and I had jobs. Our only son went to study in an American university after his high school graduation. My mother might have felt very lonely when she was on her own at home. So she gradually became weird. My wife had to quit her job to look after my mother for two years. It was really hard to take care of a demented parent at home. We felt not only physically but psychologically burdened. If we hadn't sent my mother to a home, either my wife or I would have become a neurotic. Although it was painful to have my own mother institutionalised, now I think we have made the right decision. You see, she seems to be very happy here. She is calm and her senility has stopped advancing. The matrons are kind. They do everything, from serving meals to helping her go to the toilet. I am grateful to them. And I am impressed that so many young staff are dedicating themselves to the kind of job most Japanese young persons do not want to do. Thanks to their help, we family members are relieved of the heavy burden of care. Cared for wholeheartedly by the matrons in this way, my mother will live longer than I do, I am afraid.

Mr Minezawa was satisfied with the services his mother received in the home. He said that he would like to become a volunteer of the city after he retired. By participating in volunteer activities of the city and providing services for other needy persons, he wanted to repay the kindness the government and the home had shown his mother.

In the room next door, Mrs Ōshima's eldest daughter, Mrs Ogawa, was paying her monthly visit to her mother. Mrs Ōshima was a 73-year-old widow from the local community. Her husband died some 30 years ago, leaving her with two daughters and a son. Four years before, she had fallen because of a cerebral infarction and was paralysed on her left side. She was hospitalised for two to three years. During her stay in the hospital, although her illness was not very serious, she was given intravenous injections everyday. Mrs Ogawa could not bear to see her mother become thinner and thinner, so she talked with her sister and brother about what to do with their mother.

Her brother, the heir of the Ōshima family, remained unmarried and was afflicted with depression. He could not shoulder the responsibility of looking after his mother. Her younger sister, who had married a salary-man in Chiba Prefecture, was unable to care for her mother because she had two small children to look after. Living and working in Kawasaki City, and with her mother-in-law already living with her family, Mrs Ogawa was also unable to look after her own mother. In early 1998, she applied for entrance to a *tokuyō* home for her mother and, some months later, Mrs Ōshima came to live in Aoba directly from the hospital. Mrs Ogawa and her sister took turns to visit their mother, bringing with them some of their mother's favourite foods. This time Mrs Ogawa brought some seasonal cherries and loquats for her mother, who was obviously cheered up by her daughter's coming.

Mrs Ogawa said that compared with the life in the hospital, living in a nursing home was much better. First of all, the staff members took good care of the residents. They were more patient, kind-hearted and dedicated to the elderly than the nurses in the hospital. The environment was also better than that of a hospital. The room was more spacious so that visitors could sit and talk at the resident's bedside. Actually, after her mother came to live in Aoba, she looked like a changed person. She became brighter than before, and loved to talk and laugh. Her skin regained its lustre, and she gained weight as well. Although she was gradually moving toward dementia, her overall health condition was good. Mrs Ogawa said:

> I have never seen my mother so happy and so talkative. She is always laughing. Maybe this is the right place for her to live in. Sometimes I think she might be lonely here, but when I heard what she told me, I feel that my mother has identified every resident here as our relatives. Her brothers are sitting two tables away from her, the male care worker who brings her the meal tray is her nephew, and the cook in the kitchen is her neighbour. It seems that she is living with many familiar people. As long as she feels happy, I think the home is a good place for her. To us children, since we live far away and cannot care for our mother by

ourselves, we are very grateful to the matrons for their dedicated services. We feel at ease leaving our mother here. What we need to do is to come to see our mother as often as possible.

I thought of bringing my mother home for holidays such as New Year's Day. I did this last year and found it was really hard work. My husband and I drove a long distance from Kawasaki to pick up my mother. Setting aside the questions of moving her from the wheelchair to the car and taking care of her diapers on the way home, there were the big problems of transporting her inside our house and bathing her in our small bathtub. You know, the stairs and doors of our house are not wide enough for a wheelchair and we haven't a special bathtub to bath a disabled elderly person. And I am not good at changing diapers for an adult. Although my mother only stayed at my home for two days, I was exhausted. I would rather come to see her here than take her home. My mother may also think it more comfortable to be cared for by the matrons than by me.

Not only Mr Minezawa and Mrs Ogawa, but also other family members of the residents I met in the home said that their elderly relatives were leading a carefree life in Aoba. Many of them had a hard time deciding whether or not to institutionalise their parents, because of the norm of filial piety. However, after their parent really came to live in the home, they found institutionalisation a good choice both for their parents and themselves. With the professional care of staff members, their parents could live a more comfortable and safer life than in their own home. They themselves were relieved of stress and restored to their normal daily life. They were grateful to the home for the care service it provided. And they came to visit their old family members as often as possible to compensate for their remorse for being unable to care for their older relatives by themselves.

Trainee students and other visitors

There were other temporary visitors at the home. These were students from the nursing department in welfare vocational schools who came to fulfil their field-training requirement. During their two- or three-year study period, in addition to their course work, students are also required to have field training each term, lasting about three weeks to 40 days. They are required to set up their own study objectives and to follow a matron, both to accomplish the targets and help with care tasks. Based on the comments given by the matron who supervises the student, the director of the nursing department gives the overall field training score for the student. Some female adults who are pursuing qualifications for home-helps also come to the home to have their field training. Mr Ōmura, Miss Nakayama and Mrs Nakano are the three with whom I had the most conversations.

Having failed in the university entrance examination, Mr Ōmura entered the Nerima Nursing College after he graduated from high school. He chose to study in the Nursing section for two reasons. First, he could get the qualification as a certified care worker after three years' study. With this qualification, it would be easier for him to be employed by a *tokuyō* home or an institution for handicapped persons, where the salary is more stable than that of other business sectors. The second reason was related to his grandfather, the person who cared for him most and who died just before his university entrance examination. Being unable to visit his grandfather often before his death left with him a sense of deep regret. He needed a way to make compensation. As a result he chose to enter a career where he could serve the elderly. Among the 16 students in his class, he was one of the few male students. His main purpose in field training this time was to communicate with senile elderly, in addition to acquiring the basic care-taking techniques.

As the only son in the family, Mr Ōmura seldom helped to do housework at his own home. He regarded field training as a tough job. Before he went to work as a trainee in a nursing home, he had never imagined the real conditions of elderly people. Although he understood that transporting, feeding, bathing and changing diapers for the elderly were the main tasks of a care worker, he did not know how to do them in practice. He said:

> I had never imagined that care-taking in a *tokuyō* home was such a kind of job. When I observed diaper changing for the first time, I was unable to eat anything for several days. The offensive smell and large quantity of faeces of an adult elderly person made me feel sick. I became unable to eat curry rice. And I felt embarrassed to help with bathing and diapering the older women. Although one month's field training does not sound very long, it is laborious and stressful. Everyday I have to spend three hours travelling between the institution and my home. I work in shifts as the full-time workers do. The break time is only long enough to finish my lunch. The matron supervising me tends to be too busy to spare the time to look after me, so I have to find and solve problems by myself. After a day's work, I become so exhausted that I count the number of the remaining days, hoping it will be finished soon.

Although Mr Ōmura was happy to be appreciated by the elderly for the help he provided, if possible, he would prefer not to work in a *tokuyō* home. He said:

> Not for the labour the work requires, but for the disgust and hopelessness that old age reminds you of. Do you see the persons on NG tube? And those Alzheimer's victims? How will you feel when you can't make yourself understood to these persons? I just can't tolerate to see the decay of old age.

Despite his desire to communicate with the residents and his attempts to engage with them, he came to realise with reluctance that keeping silent and listening to what the elderly said were good strategies for some residents.

Some people, such as Mrs Tanabe, are always smiling when you greet them. She will tell you about her parents, her arranged marriage, her daughter and her home. But next day you will hear something different. She will say that she is still a virgin and will marry a policeman. Each time you meet her, she will have something different to tell you. It seems as if she is an inventor who can create different kinds of histories. I don't know who she really is.

He was a little bit puzzled. And for residents such as Mrs Minezawa and Mrs Miura, there was no carry-over from week to week. In their eyes, no matter how hard Mr Ōmura tried to feed them, walked them, and changed diapers for them, he was a first-time visitor each time, a person who had never been there before. His interactions with them were a recurring novelty that made the present pleasant, but did not build into a coherent past.

Having witnessed the captivity of the residents and the ways the staff members treated them, Mr Ōmura realised the differences of what it was like to live and to work in such a setting. 'They are so feeble and powerless that they have to depend on the staff', he commented. He had considerable respect for the staff, most of whom he found to be genuinely concerned about the residents they cared for. But their ways of handling some of the residents disturbed him. For instance, he was perplexed about why they would not let Mrs Kondō go to the toilet as she requested; and why Mrs Nakamura was prohibited from eating her favourite *umeboshi*. 'Matrons says that they are doing so for the good of the residents. But being robbed of their rights, can the elderly feel happy?' he continued, 'if I am bedridden, I will not enter an institution where I can't live in my own way.'

With respect to institutionalisation, Mr Ōmura said that people who lived in former times tended to think it was shameful to receive public assistance. 'They thought that one should be responsible for one's own affairs. Even though one might die by the roadside, one should not depend on welfare. Public welfare was thought to be an unnecessary helping hand', he reiterated. It was because of such stubborn notions that people who should not be bedridden became bedridden or malnourished, and that family caretakers were forced to shoulder the care labour. Mr Ōmura thought it was narrow-minded for people to stick to the idea that welfare was charity. In his eyes, welfare service was a kind of human right that everybody should enjoy. People pay their taxes. It is a matter of course that they should receive welfare services. If one has money to purchase care service, he/she should be able to receive it rationally. So he thought it reasonable to regard welfare service as a kind of commodity that could be bought by money.

Miss Nakayama was a student from another welfare vocational school. She had worked as a teacher in a nursery for five years. Although she loved children, she quit her job because of the complicated human relationships in the school. As she was interested in ageing issues, she went to study in the Nursing Department of the Tokyo Metropolitan Welfare School. 'Japan is in a recession, so it is quite difficult to find a job if you haven't any skills', she said, 'however, in the field of social services for elderly persons, because of the increasing number of elderly people, care workers are still needed.' This was the main reason why she studied for the qualification of a certified care worker.

During her six-week field training in Kotobuki, Miss Nakayama spent half in Aoba and the other half in Sazanka. After experiencing the care tasks in practice and witnessing the vulnerability of the old residents, she thought the care job itself was worth doing because it gave her the satisfaction of being useful. She later turned to Sazanka to have another kind of experience. 'The residents here are living a more autonomous life than those in a *tokuyō* home. But compared with the elderly living in their own home, these healthy old residents are much more isolated and have less freedom.' She commented. First of all they could not choose their favourite meals and they were unable to make dishes for themselves as well. Some residents told her that although the food in the home was delicious, the meals they really liked were not so many. As they only have a moderate income, they could not afford to eat outside. And although they did not like the dishes, they had to eat them as staff members would say things like 'The dietary workers worked hard to cook for you...' etc.

When I was working in the *tokuyō* home, I found the privacy of the residents was sometimes not protected. For instance, some matrons did not close the curtain when they changed the diapers for the elderly. Here I also find that the privacy of the residents is limited. A few days ago, I went for a walk with two residents. I found that both their topics of conversation and way of talking changed entirely when they stepped out the home. They aired a lot of dissatisfactions with their room-mates and said that they felt better breathing the fresh air outside. Inside the home, as every person has to share his/her room with a room-mate, they have to restrain themselves and be patient. The elderly feel secure living in the home but they are unable to live a free life. And it is difficult for old persons to change their personalities formed a long time ago. They have no choice but to follow others.

Maybe because I am taught in my school that receiving welfare services is the basic right of every elderly person, I haven't any bad image of old-age homes. But in the wider society, there is still a bad image of institutions for the elderly. You see, when I told my friends that I was having field training in a home, some frowned. And when I brought back Sazanka's chow mein to let my grandmother have a try, she refused. To her, the food in a home for the elderly is dirty. There is still prejudice toward institutions.

Mrs Nakano was a 55-year-old housewife who had some part-time work experience in a supermarket. Last year her elder sister got a first-class certificate as a home-helper after studying in the classes held by the city Social Welfare Council. Encouraged by her sister that getting a certificate was not only useful, in order to become a semi-paid volunteer in the council or a paid home helper in private silver services businesses, but also pragmatic in terms of caring for one's own old family members, Mrs Nakano started to study in the same class as her sister. Now she was living separately from her parents-in-law, but as her husband was the eldest son, she thought she had the responsibility to care for them in the future. Before she came to have a two-day field training in Aoba, she had passed the paper examination and had been to a day care centre for the elderly. Since she had never been to a *tokuyō* home before, she did not know the real life of the elderly residents. Supervised by a matron and observing the work the staff was doing, what impressed her most was that all staff members were caring for the elderly kind-heartedly and tidily. She said,

> Although I have never been a volunteer, I feel sympathetic when I see these vulnerable elderly and I am willing to be of help to them. Today I wheeled an old woman out for a walk in the park. I took her around to see the flowers and the kids playing with the sand and water and gave her a small piece of cake to feed the pigeons. Both her eyes and face lit up. She said she hadn't been out for a while. She was so delighted that she thanked me again and again. It was the first time I was so appreciated by others. We ordinary people never find that a flower or a bird is special, but to those elderly who are confined by disabilities, nature has a big meaning.

Mrs Nakano showed deep sympathy to the elderly residents who were captives of the home due to their physical handicaps. She had not imagined that natural things such as fresh air, flowers and children would become so meaningful to the residents. And she was satisfied that she had been a help to those older people who were in such a pitiful state. From the happiness generated in her training experience, she considered becoming a volunteer in the *tokuyō* home near her home.

Motives, rewards and emotional costs

Motivation: reciprocity and altruism

What pushes an individual to volunteer, or to give time and energy with little or no expectation of reward? No matter how busy they might be or how far away they lived, family members of residents such as Mr Minezawa and Mrs Ogawa came to visit their old parents. They helped to put their parents' affairs in order. They sat at the bedside talking with them. And they washed their faces and applied cream on them. For the families, their visits were not only chances to provide emotional support to their parents but also opportunities to repay the debts they owed to their parents as well as to compensate for the remorse of being unable to care for them at home.

For families with good relationships with the home, their visits to Kotobuki also mean another kind of reciprocity. For instance, Mr Minezawa sometimes brought presents such as cake for the matrons, or he sent midyear gifts (*Ochūgen*) to the home for the care his mother received and the debt he owed to the institution. He also took part in all kinds of recreational activities such as day trips or overnight trips the home arranged.

> The staff have arranged such a good opportunity for us family members to join and are so kind to have invited me, so no matter how busy I am and no matter how many troubles I will have during the trip, I will try my best to cooperate.

He thought his participation in the activities of the home was not only a symbol of his filial piety but also a repayment of the benefits the home provided. His willingness to become a volunteer after retirement represented a good example of reciprocal interaction in Japanese social life.

In fact, it was to repay to other old persons the obligation incurred by their parents in institutions that some family members became volunteers or 'teachers' of the recreational clubs in Kotobuki. A voluntary teacher of the handicraft club in Aoba said that she had become utterly familiar with the elderly on the floor where her father had resided. She said:

> Even after my father passed away, I continue coming here. The warm greetings by the residents each time I am here let me feel that I am a part of their significant others such as families or acquaintances. These old people seem to have become my missing parents.

Thus the devotion of her time and craft skills to the old persons was evaluated as a surrogate family visit.

Among the other volunteers, their purposes for working with the residents were similar to those of the volunteers in the pet therapy programme in Elmwood Grove Nursing Home which Savishinsky (1991) studied. Mr Tanizaki and his wife wanted to make the elderly residents happy and at the same time to enjoy their own retirement life. Retired people came to seek some 'new source of usefulness' in their life. Housewives wanted to have some variation to 'the routine of their lives' (Savinshinsky 1991: 228–9). Most said that their initial intention was to help make the life of the residents enjoyable and their own life worthwhile. Many said that they had received more from the residents than they had given. They admitted that it was the good feeling of being appreciated and the self-satisfaction accompanying their volunteer activities that had kept them coming. As self-satisfaction, self-realisation and self-award are emphasised, these volunteers' action could be regarded as 'self-interested' altruism (Myers 1988: 445).

Strictly speaking, college students and quasi home-helpers are not volunteers because they come to fulfil their field tasks. But considering the nature of their act, to work without reimbursement, it would be proper to regard their conduct as an altruistic activity. College students saw their experience as a preparation for their chosen career in geriatric health care facilities or welfare institutions. A number of them were living with their grandparents or had good memories of their deceased grandparents. And the quasi home-helpers thought it a useful experience to become volunteers in order to enter a possible career, or on a personal level. Some had the experience of caring for their mothers-in-law at home. Others had the regret of being unable to care for their parents when they were alive. As the direct result of their field training, they obtain the skills and knowledge that are needed for their qualifications. Their altruistic activity is bound up with reciprocity.

In short, the initial motivation for the visitor to visit, or to engage in something that is of benefit to both others and oneself, was often combined with a number of other reasons related to careers, repayment of obligation, regrets and the pursuit of self-worth. It was an integration of reciprocity, self-serving and altruistic consideration.

Rewards and emotional cost

Volunteering is not a 'pure gift' (Befu 1977: 257; Stevens 1997: 232). It is a kind of reciprocity where intangible rewards such as emotional feelings are in play. Volunteers in Kotobuki found substantial benefits generated from their work. When Mr Tanizaki and his wife recalled their original motive for volunteering, they admitted that they had never thought they would commit to the club for such a long time, and that they had not foreseen the many meanings that volunteering would have for their life. As time went by, they found that volunteering had become a part of their life. The happiness and satisfaction gained from their experience at the home led to their further involvement in volunteer activities in the community. Through volunteer activities, they experienced the real fun in life and understood the real value of life. One could only realise his/her self-accomplishment and get the highest life satisfaction through constructing rapport relations with others.

For other volunteers, interacting with the elderly people in Kotobuki provided a chance to come to know about other aspects of society, the process of ageing and the prospect of one's own old age. Some were surprised to find that their clubs had therapeutic functions for some residents and that they themselves had the ability to appease someone's soul.

The trainee students and the people who wanted to get care certificates gained the practical knowledge and skills their profession required. The institution for the elderly was a place where various lives assembled and a variety of disabilities as well as conflicts, and interactions were exposed nakedly before people. As Miss Nakayama said, 'It's a good place to learn about life.' Not only young students but also older visitors could learn a great deal about life and the ageing process in addition to their field study benefits.

Savishinsky mentions 'functioned as a therapist', coming across many 'positive and negative encounters', 'giving and receiving affection' (Savishinsky 1991: 230), as the collective experiences of visitors, and this indicates that volunteer activity offers people a wide range of benefits. Volunteering also generates various kinds of emotions. Some were benefits and others were costs.

In Aoba, both the students and volunteers had to handle different levels of disability. People were separated into two groups when they set out to help the residents. One group included students such as Mr Ōmura who liked to help the more capable elderly persons. Because these residents could express themselves and move about, it was easy for volunteers to understand their needs and share some experiences.

People like Miss Nakayama, on the other hand, felt empathy with individuals who were bedridden, confined to a wheelchair, or suffering from dementia. She identified these 'pitiful elderly' with her older family kin. Thus the 'altruistic motive'[3] and the feeling of 'empathy' (Batson *et al.* 1987) resulted in her attachment to the more vulnerable persons. And it was Mrs Nakano's compassion for residents being deprived of their freedom to enjoy nature that drove her to wheel them out for a walk. So people's emotions, especially empathy, played a big part in their helping action.

People's feelings towards institutional life also changed during the time of their commitment to the institution and the people inside it. New trainee students at Aoba were often puzzled by the way some elderly repeated the same topics or asked the same questions. And they felt dreadful at the sight of the decay of old age: emotionless faces like living plants, skinny bodies like living skeletons, the continuous yells of the senile, the powerless moans of the sick, and the bewildering behaviours of the demented.

Stable or long-term relationships generate reciprocity. Week by week, students became familiar with the residents and their intensive contact with particular individuals yielded new findings and rapport. Mr Ōmura made a personal care plan, aiming to develop communication with Mr Kumagaya, who suffered from Alzheimer's disease. During the first week, no matter how hard he tried, he failed to make the old man talk about something. He was frustrated and began to think that it was impossible to communicate with senile elderly people. However, the next week he found Mr Kumagaya became very concentrated on the TV screen whenever there were baseball games. After discovering this, baseball became their common topic and Mr Ōmura amazingly found that he could communicate with the old man. On the day when he finished his training, he went to say goodbye to Mr Kumagaya. He was surprised to encounter the warm remark of 'Although study is very important, please be careful with your health.' It turned out that even senile elderly had the potential to communicate with others. This surprising finding and the rapport with the old man in the last period of his field experience changed his passive attitude towards institutional work a great deal.

In Sazanka, Miss Nakayama also felt close to a number of residents after two weeks' interaction with them. Several days before she finished her field training, she had the idea that she would leave something for the residents to remember her by. She bought some *Origami* and bamboo backing, and she asked those who treated her kindly to create a work together. With the ideas and talent of all (two old grannies among them were good at handicraft), they completed an excellent work of art: a full-blown orchid on the grass. It was hung up on the wall of the dining hall after Miss Nakayama was gone. She was presented with dolls, small purses or bags made of Japanese fabric and a lot of candies on the day she left the home. And she could not help shedding tears while promising that she would come to visit again. Volunteering could generate 'unexpected intimacy' (Savishinsky 1991: 225).

Visitors generally thought it was a good thing to find their relationship with residents deepened as time went by. Sometimes they found themselves in an ambivalent situation with regard to this intimacy. Probably because residents had suppressed their emotions for too long and there were too few companions in the home, some elderly persons were eager to unleash their displeasure towards someone who showed concern and compassion for them. Miss Nakayama felt sympathy with the miserable elderly who had to share with someone whose character they found intolerable, but she was sometimes frustrated with the repeated stories and the long time the elderly engaged her, because she also wanted to reach out to other residents during the short period of her field training.

In the table tennis club, Mrs Matsumoto, a resident of Sazanka who had been a member from the very beginning, suddenly stopped coming. The matron told Mr Tanizaki that Mrs Matsumoto wanted to resign because of her declining health. He wondered whether to believe this because, as far as he knew, Mrs Matsumoto was quite healthy. He guessed it was because of Mrs Sugiyama, one of the three elderly who initiated the club and also the person who had been in charge of broadcasting, coordinating and arranging the schedule of club for more than six years. She announced that she would like to have another person replace her at the club's gathering and suggested a male member take the responsibility. Most junior club members said that a senior one should take the responsibility. But the three senior male members refused politely because they were serving as the responsible persons in other clubs or that they had done it before. According to the conventional way[4] of determining one's role in a group, Mrs Matsumoto was a suitable choice because she was one of the five people who had played table tennis the longest and the only one who had no responsibility in other clubs. However, Mrs Sugiyama said that it would be better if a younger person did it. Eventually a younger female member from Akashia promised to take the responsibility.

The following week Mrs Matsumoto did not show up in the club. Mr Tanizaki sensed that there might be some rift between Mrs Matsumoto and Mrs Sugiyama because the two seldom talked to each other. And he was told that residents in Akashia tended to despise those in Sazanka. So he guessed it was because Mrs Matsumoto wanted to avoid meeting Mrs Sugiyama. Mr Tanizaki felt regret for Mrs Matsumoto's resignation, for he would miss a familiar face in his club. But he had no idea of how to deal with the relationship between the two old women; it was beyond his ability as a table tennis coach. He had a good relationship with both, so whom should he blame?

Ongoing relationships also required commitment as well as expectations on the side of volunteers, sometimes leaving them feeling obliged to go to the home or feeling guilty if they failed to drop in because of their own vacation, illness or other personal reasons.[5] Miss Nakayama said she had to give up attending a classmates gathering because she had promised to go with some residents to see their works at the handicraft exhibition held yearly in the city's civil hall, although in her heart she preferred the former. So, as in personal life, 'intimacy could be a pleasure and a burden'. Such emotional ambivalence also could be found in the volunteers in Elmwood Grove (Savishinsky 1991: 226).

Working with the elderly also had other emotional effects on people. A number of visitors to Kotobuki had little or no prior experience in a *tokuyō* home, so they found their involvement either so depressing or shocking that they thought themselves insufficiently trained to deal with the realities of nursing home life and the conditions presented by the frail and the impaired. Some young students thought they were unprepared to be human resources for old residents. Some found it impossible to separate the elderly from the image of their own parents or grandparents. Be it good or bad, an institution for the elderly is a place that can provoke all kinds of human feelings of visitors. No one was left untouched by the following feelings in their volunteer experience: empathy, compassion, bewilderment, pleasure, sadness and irritation.

Attitude towards institutional life

No visitor coming to Kotobuki would omit talking about their image of institutions for elderly persons and how they think about institutionalisation. Mr Tanizaki and Miss Nakayama saw Sazanka and Akashia as 'a place for a group of elderly living together' and they thought the people inside were somehow isolated from the society and their lives were over-administrated as well. Aoba, on the other hand, according to Mrs Nakano, was 'a place similar to a long-term-care geriatric hospital' but was better than a hospital in the eyes of Mrs Ogawa. Whatever it might be, an institution could never be a real home for the elderly in the eyes of the visitors. Most volunteer teachers and trainee students thought residents in Sazanka and Akashia were 'nice old persons' but they were 'unfortunate' because 'mishaps in their life had made them unable to live in their own homes'. The residents in Aoba were 'ordinary elderly persons with severe impairments that cannot be cared for at home'.

The idea of institutionalisation evoked several kinds of judgement from visitors. Most volunteers were impressed by the services that residents received and by the overall quality of institutional life they had witnessed. They thought the residents in the *tokuyō* home were leading a safer life than the elderly with similar illnesses being cared for in their own homes. The college students, especially, felt that Kotobuki was a far better place to be in than the other facilities they had been to or had heard of. Most volunteers thought institutions should be run with concern and humanity. They acknowledged that living standards as well as care services in institutions had been improved greatly, and people's image of institutions had changed for the better. Yet quite a number admitted that there still exist many inhumane aspects of the home. In Sazanka, privacy was not ensured and decision-making power was limited. And the public welfare policy towards welfare institutions itself has defined elderly persons as a marginal population. In Aoba, to greater or lesser degree, there were problems regarding privacy and basic rights of the residents. Due to the disability of the residents, staff members' will tended to prevail over that of the residents.

Most older volunteers saw *tokuyō* homes as a necessary alternative to elderly care by the family while regretting the declining ability of the family to care for the elderly. They expressed respect for the people who worked in such facilities. With respect to caring for their own old parents, most said they would prefer to care for them at home. For themselves, they would like to live in their own home as long as possible. If they became disabled, they would choose to enter a nursing home rather than rely on their children. Their attitude towards institutionalisation or welfare seemed to be ambivalent. On one hand, they wanted to live with their children. But they acknowledged this was only a dream or ideal that could not be realised. On the other hand, they would rather choose public service than become a burden to their children. 'If public service is available, as we pay into the LTCI programme and are entitled to receive services, why not save the suffering of our own children?' was their common opinion.

Instilled with basic theories of personal social service and an ethic of social welfare, young college students thought it was everybody's right to receive welfare services. To them, it was normal that impaired elderly lived in an institution. Their ideal institution for elderly was a kind of mini-home, where everyone could not only enjoy privacy in their private room but could also enjoy rapport with others. There was a youth-oriented tendency among the young students. Witnessing the decay of old age, few expressed their willingness to work in a *tokuyō* home because they lacked the excitement and fun ordinary young people yearned for. Their entrance into the social welfare field was pragmatic: it was the career not the elderly they had chosen. They never thought about their own old age because it was so far away from them. But they were emphatic about not wanting to finish their own life in such settings.

For family members, they acknowledged it was painful to make the decision to have their own parents institutionalised and they acknowledged as well their own inability to care for an aged relative at home if the need arose. They appreciated the ease and relief the home provided for them, as well as the good care services for their old relatives. They thought *tokuyō* homes for the elderly were an inevitable substitute for family care for the elderly when home care was unavailable. Due to the small number of welfare institutions, it was quite difficult for elderly persons to enter a *tokuyō* home and it was impossible for families to choose a home for their parents. Tending to think they were indebted to the home for the services their old relatives received, the families were unlikely to become advocates for their old kin in the same way as families in Western countries did. Even when they felt dissatisfied with the care or treatment their old parents received, they were resigned and did not speak out. So there remained a question of whether or not they have given their real opinion.

The experiences of the visitors to Kotobuki were a product of both self-serving and altruistic motives. Devoting their time, talent and energy to the elderly residents was not a pure gift. Family members, volunteer teachers, college students or other visitors all received a broad spectrum of benefits and feelings from their involvement with the institution and the people inside.

Visitors' views of institutional life and their attitude towards institutionalisation indicate that attitudes towards care of the elderly in Japan are undergoing a transition. With the permeation of consumerism and the enhanced awareness of basic rights, institutionalisation is gradually coming to be regarded as a basic right rather than a social stigma. The younger the generation, the more strongly they take it for granted that an elderly person should receive institutional care when bedridden or senile.

In a word, the amalgam of age, gender, motivation, emotional resilience and their attitudes towards old age and institutional life represents a third kind of reality: the visitors' view of life and elderly care in institutions.

Notes

1 Institutional human being (*shisetsu ningen*) is a word used by staff members to indicate some characteristics of the elderly residents: having long lived in the institution, voluntarily following the routines to maintain the harmony of the home, depending on the home administration, and lacking self-determination.

2 The welfare cooperator system is a unique voluntary organisation established in 1972 under the leadership of the Higashimurayama City Social Welfare Council. Its members consist of volunteers, welfare commissioners, those recommended by the residents' associations and members of the Social Welfare Council. Originally this organisation was established to help the council with its fund-raising and to organise bazaars. Now this organisation is divided into seven

sub-groups. Each group plans their own volunteer activities ranging from publishing mini-newspapers, providing meals-on-wheel services and organising events to enhancing the communication between children and the elderly, holding rapport concerts (*fureai consāto*) for elderly and handicapped persons living in institutions, to opening a citizens' welfare college. One of the tasks of the welfare cooperators is to keep a close watch on elderly persons and handicapped persons living alone in the community.

Fureai comes from the verb *fureau*. Literally it means 'to touch each other by the hand', 'to come into contact with' or 'to sympathise with others'. *Fureai* implies an ideal form of open-hearted encounter between people, or a spontaneous interaction involving feelings and emotions. Here I translate *fureai* as 'rapport'.

3 Batson and his colleagues (1987) point out that an individual may have two reactions when confronted with the personal suffering of another. One reaction is distress; that is, the individual feels upset and compassionate at the sight of the suffering. In order to relieve his /her own distress, the person sets out to help the sufferer. This is termed an 'egoistic motive' for altruism, because the action serves to benefit the altruist him/herself. Another reaction is empathy. In this case, one feels sympathy for the sufferer and does not emphasise one's own feeling but that of the other. This is called an 'altruistic motive'.

4 Here it means the age grade or age hierarchy system that anthropologists such as Norbeck (1953), Lebra (1976), Bethel (1992b) and Traphagan (2000) describe in their studies on Japanese social organisation, community social structure and social interactions.

In her study of the social life of the residents in a Japanese old-age home, Bethel indicates that both a seniority structure and a horizontal age grade identification exist in the social relationship of the residents in the home. The age hierarchical or seniority system, which supposes that 'authority and prestige accompany with the length of residence' (1992b: 116), is a cultural format that regulates new residents' integration in institutional life and shapes the social relationships of the room-mates.

In Kotobuki, the seniority structure could be found in examples such as younger residents running errands for their senior neighbours, and junior roommates tended to be more restrained or modest in interaction with the senior ones, but in general it was not so significant as in the Aotani community. One possible explanation for this, I think, would be that the age hierarchy system might be more significant in a rural community such as the one Bethel depicts, than in suburbs of Tokyo where the Kotobuki home is.

In Kotobuki, when the younger residents did favours for the older ones, it was either because of the age seniority notion or the feebleness of the senior. Staff members said that many years ago the hierarchical relationships among the residents were more evident, but at present they had become more equal. In recreational clubs, there was a tendency that for the senior members to be respected by the juniors. In the 'responsible person selection affair' in the table tennis club, Mrs Matsumoto confessed that the reason for her resignation from the club was not because she wanted to serve as the responsible person, but because she could not bear the overbearing ways of Mrs Sugiyama.

5 Take myself as an example, during the period of my volunteering in Kotobuki, I was often asked by the residents questions such as 'Will you come this Sunday?' or 'Will you have time to play *go* with us this Sunday?' or 'There is a gateball game this Saturday, will you come to support us?' I knew they expected me to be with them because they wanted companionship. Normally I would go to enjoy their voluntary recreational activities such as *Karaoke*, and playing *gobang*, but sometimes I really wanted to take a break and have a holiday to recover. To work

and volunteer in three different institutions six days a week was not a light thing for me. I had to deal with the same frustrations and puzzles as the trainee students such as Mr Ōmura had in their field experience. In addition I had to take care of my study. So I wanted to skip going to the home occasionally. At times when I was tired, I felt obliged to visit the old residents on holidays. But at times when I was not fatigued, but failed to keep the promise that I would visit them on account of other reasons, I felt guilty that I had not satisfied the expectations of the old people.

Mr Tanizaki said he still went to play table tennis with the residents on occasions when he did not feel well because he knew that the elderly were waiting for him. Though he did not indicate whether or not he really wanted to go coaching at the club at such times, I guess he would be in the same ambivalent situation as I was.

6 A problematic issue in Kotobuki
Conflicts

According to Krauss *et al.* (1984) social science research on Japan for most of
the post-war period has emphasised the collective, hierarchically ordered interpersonal relations and the consensual decision-making characteristics in social
organisations. Many micro-level studies of individual and small groups have
portrayed Japanese as 'polite people seeking the social harmony idealised in
traditional Japanese culture' (Krauss *et al.* 1984: 3). Furthermore, De Vos
suggests there exists 'a Japanese pattern of relatively non-conflictful emotional
interaction' in the traditional 'hierarchical social structure' (1992: 16), where
everyone had their place within a harmonious, age-graded hierarchical status
system (1992: 20).

However, the harmony model has been criticised for ignoring areas in
Japanese society where internal conflicts are persistent, as well as for its
predisposition to look at small groups, rural communities and single firms
or factories. Studies indicate that post-war Japanese society has a great deal
of conflict in social movements, organisations and political processes (Befu
1990; Krauss *et al.* 1984; Mouer and Sugimoto 1986). Lebra believes that
the Japanese put more value on social interdependence, cooperation and
solidarity than in the West, but this does not mean that the 'Japanese never
risk confrontation but that, as long as harmony, or the appearance of
harmony, is to be maintained, nonconfrontational modes must be exhausted
first' (1984: 42). Providing four models of Japanese society with relevance to
conflicts, Befu suggests that 'Japan is not in reality a harmonious society,
even though harmony may be its motto' (1990: 233). Bethel, in her study on
the institutional life of the elderly residents in a home for the aged, indicates
that interpersonal relationships are harmonious when the age and seniority
system functions well in interactions, while irresolvable conflicts arise when
'residents do not take their proper place in the social hierarchy based on age,
sex, and seniority' (1992b: 119). These studies suggest that although
conflicts may not be as noticeable as in Western societies, and although they
may be expressed and handled in different ways than in other societies, still,
conflicts exist ubiquitously at all levels of Japanese society.

In the small community of Kotobuki, the home administration asked
every resident to be considerate towards each other and lead a harmonious

group life. Most residents were trying their best to get along with their peers, but both confrontational and non-confrontational conflicts could be found in interpersonal interactions. The direct clash between Miss Nishikawa and Mrs Takagi mentioned by Ms Shinozaki, the head matron, in Chapter 4 is an example of a confrontational conflict. This case, in the eyes of the staff members, was a combined result of prejudice towards mental patients, and lack of consideration and overstatement of self-assertion of the ordinary residents in Akashia. In Sazanka, where two residents had to share a room, it was true that direct confrontations were almost invisible because most residents tended to be more restrained or more considerate with each other than those in Akashia. However, this surface of interpersonal harmony concealed many non-confrontational hostilities that took the form of negative communication and alienation, especially between new residents and their 'senior'[1] room-mates.

This chapter deals with these two kinds of conflicts in the interactions of the residents by illustrating how they were initiated, extended and terminated. Through the analysis of the problematic cases, I shall discuss how the limitations of the home, such as the lack of a therapeutic environment and privacy, affected the quality of life of mental patients as well as the normal elderly.

Problem 1: Discrimination

Conflicts between psychiatric patients and normal elderly residents

A Japanese professor in the Social Work Research Institute of the Japan College of Social Work said in his class that Japan is a nation that discriminates against its minorities. Not only foreign labourers working in Japan and ethnic groups such as Koreans and *burakumin* were alienated by the larger society, but also the victims of diseases such as Hansen's disease and mental illnesses were treated as social outcasts by the majority of Japanese people. The experience of Miss Nishikawa Fumiko in Akashia demonstrates why it is difficult for psychiatric patients to live together with ordinary elderly people in an institution, and how a mental patient becomes a social outcast alienated by others.

Miss Nishikawa was a 69-year-old schizophrenia patient who came to live on the fourth floor of Akashia in mid-1997. She fell ill in her 20s and was taken care of at home by her parents. After the death of her parents, as her only sister could not look after her, Miss Nishikawa had been hospitalised in a private mental hospital. The same thing happened to her that happened to many in-patients of psychiatric hospitals in recent years: she ended up staying for a longer period because the hospital needed to discharge some old patients with minor symptoms to solve its difficulty in accepting new patients (Harding *et al.* 1985). With no home to return to and no community rehabilitation facilities she could utilise, she came to live in Akashia with her sister as her guardian.

After she became a resident of Akashia, she apparently had many difficulties in adapting herself to the new environment. She frequented the matrons' room several times a day to complain about her poor health condition. She said that she was suffering from stomach troubles, bowel problems and having fits. For these reasons she went to see doctors frequently but tended to be suspicious about the diagnosis and changed hospitals very often. However, her main problem in the home was not her health condition but the discrimination against her by other residents on the floor. The person who was most unkind to her, in her eyes, was Mrs Takagi, a senior resident who had lived in Akashia for more than ten years.

Mrs Takagi had lived with a man for ten years after her husband died. As she could not get along well with the man's eldest son and his family, she was driven out. With nowhere to go, she came to Akashia. Mrs Takagi was the kind of person who was always carping at others. She often spoke ill of her peers, saying that Mrs Chiba's mouth smelled offensive, that Mrs Kobayashi wore the same clothes every day, and that Mr Shiraishi's daughter should teach her father how to clean. Her conflicts with Miss Nishikawa began soon after the latter entered Akashia. The first complaint Mrs Takagi made to the matrons was that she wanted Miss Nishikawa not to distribute food to others. 'We don't accept presents from absurd persons', she said, 'we all have our own ways of enjoying our lives here. Could she find something to do such as reading books to enjoy her life rather than disturbing others?' And she often complained of Miss Nishikawa's misconduct, for example, forgetting to flush the toilet after using it. Even though she had not witnessed it with her own eyes, she would report to the staff members that someone else had told her that Miss Nishikawa was 'unbelievably' washing her hair in the washroom naked from the waist up. She also showed such a great interest in Miss Nishikawa's outings that she often searched for her on ordinary days. If she could not find Miss Nishikawa on the floor, she would go to ask the matrons where she had gone. After she had hinted by innuendo among the residents that Miss Nishikawa had dirtied the toilet, she would go to tell the latter purposely that she was not pointing to her. She also advocated that abnormal persons such as mental patients on the floor should be hospitalised.

Miss Nishikawa, on the other hand, frequently told the matrons that Mrs Takagi was going to oust her from the floor. She said 'Mrs Takagi is bossy and always speaks evil of me behind my back.' As she was obsessed with the idea that Mrs Takagi was treating her badly, she tended to have the impression that everything Mrs Takagi did was to persecute her. So when she saw Mrs Takagi talking to others, she imagined that the 'spiteful old woman' was speaking ill of her. Although she went to complain to the matrons, she could not make clear what she was saying or she would forget what she wanted to say halfway through. Then she would stop speaking, keep silent for a while and return to her room with her head hanging down. A minute later, she would appear again at the matrons' room. As she repeated such behaviour all the time, Mrs Takagi and the other residents thought her weird and deliberately isolated her by not interacting with her. Feeling alienated by others, Miss Nishikawa spoke of her dissatisfaction at the gatherings of clubs and recreational activities. At first she gained some sympathy from the others. However her unclear statements as well as her repeated laments about being socially ostracised (*murahachibu*)[2] gradually upset the other members. As a result, she became an unwelcome person in the clubs. She was gloomy, angry and disappointed. Eventually she developed a persecution mania and was hospitalised for a while.

During Miss Nishikawa's hospitalisation, Mrs Takagi led the residents on the floor in an appeal to the matrons to protect their lives. The claims were: 'Though she has no business there, Miss Nishikawa often stands in front of our doors', 'Whenever we are talking about something with each other which has nothing to do with her, she will come to accuse us of speaking ill of her', 'We will become neurotics if her abnormal behaviour continues disturbing us', 'If you do not take any steps, we will be beaten and become strange', and so on. They said that regular hospitalisation of Miss Nishikawa was necessary for the psychological well-being of both the patient and the other residents.

Ms Shinozaki and other staff members expressed their gratitude for the patience of Mrs Takagi and other residents, and the attention they paid to Miss Nishikawa. 'We understand your frustrated feelings and the inconvenience Miss Nishikawa and other mental patients cause to your daily life', Ms Shinozaki said, 'But as Miss Nishikawa is a sick person, she is different from normal people who can control their own behaviour. I hope you can understand that she is unable to fulfil what you expect of her. As you are living under the same roof like a family (*hitotsu kama no meshi wo tabeteiru*), I hope you can overlook her misdeeds and lead a harmonious life here.'

Unsatisfied with the response of the matrons, Mrs Takagi asked four other residents to go to the warden's office to make some demands. They inquired why the home had accepted so many strange persons such as Miss Nishikawa, who had ruined their regular lives and imposed stress on them. They hoped persons with mental illnesses would not be admitted any more. To the wishes of these five residents, the home administration gave the following response.

(1) The home can listen to residents' demands and opinions regarding their daily life as well as operations related to recreational activities and events, but it cannot listen to opinions related to other persons' admission or discharge, individuals' privacy as well as personnel affairs concerning the staff members.

(2) The home understands that the presence of mental patients may have affected the lives of the residents on the floor and that some might become irritated. However, the home cannot dismiss the persons who cause problems in order to appease others' dissatisfaction. Regarding new entrants, as the home has its own problems in operation, it cannot always choose people who are like prize pupils.

(3) A recent trend in the social service field is that both the number of *keihi* homes and the elderly clients are decreasing, while the new entrants tend to be older and have severe disabilities. If the home does not admit persons with mental illnesses or other kinds of disabilities to fill up vacancies, it will fall into financial difficulties. If this happens, the home will probably be closed down or be consolidated by the *yōgo* home, and the lives of the residents will be affected.

(4) The home will do its utmost to ensure everyone leads a comfortable life. Yet it also hopes that all residents will be considerate of the feelings of others and be patient with the troubles arising from group life.

To this correspondence, the majority of the five female 'advocates' showed their understanding to some extent. Mrs Takagi accepted it reluctantly, however, because she did not achieve her aim of ousting her 'enemy'. But she admitted that through the direct dialogue with the warden, she was somehow able to dispel her gloom.

The home, on the other hand, attempted to solve this problem by seeking the cooperation of the patient's family. The warden had a talk with Miss Nishikawa's sister about her future. The two came to an agreement that, considering Miss Nishikawa's mental stability, the social environment surrounding her, as well as the other residents' lives, it was difficult for her to continue living in Akashia. It would be better for her to live in a *yōgo* home or a mental hospital. However it was difficult for a psychiatric patient to enter a *yōgo* home because a great number of applicants on the waiting list were victims of mental illnesses. Nor was it possible for Miss Nishikawa to become a permanent in-patient in the mental hospital because her symptoms were not so serious and she herself disliked the hospital. It was obvious that this problem could not be solved immediately. So there was no other choice than to have Miss Nishikawa go back and forth between the home and the hospital.

When Miss Nishikawa knew she was able to stay in Akashia continuously, she became a bit brighter. After she was discharged from the hospital, maybe because she had gradually become used to institutional life, she complained less than before and became more composed. Being a Christian, she went to her church every week. In addition to participating in club activities regularly, she became close to a resident on the second floor who was sympathetic to her. However, her hostility towards Mrs Takagi did not abate. Neither did Mrs Takagi's resentment of Miss Nishikawa. The two persons took turns to go to the matrons' station or the nurses' station to blame each other. As people tended to be more sympathetic towards the weak, the staff treated Miss Nishikawa as a powerless child who needed protection. This, in the eyes of Mrs Takagi, might be explained as the matrons taking the side of her enemy. Eventually the accumulated animosity between the two escalated into an overt clash.

One afternoon, Miss Nishikawa came back from a check-up in the Kichijōji Hospital. Mrs Takagi asked her whether she had just come back from Ryokufusō hospital, a general hospital in the city. Miss Nishikawa did not answer and returned to her room silently. As she had been ill-treated by Mrs Takagi several times, she was unwilling to talk to the very person who had bullied her and whose intentions were unkind. Just before dinner, she came out of her room to speak to Mrs Takagi who was then in the hallway, 'Isn't it you who spread the tale about my being in the mental hospital?' At this, Mrs Takagi became angry. She replied in a loud voice 'I didn't say that. Who has said so, you bring him/her here. Let's go and speak to the warden. People in your rooms please come out to be witnesses.' With this, she gathered two or three other residents who were uneasy with the presence of Miss Nishikawa. Circling the latter in the hallway, maybe because they had built up too much anger and stress, Mrs Takagi and her 'comrades' heaped their accumulated resentment on Miss Nishikawa. Attacked vehemently by her neighbours, Miss Nishikawa was so shocked that she could not say a word to defend herself. She became pale as if she was going to faint.

Ms Shinozaki, a welfare supervisor and a nurse came to the spot to see what had happened as soon as they heard the noises. To the staff members, Mrs Takagi said in a low voice, 'It is unnecessary for us residents on the fourth floor to be patient with such an insane person. There is a vacancy on the second floor and she was getting along well with an old woman there, it's better to transfer her to that floor.' Looking at the poor Miss Nishikawa, both the nurse and Ms Shinozaki could not help shedding tears. They were unable to understand why, despite the fact that staff members had interfered in the conflicts between the two several times, the normal one still could not put herself in the patient's shoes, and why people could not treat the weak more kindly but would rather exclude them and make them more unfortunate. 'We have no choice but to change the rooms of the two. I think both should be transferred to other rooms. Otherwise it is unfair.' Ms Shinozaki said to the welfare supervisor.

At dinnertime, although Miss Nishikawa was accompanied by the nurse to the dining hall, she was so shocked that she squatted down on the floor. Seeing that she was in an unstable condition, the nurse led her back to her room. Her meal was carried in but she did not eat anything except for some *tofu*. Bending down her head speechless, she sat on her bed contemplating.

At about eight o'clock that night, Miss Nishikawa came to the matrons' room to take her medicine as usual, seeming to have calmed down. She said to Ms Shinozaki who was on night shift that day. 'If only had I answered yes upon being asked whether I had been to the hospital, there would not have been such a big trouble. But I have a resistance toward that person in my heart. If you had not been there, I would have had a terrible experience.' Miss Nishikawa was grateful to Ms Shinozaki. At the same time she was perplexed as to why people on the other floors were kind to her while her neighbours were so cruel, and why she could be respected as a 'mother' by younger inmates in the hospital but had to be abused in the home. Also, she did not know how to face Mrs Takagi and other residents who had maltreated her the next day.

This conflict was finally resolved by transferring Miss Nishikawa to the second floor, on which 'weak persons' such as demented elderly persons and psychiatric patients were relatively concentrated. The nurses said, 'As many residents who have similar illnesses were living on the second floor, the environment there may be more suitable to Miss Nishikawa. At least she will not be regarded as abnormal there. We hope she will find her peace there.' But they agreed with the matrons that this solution was an unfair one, because the other person in the affair, Mrs Takagi, who had taken the role as a 'prosecutor' was not punished at all. She achieved her objective of ostracising her enemy and was able to continue living on the floor without any change. 'Ultimately, the loser will be the weak person because she is unable to defend her own rights', Ms Shinozaki concluded, 'I don't think transferring the weak is a final solution to dealing with the conflicts between the mental patients and the so-called normal persons. What shall we do if the next entrant is also a patient? Can we promise such a clash will not happen again?' She thought that, as long as other residents could not understand that mental illness was a kind of impediment like a physical disability, neither the living environment for mental patients in Akashia nor the quality of their life could be improved.

Mental patients and prejudice towards them in institutions

During the period I conducted fieldwork in Kotobuki, there were about 20 psychiatric elderly patients living in Sazanka and Akashia. About half were taken ill when they were quite young, and had long histories of hospitalisation. Mr Aoki, the schizophrenia patient who narrated his story in Chapter 3, was an example of such a person. Others became depressives or schizophrenics quite late in life because of shock or the loss of their loved ones. All of them regularly went to see their doctors in mental hospitals. Since all were taking medicine, the mental state of most patients was stable. But at the start of their institutional life, because they were suddenly put into an unfamiliar environment, and because quite a number had become adults without reaching maturity due to their long isolated life in hospitals, they were observed to be unable to adapt themselves to life in the home as well as to the human relationships. Some suffered relapses. Miss Nishikawa was one of several whose state was not so stable. Most of these patients were harmless.

According to the staff members, in Sazanka, the old people were relatively more sympathetic and tolerant towards these elderly with problems, because they had long lived a group life with both psychiatric patients and physically handicapped persons, and they had witnessed the horrible fate of some of those who suffered from senility. Even when they felt uncomfortable with mental patients, they would rather keep themselves away from them than confront them directly. So there were rarely conflicts between mental patients and the normal elderly residents. However, the residents in Akashia tended to be more aware of their rights. They were less considerate and more prejudiced towards mental patients, even though they had been cured. This could be represented in the words: 'I am paying for my stay in the home, so I do not want to have any odd persons as my neighbours.' Miss Nishikawa was a victim of discrimination and the selfishness of such residents.

It was true that mental patients had more problematic behaviours than normal persons. For example, the two suicides in the history of Sazanka were both committed by psychiatric patients. In a public *yōgo* home in the same city, a couple of years earlier a horrible murder incident had been caused by a mental patient resident. Thus, how to take care of such patients under the same roof as many ordinary residents had become a big challenge facing the institution's administration.

On one hand, as the psychiatric patients were cared for under the medical care regulations in Japan, there was no welfare institution for which they were eligible, and community rehabilitation facilities for such patients were poorly developed, so when the patients became old and were discharged from hospitals without any homes to return to, welfare institutions for the elderly had to take in some of them. Mr Itō said in Chapter 4 that Sazanka should be fair to all applicants, so it had to admit mental patients who had been on the waiting list for a long time. In addition, the improved housing conditions for the elderly as well as the emergence of the re-examination of whether the institutional provision of both accommodation and three meals a day was really good for promoting the autonomy of the healthy elderly in the welfare field had led to decreasing numbers in *keihi* homes and its applicants (Miura 1996). As a result, existing homes of this kind fell into financial problems. In order to keep the institution operating, Akashia chose to recruit elderly mental patients. These were the 'push' factors causing institutions to accept elderly with psychiatric problems.

On the other hand, after the homes admitted these patients, they found themselves having to deal with various kinds of problems resulting from the admissions. Staff members lacked both professional knowledge about mental illnesses and training in caring for these patients. More problematic, the other residents showed strong prejudice or discrimination towards mentally disabled persons.

Munakata (1986), in his study on mental illness and the mental health care system, as well as Harding *et al.* (1985) and Reilly (1996), in their investigation of human rights of mental patients, all mention Japanese people's prejudice towards psychiatric patients. According to these studies, it had been the practice prior to the Second World War for mental patients to be locked up in asylums under police custody or left alone in cold, dark rooms by their own families, and 'the prevalent attitude was stigmatisation of mental patients, a belief that mental illness was hereditary, and a feeling of shame if such a patient turned up within one's own family' (Harding *et al.* 1985: 10). The general expectation in society of the mental health care system is the maintenance of society rather than the well-being of the patients. So the mental hospitals are always overcrowded and the average length of stay is long. And the 'particular Japanese social problem of non-acceptance of mental patients by their families' (1985: 24) is a contributing factor to the above features in the mental health care system. Psychiatric patients are also discriminated against in the field of employment, social services and training opportunities offered to the physically disabled (1985: 36).

In Kotobuki, the clash between Miss Nishikawa and Mrs Takagi was a good example illustrating the discrimination issue. Besides this, social discrimination towards mental patients was presented in many other forms. First, most such patients were 'abandoned' by their families. Mr Aoki, for example, although he wanted to go home to eat homemade food or spend holidays with his family, was not allowed to do so by his own mother and brother. Miss Nishikawa's sister was reluctant to be involved in the affairs of her sibling and entrusted to the home the whole responsibility for dealing with her sister.

Inside the home, people referred to mental patients as feeble-minded persons. Elderly persons who shared a room with such patients said that they seldom talked to their room-mates, because these persons were either fearful or uncommunicative. Mr Hagiwara, a schizophrenic on the second floor, said that although the food and other provisions in the home were better than in a mental hospital, and there was much freedom, people's attitude and expectations towards him were different. In general, except for daily greetings, residents tended to keep themselves away from psychiatric patients. So the latter were actually an isolated presence in the home. Thus, the invisibility of conflicts in Sazanka could also be explained as the result of the deliberate strategy of avoidance on the part of the ordinary elderly residents.

In short, in Sazanka and Akashia, residents could show their sympathy towards physically disabled persons and victims suffering from senile dementia, and express their understanding towards depression, but psychiatric disorders were regarded as dangerous. 'Generally people feel uncomfortable if there is a mental patient nearby' (words from the head nurse), and this attitude, together with people's lack of knowledge about mental illnesses, created a less therapeutic environment for psychiatric patients in institutions.

Welfare homes for the elderly are places for old persons to live their later lives, and they are also places where older mental patients can live after they return to society. People may say that it is a great development that mental patients can live with ordinary elderly persons in institutions because it demonstrates that discrimination towards mental patients is diminishing. However the reality is that such old patients could not go back to their own homes, they were transferred from one institution to another. In welfare institutions, staff members, even the professionals such as welfare supervisors and nurses, are not well trained to deal with mental patients and their demands. In addition, there is no psychiatrist who can provide medical services. Under such conditions, even though the number of mental patients is small, it remains in doubt whether welfare institutions for the elderly are a suitable choice for mental patients to live in peace. As Ms Shinozaki put it, 'environment is very important for mental patients', and as long as people's prejudice towards them persists, the lives of mental patients in institutions will not be improved. It would be better to establish a special kind of facility for older mental patients to live in.

Problem 2: Silent resistance

Interpersonal conflicts in Sazanka: two examples

The room is the basic social unit of the Kotobuki community. In Aoba, four persons shared a room, but since most of them were either bedridden or demented, little interaction was observed among them. In Akashia, each resident could enjoy his/her freedom and privacy in his/her private room. In Sazanka, where two residents lived in the same room, there was, inevitably, interaction between the two persons. Relationships between room-mates were basically regulated by self-administration and a sense of mutual assistance. When a new resident came, his/her room-mate helped to integrate the new person by serving as a guide to institutional life. Thus there existed a kind of senior–junior relationship between them.

As with Bethel's findings in her studies of the relationships between the residents in the Aotani home for the elderly (Bethel 1992b), when the seniority system functioned well and two residents conducted their actions by mutual concessions, the relationship of the room-mates was harmonious. However, not all room-mates got along well with each other. As new residents could not choose their room-mates, they had to fit themselves into the room environment the senior person had already established, and the two tended to have different living habits, so there were times when the junior could not get in tune with the senior. Latent tension always existed between the two people in the same room. Basically, the new resident did not want direct confrontation or explicit expressions to show his/her objection towards the senior, but rather he/she used 'non-confrontational' (Lebra 1984: 42) techniques such as negative communication, or emotional and behavioural cues to signal a conflict. A 'peaceful' surface usually covered strong emotions generated by latent conflicts: frustration, anxiety, anger, grudge, hatred, guilt and contempt. The narratives of Mrs Fukushima and Miss Hiraoka exemplify the silent conflicts in the relationships of room-mates and show how two new residents managed conflicts.

Mrs Fukushima

On the fourth floor of Sazanka, the dining hall was one of the few places where residents could take refuge from the room-mates they disliked. It was also a place where friendships between people who were in the same boat formed. Mrs Fukushima and Miss Hiraoka were two old women I found to be always in the dining hall talking with each other using a hearing aid. At first, I wondered why the two were always there, why they did not go back to their own rooms and why they looked so vigilant while talking and quickly changed topics when someone approached the hall.

One morning I went to Mrs Fukushima's room to give her room-mate some pictures I took of an event. Mrs Fukushima was not in, only her room-mate was there watching TV. Seeing my appearance at the door, the old woman showed by her expression that I was not welcome. I thought it might be because I had disturbed her watching TV, so I made an excuse and gave the photos to her. The old woman accepted them and said thanks after I told her the pictures were free of charge. The cold look in her eyes as well as her apathetic tone left with me the idea that she was not a stereotypical sweet granny. When I was leaving her room, Mrs Fukushima came back. I gave her pictures too. Later I was called out by Mrs Fukushima, who was having a conversation with Miss Hiraoka in the dining hall. The former asked what I thought about her room-mate. I said she seemed to be an unkind person. At this Mrs Fukushima began to complain of her anguish in living with her room-mate.

Mrs Fukushima was 83 years old. About a year before, she had been widowed. The welfare commissioner in her district came to visit her when he saw the demise of her husband on their family register. He thought it was unsafe for an old woman over 80 to live alone, so he suggested she enter a *yōgo* home. A couple of months after the welfare commissioner reported her condition to the ward welfare office, she was asked whether she would like to live in Sazanka where a vacancy was available. Considering the insecurity of living by herself, she agreed to move into Sazanka. At first, she was placed with a room-mate who was sensitive to cold. The time she came to Sazanka was exactly in mid-summer, August. Yet her room-mate did not turn on the air conditioner and put a thick quilt over herself every day. With the room temperature as high as 33 to 36 degrees centigrade, Mrs Fukushima felt very uncomfortable. However as she was a newcomer, she was too reserved to ask the staff members to change her room. She had no choice but to endure. Eventually she was unable to stand the heat and fell ill. In the hospital she told the truth to the doctor when asked. After her discharge, she was put in another room. 'Maybe I am an unfortunate person so I have to live with persons with bad characters,' Mrs Fukushima sighed over her bad luck.

According to Mrs Fukushima, the room-mate with whom she was living was a self-centred person. Day and night, she stayed in the room watching TV. When she was displeased with something, she yelled at the TV set. She was irritable and spoke to herself loudly all the time. As soon as she got up, she had a snack, leaving the crumbs all over the room without cleaning it. After lunch she watched TV, spoke to herself and took a nap. At seven o'clock at night, she turned off both the light and the TV without considering Mrs Fukushima's convenience. And she would get angry if Mrs Fukushima did something ahead of her. For example, Mrs Fukushima could not get up even if she had been awake for some time but had to wait on her bed until her room-mate got up first. The latter tended to spend 20 minutes putting on her clothes. During the period her room-mate went to wash her face, Mrs Fukushima got up and cleaned the room very quickly. Living with such a room-mate, Mrs Fukushima was obviously very angry. She said:

> She never thinks that there is another person living with her. She turns the TV set towards her alone, never cleans the room, always makes rattling noises and closes the curtain at her own convenience. In a word, she behaves as if she alone is the owner of the room. I am enduring as if I am an inferior. It is the first time that I have met such a person. I cannot understand at all how she was brought up. She is selfish, mischievous, and she does not know proper etiquette. She must have been brought up with tender care and cherished as a treasure. Sometimes I am so angry that I want to slap her in the face. However I am not the type to quarrel with others, so I restrain my rage. Since I have no place to go, I have to endure.

Mrs Fukushima said she was reluctant to tell the matrons about her frustration. First, she did not want to become a problematic person in the eyes of staff members as she had just changed rooms. She knew it was difficult for matrons to deal with the residents. 'Just like the son who is sandwiched between his mother and his wife, they have to take the sides of both. It is difficult for them to find a balance', she said, showing understanding towards the staff. But Mrs Fukushima also indicated that as her room-mate had lived in the home for more than 15 years and she was good at currying favour with the matrons, she herself would be in a disadvantaged position if she went to complain of her room-mate. And she commented on her room-mate:

> I don't think flawless people will come to live in a home like this. Among the 40 persons on this floor, about 16 or 17 are not right-minded people. I heard that the lady in my room (*uchi no ojōsan*) has changed her room-mate many times and no one could get along with her. No one would like to be friends with her, you see. I think people like her should be put into a private room.

Mrs Fukushima used '*ojōsan*' (a young lady from good family) to talk cynically about her room-mate. While sitting on her seat in the dining hall which was right opposite to her room, she always looked in the direction of her room to observe whether there was something happening in front of the matrons' room. She said as she could not quarrel with the '*ojōsan*' directly, the only means she used to show her ill feeling towards the latter was to deliberately rustle the laundry clothes-peg holder continuously when she brought back her clothes from the veranda.

As she was a newcomer, she had no friend in the home to talk with until Miss Hiraoka came. 'I will become crazy if I continue living with this *ojōsan*. I wish we two could live together but here we are unable to choose our own partner', Mrs Fukushima showed her dissatisfaction with a sigh. While she was talking, Miss Hiraoka did not make any comment but nodded her head now and then. Ten years younger than Mrs Fukushima, she came to live in Sazanka a few months after the former's entrance. The same status as a junior resident and the same fate of being put into a situation of having to live with a senior room-mate who was disliked by all bound the two together. They became friends and often had conversations together to dispel their gloom.

Miss Hiraoka

Miss Hiraoka had come to live in Sazanka six months before, after she was discharged from a hospital where she was hospitalised for malnutrition and became a recipient of Livelihood Protection. She had never thought that she would end up in a home. She had taken it for granted that she would be able to receive care from her divorced friend whose children she had helped to bring up and whose apartment she had put some money in to buy. And she had thought that she would be able to be buried in the grave of that family with whom she had lived for more than 40 years. Because when young, Miss Hiraoka moved into her divorced friend's home to help take care of her two children, she did not have a formal job except for some side jobs. In addition, she did not join in the National Pension Scheme. As a result, she had neither her own home nor income when she became older. Becoming less and less important after the children reached adulthood, Miss Hiraoka was often criticised for being a financial burden after her friend retired, which worsened the relationship between the two.

The elder son whom Miss Hiraoka brought up took the responsibility for looking after her after obtaining agreement from his wife. But since she was not related to the young couple by blood and the young generation's living habits were different from hers, Miss Hiraoka could not get along well with them. As the daughter-in-law only cooked for dinner, and the poor old woman did not have the money to buy a lunch box, she could only eat once a day. And she was unwilling to tell the son that she was hungry and that she needed some money. Having nothing to do at home, she began to commute to the day service centre in the city welfare hall at the suggestion of the officials in the city office. The daughter-in-law was angry at Miss Hiraoka's going to the city office because an officer called to ask the family to give the old woman some money to buy lunch. With the 500 yen a day she got from the son, Miss Hiraoka went to the day service centre for eight months. As the nurse there thought Miss Hiraoka's leanness unnatural, she took her to the hospital to have a health check. She was diagnosed as suffering from malnutrition. The son was called by the city welfare office for information and was criticised by the officials there. He was so angry when he got back home that he said Miss Hiraoka had disgraced him in public and that he had no responsibility to take care of her. As a result, the poor old woman had her connection with the son cut and was evicted from the family. With no home and no money, she became so worried that she had a fall. After she was discharged from the hospital, she found herself in Sazanka.

The room-mate Miss Hiraoka lived with was about 20 years older than she was. She was said to be the oldest person in the home, and the person who had lived in Sazanka the longest. Although she was not a bad person, she was nagging and didactic. She directed the way things were done in the room. And she berated Miss Hiraoka constantly for her not doing things her way. Living in such an atmosphere, Miss Hiraoka was stressed and disgruntled. She chafed at her room-mate like this:

> She always thinks she is right. Who has done wrong? She behaves as if she was my mother-in-law. Actually I call her 'my mother' (*uchi no okāsan*) secretly. She criticises how I put away the cleaning bucket. She demands that I do everything her way. If I do not follow her, she will point at me and say 'You, you don't listen to me!' or 'I will report all you have done to the matron.' If I pretend not to hear her and turn my back on her, she will seize my shoulder and say loudly 'Listen to me' or 'Can you hear me?' As she is as old as my own mother, there is nothing for me to do but say 'yes, yes'. I am new and junior, so it is reasonable for me to follow the opinions of the senior ones. I can listen to her occasional sermon but it is impossible for me to tolerate all the time. Anyway she is not my mother. I was unable to bear her imperative tone, repeated criticism and endless fastidiousness so I haven't talked to her for three months. I just keep myself outside of the room.

Miss Hiraoka chose keeping silent and avoiding speaking to her room-mate as a means of resistance. Sometimes she wanted to reply with a 'you idiot' to show her disgust. However, when she thought about the commotion that would result, she restrained herself. In addition as she was indebted to the home, she thought she should not make trouble:

> Ms Shinozaki said we could go to talk with her or the matron assigned to our room when we had problems. It is very kind of her to say so. But there are many problems in the home that matrons are unable to solve. I don't want to trouble them, so I don't express my dissatisfaction or my wish to change rooms.

She just resisted silently. Except for bedtime and other occasions when she had to stay in her room, she kept herself in the dining hall or the reading room, or went for a walk in the park. It was during the three months she fought silently with her 'mother' that she became close to Mrs Fukushima. They often sat together to grumble at their room-mates and to comfort each other. They hoped that there would be a professional counsellor who could listen to their anguish. Sometimes a trainee student who showed sympathy to them performed this role.

Basically, staff members would not meddle in the relationship of the room-mates as long as no one came to complain. One day when Miss Hiraoka was washing clothes in the washroom, Ms Shinozaki came to ask her to consider making up with her room-mate. As Miss Hiraoka seldom stayed at her room and did not talk with her room-mate, the latter went to tell the matrons that if Miss Hiraoka disliked living with her, she could change a room-mate. And she hoped the staff would ask Miss Hiraoka what she was thinking. Listening to Ms Shinozaki's sincere words that she hoped everyone could live a happy life in the last stage of their life, Miss Hiraoka reflected on her past behaviour and thought she might have been too cruel to her room-mate. She promised to reconcile with her room-mate from her side first. She did it. Her room-mate was happy and reported to the matrons about their reconciliation right away.

However their harmony did not last long. Her room-mate's incessant criticism as well as her dictatorial will to control made Miss Hiraoka feel fed up. She refused to speak to her room-mate again. The matron in charge of her room observed that the two old women were not getting along, so she asked Miss Hiraoka informally over dinner whether 'your house was shaking again'. That night Miss Hiraoka heard her room-mate whimpering in the dark. The sobbing weighed heavily on her heart. She suddenly understood that her room-mate was actually a lonely person. She reprimanded herself for alienating an old person as pitiful as herself. She could not fall asleep and felt wretched for being a woman. She did not know what she should do when she woke up the next morning: make up or continue the silent fight.

In fact there were few residents in Sazanka who had not experienced the same feelings such as frustration, anger, resentment, hatred and guilt that Mrs Fukushima and Miss Hiraoka had experienced in the process of adapting themselves to institutional life, especially in their human relationships in the early period. Sudden change in environment, difficulties and failures in dealing with new relationships and few resources of emotional support could account for these kinds of conflictual emotions. However, on the surface, direct confrontations were rarely observed. Various kinds of conflicts were ubiquitous in each room, some minor, others serious. And the latent tension between the room-mates was usually further escalated by the limitations of institutional life such as lack of privacy, no choices in selecting a room-mate, and the pressure of the notion of harmony the home promoted, which taxed individuals to their limits of personal capability of perseverance. In conflictual relationships, the seniority system regulating human behaviour was usually breached.

Strategies for interpersonal conflict management

The methods the residents used in dealing with conflicts were basically non-confrontational. Both Mrs Fukushima and Miss Hiraoka used 'negative communication' (Lebra 1984: 43) to manage conflicts with their room-mates. That is, they expressed their frustration or anger to the source, their room-mates, in a negative manner by not communicating with them. Instead of confronting their room-mates, both Mrs Fukushima and Miss Hiraoka avoided seeing or contacting their room-mates by not staying in their rooms, thereby letting the room-mates know how upset they were with them or how strongly they disliked them. Mrs Fukushima never talked to the '*ojōsan*' in her room and always showed a sulking face. And she produced intentionally nasty noises to express her dislike towards the '*ojōsan*'. Miss Hiraoka's 'mother' liked to talk. However, in a face-to-face conversation, Miss Hiraoka refused to respond to her either by turning her back on her 'mother' or by feigning deafness. She always removed her hearing aid when she was in her room. She also signalled her objection to her room-mate by sulking. In the period when she made reconciliation with her 'mother', she followed the old lady's orders to do tasks in the room, silently. As she expressed it, 'If I do not follow her way, she will keep on nagging. So I tolerate doing it this way'; this silence meant a mixture of endurance, grudge and grievance.

Lebra suggests that the Japanese often create a triad to avoid confrontation between two parties. Conflict between A and B may be communicated indirectly through the third party X who, as a go-between or an arbiter, represents A or B or both in conflict. 'When a conflict is at a stalemate, X, who commands respect from both parties, may provide a breakthrough by presenting himself as the person on whose behalf A and B are advised to forgive each other' (1984: 45). In Sazanka, the matrons played the role of go-between or arbiter. For example, taking a surrogate role, Ms Shinozaki first offered a vicarious apology to Miss Hiraoka for the inconvenience her 'mother' had caused and then she urged the latter to relent. Miss Hiraoka gave in and considered reconciliation with her 'mother' in order to save face for Ms Shinozaki.

However the presence of the arbiter could not always be effective in mediating the conflicts between the room-mates. Sometimes it became pressure on both parties, or even a dramatic conflict. Miss Hiraoka felt pressed whether to make up with her room-mate or not after the matron perceived her second discord with her 'mother'. As she perceived the '*ojōsan*' as a person who was good at flattering the staff, Mrs Fukushima thought the matrons might be her room-mate's allies, so she thought it useless to complain. In the case of Mrs Takagi and Miss Nishikawa, as the staff members were more protective toward the latter, the former thought the matrons on her floor all took sides with her opponent. She reproached Miss Nishikawa in the confrontation that it was because of her existence that it had become difficult for her to make demands of the staff members.

A variant of triadic conflict management is displacement. In an attempt to convey his/her anger or disapproval to B, party A may release all his or her frustration with B upon X, when confident that X will not relay them to

B, the source of frustration (Lebra 1984: 46). In Sazanka, close friends and trainee students often acted as sympathetic listeners who could offer a dumping ground for A's *guchi* (personal laments). Female residents in particular liked to exchange their *guchi* regarding their room-mates. After Mrs Fukushima and Miss Hiraoka became friends, the two often sat in the dining hall enumerating the wrongdoings of their room-mates. After I showed sympathy to Mrs Fukushima, she would release her *guchi* to me each time I went to Sazanka. She said she was able to drive away some of her gloom after I had listened to her. In displacement management, as the sympathetic listener does not have the power or ability to eliminate the source of A's dissatisfaction, that is, he/she is unable to provide a private room or change a room-mate for party A, he/she can only appease the discontented temporarily. *Guchi* release, thus, in Lebra's words, is meant not for 'counselling but for catharsis or emotional exorcism' (1984: 46).

Self-accusation as well as acceptance of reality was also employed internally by individuals to deal with conflict. Miss Hiraoka felt guilty that she had alienated her 'mother' when she heard the latter sobbing in the dark. She considered forgiving her 'mother's' bossiness and fussiness. Mrs Fukushima accepted her fate of always having to live with 'bad people' by persuading herself to believe that she was an unfortunate person. Realising that her problems were also shared by newcomers in other rooms, she said she had no choice but to put up with the inconvenience.

This chapter deals with conflicts at interpersonal level among the residents in Kotobuki. The three cases introduced here indicate that not only confrontations but also non-confrontational conflicts exist in the interaction among the residents. Thus it affirms the claim Krauss *et al.* made that the harmony model alone is not sufficient to explain the social structure in Japan and that a conflict model must be added (1984: 376–9). Through the examples described in the chapter, we can find that the ideal of harmony is still strong in the small social organisation of Kotobuki. For example, the institution promotes cooperation, rapport and consideration of each resident in creating a peaceful atmosphere easy for everyone to live in. Consideration, endurance and mutual concession are seen as the common values among the residents in maintaining harmonious relationships.

Oriented by such cultural norms, individuals attempt to avoid conflict and open confrontation by using 'non-confrontational' strategies. These strategies, as Lebra (1984) has suggested, include negative communication, triadic management, displacement, self-accusation and conflict acceptance. Open confrontations happen only when these non-confrontational resources are exhausted. Although residents use such methods to avoid confrontations, they tend to maintain a harmonious surface at the price of suppressing their own emotions. Latent tension as well as hostility is always concealed beneath the surface of harmony. This kind of interpersonal tension is usually observed in the relationship between newcomers and their senior room-mates, especially when the age hierarchical system does not function effectively.

The conflict between mental patients and other residents is one of the major problems in Kotobuki. Due to the prejudice towards mental illnesses, most of the psychiatric patients are actually alienated from the ordinary residents. Although welfare institutions for the elderly have become a refuge for mental patients in recent years, with resistance towards these patients from both their families and their fellow residents, it is difficult to say that the quality of life of these patients can be ensured in homes where a therapeutic environment is lacking. How to improve the living environment for the patients under the existing system and empower the staff members with professional knowledge and skills to deal with psychiatric residents remains the big challenge of institutional management.

The lack of privacy and choice in selecting a room-mate are the main limitations of institutional life in Sazanka. They are also the sources of conflicts between room-mates. As long as private rooms are unavailable, the conflicts between room-mates cannot be avoided.

Notes

1 'A senior' here refers to a resident who came to live in Kotobuki earlier than a new resident. He/she was not necessary chronologically older than the newcomer.
2 Village ostracism (*mura hachibu*) based on conformity to the group norm was enforced in Japanese rural areas towards nonconformist families in the past. In *mura hachibu*, the community made an agreement not to cooperate with and lend help to transgressors in times of rice transplanting, harvesting, funerals and so on. As a result, the family was socially exiled without being forced to move out of the community (Befu 1990).

7 Beyond the homes
Towards the LTCI system

Welfare institutions for the elderly are operated under the regulation of welfare policies. Changes in social policies for the elderly usually have an impact on the operation of institutions, and thus inevitably affect the lives of the people who live and work in them. The 'Long-term Care Insurance' (LTCI) scheme is the newest Japanese public policy intending to meet the expanding needs for long-term care and to secure a decent later life for every old person.

Under this LTCI system, local municipalities (cities, towns and villages) are the insurers. They are responsible for collecting resources to develop the necessary social services for their citizens, organising professional teams to assess the care needs of elderly individuals, create the necessary care packages and distribute services for the persons in need. In order that everyone can receive care services when he/she needs them, all Japanese people aged 40 and above must pay premiums into the system: the employed through payroll deductions, the self-employed through a health insurance premium, and the retired through deductions from pensions. Deductions or waivers of the monthly premium and the 10 per cent co-payment are available subject to one's income status.

The benefits include institutional care in geriatric hospitals and units of general hospitals designed for the elderly, geriatric health care facilities, *tokuyō* homes and group homes for elderly with dementia. In-home care services ranging from home-help services, visiting nurse/rehabilitation services, day care and short stay, to loan of devices such as wheelchairs and financial assistance for improving the home, for example, making it possible to use a wheelchair at home are also included.

An elderly person who needs care services applies to the Certification Committee for Long-term Care Need in his/her municipality. The Committee makes the evaluation and judgement of care need based on the results of an investigation into the applicant's mental and physical condition, and on the opinion of a family physician. An applicant assessed as 'independent' is ineligible to receive care benefit. A person judged as from 'in need of support' to 'in need of care level 5', is entitled to receive LTCI benefits. He/she can either leave it to a care manager, usually a doctor, a nurse, an occupational or physical therapist, or a certified social worker, to select a package of services and draw up a care plan, or make the care plan by him/herself.

Ninety per cent of the cost for care services is paid by insurance (split 50/50 between the care insurance premium and the public fund). The remaining 10 per cent must be paid by the insured. Principally, benefits are paid to elderly persons aged 65 and above. Among insured persons aged between 40 and 64, only those who are in need of care because of ageing are eligible for payment.

Enactment of the LTCI policy in 2000 has resulted in fundamental changes in institutional care for the elderly. Until 1999 welfare institutional care for the elderly had been regulated by the Law for the Welfare of the Elderly. Admittance to a welfare institution was an official 'measure' taken by administrative machinery such as the prefectural and municipal welfare offices, and a mean-test approach was adopted for eligibility assessment. After the welfare administration reached a decision on the necessity of institutional care for an elderly person, it assigned a private welfare institution to provide care for the old person. There was no choice for the elderly person to select an institution by him/herself. Although social welfare corporations that run welfare institutions are technically private enterprises, they have been managed under the control of the government, which can exert influence over their hiring and decision-making processes. They are dependent on governmental funding via a system called 'welfare placement by commission' (*sochi itaku*), whereby the government assigns welfare projects to them. Welfare institutions for elderly, whether public or private, had been the so-called welfare projects assigned by the governments; they operated mainly on public subsidies which came from taxes, and their role was focused solely on implementing the measures decided by welfare offices. They were subordinated to public administration and were unable to design or create services independent from the government due to their insufficient financial capacity and the tight legal restrictions on them.

The introduction of the LTCI scheme has brought about many changes in institutional care. First, institutional care for the elderly residents in *yōgo* homes continues to be regulated by the official 'measure system'. But for *tokuyō* homes, this 'measure system' is eliminated. It becomes the elderly client's right to choose receiving nursing care in an institution. And care services are provided in the form of fulfilling the contract between the client and the *tokuyō* home.

Second, with the termination of the 'measure system', financing of care services has changed from mainly public subsidies to the combination of LTCI benefits and the 10 per cent co-payment by the clients themselves. Third, if the elderly clients want to receive additional private services besides the packages of care services provided by the LTCI, they must purchase them out of their own pockets.

Fourth, the service provision structure is changed from the municipal administrations entrusting private welfare corporations to provide services, to the clients themselves choosing services from the private enterprises in the local community. In addition to this, in order to encourage the private sector to enter the care market, there are measures liberalizing regulation, which make it possible to entice various kinds of enterprises into the social service market. Thus welfare institutions face potential competition from these kinds of private enterprises.

Finally, in contrast to the former welfare system where institutional care only concerned a few impoverished or disabled elderly persons, by paying contributions to the LTCI scheme all Japanese elderly who qualify as disabled are entitled to receive individually tailored care service packages.

Wouldn't the cut of public subsidies as well as the 10 per cent self-payment by the residents lead to difficulties in the management of the institutions and deterioration in the current quality of life of the elderly persons? Would all staff members be able to provide satisfactory services in accordance with the clients' demands? With private profit-making service providers burgeoning in the market, would the welfare institution fall into bankruptcy? This chapter intends to explain what employees in Kotobuki think about the LTCI scheme and how the enactment of this system will affect, and has affected, the operation of the home and the people in it in terms of quality of life of both the residents and staff members. From the angle of the social service providing sector, it attempts to supplement the studies that mainly emphasise the significance of the new programme from a policy-making perspective (Campbell 2000; Campbell and Ikegami 2000; Kyōgoku 1996; Maeda 2000) and those that discuss how to realise an ideal system for the care of the frail elderly from a variety of angles, including the social and family aspects of care, clinical aspects, macroeconomic and macro-political aspects, and housing design aspect (Campbell and Ikegami 1999). As a matter of fact, I should give an account of more of the changes that the LTCI programme has brought about to the home since its enactment in 2000. However, during the second short visit to Kotobuki in 2003, I was unable to meet many of my former staff informants to listen to their opinions, for some had retired and some had been transferred to work in other institutions run by the same social welfare corporation. As one main theme of the whole book deals with how the meaning of 'social welfare' has evolved over time, I would like to present here the voices I recorded in 1999 before the LTCI programme was put into force. Some new observations regarding changes in Kotobuki during my second visit will also be added.

Staff attitudes towards the LTCI programme

According to Ikegami, in a general opinion survey conducted by the Prime Minister's Office in 1995, 82 per cent of the Japanese people were in favour of the introduction of the LTCI programme (Campbell and Ikegami 2000: 227). During my stay in Kotobuki, I heard manifold opinions from the employees regarding the LTCI policy. Some approved, some objected and others worried. Quite a number of staff members extolled the concepts of welfare rights, free selection and self-determination in the new policy. Mr Fujiwara and Mr Fakuda, however, represented typical dissonant voices.

Mr Fujiwara, a care staff member in Aoba, explained the concepts of individualism, self-responsibility and basic rights, as well as citizen consciousness in Japan in order to question the workability of the LTCI. He said that in pre-war Japan it was a matter of course that children shouldered the whole responsibility for caring for their old parents. However, defeat in the war brought in the American concept of democracy. Democracy in Japan, according to Mr Fujiwara, was only a narrow sense of individualism, or egoism. It does not inquire about the responsibility of the individual in connection with the state and the general society. When children become independent, they tend to think that they are only responsible for themselves. Children and parents do not interfere in each other's affairs. As more and more younger people neglect to consider their relationship with their parents in the context of society and shift their care responsibility to the public, the government has no choice but devise a system in which the whole society shares the responsibility to care for its old citizens.

Mr Fujiwara also thought that the sense of political participation of Japanese people was low. In Europe and America civil revolutions were started by the people themselves, but it had never happened in Japan that people launched a revolution and established a national state by their own hands. The Meiji Restoration was only a power struggle between the Tokugawa Shogunate and the fief clans. It was more a top-down revolution than one carried out by the people. Thus people do not have the same strong sense of self-responsibility and roles in society as citizens in Western countries do. Because people think that politics has nothing to do with their own business, they show little interest in voting and public policies. And, as symbolised in the words 'Uncle Sam will foot the bill' (*oyakata nihonmaru*) and 'the lord' (*o-ue-sama*), Japanese people always assume a posture of complying with what the government has done or said. They accept everything bestowed on them by the government.

Mr Fujiwara assumed that the LTCI was not necessarily based on people's wishes. With regard to the extent of the acknowledgement of the programme by the Japanese people, Mr Fujiwara remarked that a lot of people did not know or even did not care about the programme. The elderly residents, especially, who were unacquainted with the notions of self-responsibility and basic rights, could comprehend neither the concepts nor the content of the programme. So it was difficult for them to choose services on their own and protect their rights. As the old people were accustomed to being submissive to public administration, they would not object to the policy but would do what they were required to do. Thus for these elderly persons, there was actually no real self-determination under the LTCI. The government was actually taking advantage of this characteristic of the old persons to introduce the LTCI programme. In addition, most residents in the Aoba were old professional housewives who belonged to the low-income category. They lived on the survivor's pension (*izoku nenkin*) of their husbands or their meagre national pension. They had bitter experiences during the war and many were deprived of their children in action. Nearly everyone had sacrificed for the sake of the national state. Under the 'measure system', these residents had been cared for by the government. However with the introduction of the LTCI system, the government had changed its policy to get rid of the responsibility for caring for its old citizens. Thus the old people were actually victims of political policies.

Another welfare supervisor, Mr Fukuda, thought that because the government did not have the necessary finance to expand social services and would meet strong objections to collecting revenue by increasing taxation, it initiated the LTCI scheme to accumulate the necessary resources. As the policy requires local governments to equip the essential welfare and health care services, in addition to subsidies from the government and premiums paid by the insured, municipalities would have to share the cost for services. In communities where revenue resources are abundant, the LTCI programme may work. However in a residential city like Higashimurayama, which has no industries, the city's revenue mainly depends on residents' tax. It is quite difficult for the city government to carry out the programme because of its weak finances. Mr Fukuda thought that welfare was a public administration issue and that the government should depend on public funds to expand social services for the elderly rather than transfer the duty on to the people themselves. The LTCI actually made citizens in cities without major industries more financially burdened, for the monthly insurance premium was higher than the national average amount.

According to Mr Fukuda, the new programme was only a gimmick of the politicians for the purpose of getting votes in the election. As the law was drafted by politicians who know little about the practical care field, there were quite a number of problematic issues in the assessment system and service provider system. He thought it was irrational for the government to enact the LTCI at such a rapid pace under these conditions where the development of care services was undesired and older people's sense of welfare and basic rights had not yet changed. To him, the LTCI programme was a kind of insurance scheme rather than a welfare policy. He doubted whether it was right to bring the marketing principle into the field of welfare and whether the programme could solve the problem of caring for old people. He thought that instead of changing all social services into commercial commodities, some welfare philosophy about life such as charity, philanthropy and mutual help should be preserved in the Japanese welfare system. He hoped the government would preserve some welfare programmes aimed at marginal elderly persons in the national administrative structure.

Yet he was not totally displeased with the LTCI programme. At least there was one good point. That is, with the abolition of the 'measure system', the elderly persons are able to have more choices in how to lead their later lives. They could choose an institution to receive care rather than be assigned to a facility by the welfare administration.

In a word, the opinions of Mr Fujiwara and Mr Fukuda represent the major doubts the Japanese public have about the LTCI programme. Mr Fujiwara raised the following big question: in a country where citizens' awareness of political participation is low, the concept of people's right to social welfare is not deeply rooted, and social welfare services have been regarded and practised as the nation's compassion in a paternalistic tradition, would the elderly be able to claim their welfare rights and demand care services? On the other hand, the viewpoint of Mr Fukuda reiterates the philosophical debate between two wings of Ministry of Health and Welfare officialdom in deciding whether the social welfare or the social insurance principle was the most applicable approach to long-tem care, in which the bureaucrats and their allies of practitioners and experts in favour of the Scandinavian Model eventually lost (Campbell 2000: 93). However, most staff members agreed that everyone should be given the right to choose care services when he/she enters old age and that the system should be user oriented. Many also thought that, although market demand and competition would endanger the operation of the institution as well as the subsistence of the employees, it would also stimulate the creation of new services, encourage active participation of private service providers, and ensure responsibility and quality of care of the staff members.

Effects on the management and the people of Kotobuki

After the LTCI came into force, the operation of Sazanka and Akashia remained the same as before. But Aoba has changed into a 'Nursing Care Welfare Institution for the Elderly' (*kaigo rōjin fukushi shisetsu*). A great deal of the home's management under the old system has been changed.

First, the financing of the home has been changed. Under the old system, Aoba was operated mainly on the 'measure fee'. When the home took in an elderly person, it was subsidised with about 350,000 yen per month. This money came from the tax revenue of the national government, Tokyo Metropolitan government and the entrusted municipalities. Despite the continuous public subsidy cuts in recent years, the home still had quite stable financial resources for operation till 1999. Under the LTCI, the home is operated mainly on care insurance benefits. The average amount paid by the insurance programme for institutional care is about 325,000 to 431,000 yen per person per case. In the case of Aoba, the monthly insurance benefit is 325,000 yen per person. The elderly residents pay 60,000–80,000 yen per month for the 10 per cent co-payment of services, meals and articles for daily living.

As mentioned in Chapter 4, in the initial years after the enactment of the new policy, Aoba continued to receive public subsidies to avoid sudden financial problems in operation. However, the amount of this public fund is dropping year by year. In 2002, the total income of Aoba was 460,000,000 yen (equivalent to $3,538,460), a reduction of 20,000,000 yen (about $153,846) reduction compared to the previous year. With public funds totally cut from 2004, the income of the home will be further reduced. According to Mr Itō, although the new policy is now being operated smoothly in Higashimurayama City, with its weak finances, the city is heavily burdened and citizen's monthly contribution to the care insurance scheme (3,250 yen = $30) is higher than the national average of 2,800 yen ($26). He had some apprehension as to the future durability of the LTCI policy in the city.

Formerly, considering the care capacity of the home and the care burden on staff members, the home took in not only old persons with the greatest care needs but also quite a number of elderly with fewer care needs. However, under the LTCI, as the most disabled patients, labelled as 'in need of care level 5' get the largest care insurance benefit of 9,980 yen or so per day (while it is 8,120 yen for patients 'in need of care level 1'), in order to collect the necessary money for operation, the home was forced to accept only elderly persons who need the highest level of care whenever vacancies are available. According to regulations under the old system, the number of beds in Aoba should be 100 and only two elderly clients in local community could come to receive short-stay services. However, currently the number of permanent residents has risen to 104, and the beds for short-stay clients have increased to six, while the number of care workers remains the same as before. Being more heavily occupied by attending to the bodily care of the elderly, care staff say that they have less time to tend to the psychological needs of the residents, and they themselves feel more easily exhausted than before. Without a balanced ratio of elderly clients with different care needs, caretakers will continue to be heavily burdened. And the quality of care will be affected.

Second, as a by-product of the financial change, public subsidies for meal provision have been cut and there are no longer funds for clubs, recreational activities and festivals. Because of the drastic cut in the subsidy for meal provision, many nursing homes have cut the dietary section from the management structure and begun to source meal provision from private businesses. In order to save labour costs, some institutions began to hire part-time dietary workers and care workers to reduce the number of full-time employees. In Aoba, although the dietary section was kept for the time being, Mrs Yoshiwara, the dietician in Chapter 4, worried about the possibility that her colleagues would lose their jobs when I interviewed her in 1999. And she was apprehensive that the quality of meals would go down if the budget for meal provision kept on declining under the LTCI. Her worry will soon become true, because Mr Itō, told me in early April in 2003 that, in order to keep costs down, the home is going to cut the dietary section and use private outsourcing for its meal provisions from 2004. This change, of course, will not only lead to the unemployment of current dietary staff but also less diversity in food provision than the residents have previously enjoyed.

The residents have also lost a lot of fun. In order to maintain the high quality of life of the residents, club activities such as flower arrangement, calligraphy, *haiku* and group work are still kept intact, and traditional festivals and events such as the New Year, cherry-blossom viewing, *Obon* and birthday parties are still held in Aoba. However, since public subsidies for club and recreational activities are cut, elderly clients participating in such activities need to bear the expense, if there is any, for example, purchasing flowers for the flower arrangement club, preparing the lunch boxes for cherry-blossom viewing trips. Thus, with almost all services turning into commodities under the LTCI, there are no free recreational activities any more. If the elderly residents want to enjoy eating outside with their peer, or to enjoy their favourite dishes, or want to go for a hot-spring trip and other kinds of fun, they have to pay from their own pockets, although the home will render some help in contacting the hotel, restaurant and so on. Judging that their self-paid expenses (co-payment for care services, fees for meals and for additional services or articles for personal use) were more of a burden than before, when they were paying nothing or small amounts under the old 'measure system', many residents are unwilling to receive these services. As a result, the residents are having less entertainment than before. Although I didn't hear many complains regarding their recreational lives at the home, as the residents had become accustomed to the various kinds of recreational activities and festivals the home offered and had enjoyed them very much, the sudden disappearance of these enjoyments, I suppose, has certainly led to some dissatisfaction with institutional life.

Third, the principle of home management has been fundamentally changed. Under the new system, care management is introduced into the practice of care provision. A *tokuyō* home becomes a kind of hotel where customers choose to receive their services. Clients enter the home on contract. The home must respect the self-determination of the elderly persons. Until recently, staff members' attitude toward the elderly residents was 'As long as you live here, we will protect you.' Matrons have cared for the residents without the concept of customer orientation. In order to get things done, it has been a practice for care workers to keep elderly persons in their wheelchairs with belts. Constraint of an elderly person had been explained as 'security', that is, preventing the clients from falling. And there was a streak of over-familiarity in the way care staff spoke to the elderly persons. The clients' feelings were not taken into consideration very much. However, under the LTCI, confinement becomes an issue of infringing the rights of the clients. As a result, the boundary between the will of the clients and the judgement of the staff is difficult to define. This has become a difficult issue in care practice.

Furthermore, there are some effects on employees. Together with the introduction of LTCI, the policy of equalisation of the public and private institutions of the Tokyo Metropolis is eliminated. The cost of employees' salaries is now mainly covered by the funds collected in the new system. For the first time in history, *tokuyō* homes have adopted the concept of 'management' in their operation and begun to keep down their labour costs. In practice, Aoba is recruiting more part-time care workers than full-time employees to save on labour costs. In addition, the current wage structure in Kotobuki, according to Mr Itō, will undergo an overall transition in 2004. That is, the seniority wage system (*nenkō joretsu chingin*) will be replaced by a new system whereby a salary consists of basic pay (*kihonkyū*) and competency wage (*nōryoku-kyū*), and a bonus is to be paid based on the assessment of an employee's performance (*jinji kōka*). Due to such changes, many staff members are worrying that their salaries will decrease.

With the implementation of the LTCI, it becomes the elderly clients' right to choose institutions where they can receive nursing care services. The quality of the staff becomes an important factor that influences the clients' decisions. As Aoba is competing with other care institutions such as hospitals with designed long-term care beds, geriatric health care facilities and other private facilities in recruiting clients, and will continue to do so, many staff members have a strong sense of crisis. Having doctors and nurses available, medical facilities can provide medical treatment and health care services better than *tokuyō* homes. Private companies, on the other hand, having the know-how to carry out thorough research into the needs of the elderly clients, are able to offer services based on the market concept of respecting the rights of customers. However, welfare institutions have been operating without such pressures under the 'measure system' for quite a long time. They are inadequate in providing either medical service or thorough care services that meet the demands of the elderly persons. In order to survive in the care market, staff members thought the home should do more to improve the quality of the employees. In addition to professional knowledge and skill in care, they thought they needed to gain more medical knowledge, especially about geriatric illnesses and their treatment. They suggested in-service training programmes be developed and a method for evaluating the work of the employees be designed.

Lastly, changes have also occurred in Sazanka and Akashia. Although the operation of the two homes has nothing to do with the LTCI, they are greatly affected by the implementation of the programme, especially in the case of Sazanka. In this home, the 'measure' policy remains in force, but the annual subsidy has been cut by 5 per cent every year from 2000 till 2002 (14,000,000 yen ($114,754) was cut in 2000 from an annual budget of 145,000,000 yen ($1,188,524)). From 2002, the home began to receive subsidy according to the new standard decided by the Tokyo Metropolitan government. Affected by this fee cut, the home had to reduce the budget for food provision, annual events, club and recreational activities, newspapers and magazines, etc. This change has certainly affected the lives of the residents. Mrs Suzuki, an old lady who came to live in Sazanka in 1997, complained to me when I dropped by on the third floor in 2003, that the food provided was beginning to taste unpleasant and the residents were enjoying fewer recreational activities.

The second influence is that some relatively independent elderly persons residing in Aoba have been transferred to Sazanka. Under the LTCI, all former *tokuyō* home residents are divided into three groups according to their care need assessment results. One group includes people who are assessed as 'independent', 'in need of support' and 'in need of care grade 1'. The second group consists of elderly people 'in need of care grade 2 and grade 3', and elderly persons in need of care grade 4 and 5 belong to the third group. When it takes in these old persons, the home receives LTCI benefits according to their assessed care need grade.

Some of the elderly belonging to the first two groups came to live in Sazanka and Akashia in late 2000. Although they were judged as 'independent' or 'in need of support' or 'in need of care 2/3', they are weaker or have more severe disabilities than other residents. A couple cannot make themselves understood because of senility, so staff members have to provide more care services for them. With no possibility of hiring new care workers due to the stringent regulations on welfare institutions, caring for these clients has become an additional burden on current staff members. In addition, both Sazanka and Akashia were built more than 15 years ago, hence they are not well equipped for elderly persons with handicaps. Both homes need a great deal of repair and maintenance due to the wear and tear of the building. So the homes had to use a large share of their budget to newly equip or refurbish some facilities for physically disabled persons who use wheelchairs and walkers. This has put additional financial pressure on the already diminished budget.

Great progress in facilitating the independent life of the elderly residents has been achieved in Akashia, however. As residents in *keihi* homes are eligible to receive in-home care services under the LTCI system, a number of elderly are hiring home-helpers to help clean their rooms, go shopping, and so on. And these home-helpers come from the Home-helper Dispatching Centre newly established by Kotobuki in 2001.

In summary, the 'Long-term Care Insurance' is the newest Japanese public policy aimed at providing both in-home services and institutional care for the elderly in the field of health care and welfare services. The attitudes of staff members in the welfare service practice field towards this new system are ambivalent. Some agree and others object. The most debated issues centre on 'whether it is right to introduce an insurance scheme into the welfare services area', 'whether the elderly clients can enjoy their welfare rights and select necessary care services by themselves in a nation where Western values such as basic rights are not deeply rooted among older persons' and 'whether welfare institutions will be able to survive in the care market'.

Considering that it entitles everyone with the privilege to receive long-term care, improves the independence and quality of life of both the frail older people and the family caregivers, and provides a legal basis for the shift from a government-based welfare system to a more plural one that includes both private and non-profit service providers, the LTCI policy can be regarded as a step forward in the formation of new relationships between the state, family and individuals, service providers and service users. It has made it clear that the Japanese-style welfare state is becoming more and more market-oriented and the meaning of 'social welfare' has changed.

In the social service providing field, whether or not the home can accumulate enough financial resources to stay in operation is the biggest worry of the staff members. The abolition of the 'measure fee' and self-responsibility for paying for meals and recreational services under the LTCI have inevitably affected both the operation of the *tokuyō* home and the work and lives of the people in it. Care staff's unfamiliarity with market principles such as the 'rights of the customer' is becoming a drawback in providing satisfactory services for the clients. Their awareness of 'a customer' is gradually forming. With weak staff capability in terms of medical treatment and health care, whether or not the nursing home can survive in competition with other care facilities for the elderly remains a big challenge in institutional care. The *yōgo* home is also under pressure to accept former nursing home residents who are ineligible to receive high-level nursing care.

8   Conclusions

As Japan has become an 'ageing society', the increasing number of elderly persons, and the declining ability of the family to care for its older members have generated a demand for the expansion of social services for the elderly. Institutionalisation, once considered as a government endowment and a social stigma, is now being redefined as the basic right of every elderly person. And it has become an inevitable alternative to home care for old parents. These trends have led to the development of long-term care services for elderly clients and the improvement of institutional care in welfare facilities. In 1995 about 1.66 per cent of Japanese elderly persons aged 65 and over were living in some kind of institution for the elderly, where a special workforce has developed to deal with their needs.

Given the fact that more elderly persons will spend some of their later life in institutions, there is a compelling need to understand the social conditions that bring individuals to institutions, what happens to them when they come to live, work, visit, or volunteer in an elderly institution, and what constitutes good quality of institutional life.

This anthropological case study has tried to achieve this aim based on six months' fieldwork in a comprehensive welfare institution named Kotobuki in a residential city of Tokyo. The main issue investigated in this study is the 'QOL' of the residents. Among the other issues I have dealt with are people's perception of institutional life and attitudes toward institutionalisation and the corporate culture of institutional work. My principal concern was what institutions mean to people when they live, visit and work in the institutions.

This final chapter summarises major findings from the previous chapters, presenting theoretical aspects of my findings and perspectives for future improvement of QOL and work in such institutions. Although the conclusions and proposals summarised here only represent one welfare institution, they not only address experiences that are common to millions of other persons who are either living or working in other institutions for the elderly, but also provide recommendations applicable to facilities which have similar problems to those of Kotobuki.

Quality of life

Most elderly informants were satisfied with the security and services the home provided and regarded the present as the most leisurely period in their lives. Employees and visitors also felt that the general QOL and care were good, with workers taking pride in Kotobuki's good reputation. Both residents and caregivers pointed to the provision of nutrition, security, shelter, care and activity programmes, as well as relationships with peers and support from families as the primary elements in good QOL. Through my observations I found that life satisfaction and quality of life also depend on the following factors: (1) quality of staff and their care, (2) health condition of the residents, (3) perceptions of institutional life, (4) decision-making about entering a home, (5) religious beliefs, (6) autonomy, (7) dealing with death, (8) limitations of institutional care and (9) governmental policy.

Provisions of the homes

Both the residents and staff members frequently mentioned the provision of accommodation, food, clothing, articles for daily living, bath, recreational and club activities, event programmes, comfortable temperatures and fully equipped care facilities as strengths of life in the home.

Through carefully examining the *fureiai* interactions between the elderly residents and nursery children in a programme in Kotoen, Thang finds the dominant feature of intergenerational programming in Japan can be characterised as 'an emphasis on the past', or 'revitalization of the traditional cultures' (2001:191). This is applicable to Kotobuki and the many other institutions I visited. It is safe to say that the main characteristic of Japanese institutional care for the elderly is its emphasis on Japanese traditions and cultural values. Food and annual events are provided in traditional ways; club and recreational activities focus on forms of traditional arts; there are traditional religious rituals for death; values such as endurance and cooperation are promoted to maintain harmonious human relationships; the norm of collectivism is promoted to form a familial atmosphere, and 'dependence on indulgence' (*amae*) of the sick elderly is acceptable when providing care. It is in this cultural environment that the residents can lead comfortable lives in the institutions. Some criticism exists, though, suggesting that in order to avoid creating segregated 'institutional beings' the constructing of home atmosphere should not always incline towards nostalgia and the past, but adopt new values and changes to help the elderly adapt to the present.

Quality of staff and their care

Staff members and the services they provide are a source of security for the residents. Except for certain disagreeable matrons, most residents thought that the staff members were kind and took good care of them. And they appreciated the services they received. Family members of the residents felt at ease about putting their old relatives into institutions because staff members were caring for them quite well. Impressed by the dedicated care offered by the caregivers, other outside visitors thought that elderly persons in a *tokuyō* home were leading a far better life than those in the community. The staff members, on the other hand, thought that not only professional skills in care, but also a spirit of teamwork as well as a loving heart for old people were prerequisites for providing good quality of care for the residents.

Health condition of the residents

Health status is one of the most important issues for elderly residents. Illnesses and declining physical functions not only affected residents' mobility and their ability to carry out activities of daily living, but also diminished their social relationships, thus casting them into a more isolated and dependent status. Those who were suffering confinement and intolerable pain lamented their status of being captives of their bodies, and they thought it a burden to live too long. The healthy elderly, on the other hand, were afraid of falling ill or becoming *boke*, a state whose cultural meanings were elaborated by John Traphagan (2000) in his ethnographic study on a rural Japanese hamlet. Like the older gateball players in the hamlet, these elderly in Kotobuki were making every effort to maintain good health in order to avoid being a burden to others.

Perceptions of the status of being institutionalised

Perceptions of their current status varied slightly among the residents in different age groups and in different types of homes. In Sazanka and Akashia, generally elderly persons who had suffered from intra-familial tension and who came to the homes because of other unfortunate circumstances felt that their current situations were better than before.

Residents born in the Meiji and Taisho periods still thought that the elderly should be cared for by their children. Those who had children felt lonely and somehow humiliated by being unable to receive care from their children, and therefore thought living in the home a situation without hope. However, the younger residents who were born in later periods, especially those who lived in Akashia, tended to have a stronger sense of basic rights and a different view of their status. Many such residents did not feel ashamed of being institutionalised. They thought they had the right to receive some welfare services to counter potential financial problems and risks in their old age, because they had paid taxes when they were working and they were also paying fees for their institutionalisation. They were satisfied with their current status.

Decision-making in entering the home

Few elderly persons chose voluntarily to live in the homes. In most cases, an elderly person was persuaded by his/her district welfare commissioners, ward welfare officers, relatives or friends to apply for entrance. The elderly persons who had expected to live in their own homes or to receive care from their families tended to have lower life satisfaction than those who had chosen to live in a home.

Religious beliefs

One of the most important invisible sources of support for many residents is religion. A number of residents admitted that their religious beliefs helped them adjust to home life. Many residents were religious followers and they believed that religion would protect them and ensure them a peaceful later life. They practised their religion by doing their daily tasks, reflecting on their conduct and participating in religious activities organised by their church. And the most common faith was the devotion to their own family ancestors. Many said that they obtained a psychological tranquillity or security after they finished doing their daily services.

Interpersonal relationships

Life in Kotobuki revolved around three kinds of relationships: resident–resident relationships, resident–staff relationships and resident–family/friends relationships. The resident–resident relationship was the most difficult issue in the process of adapting to institutional life. Whether or not residents were able to lead a happy life in the home largely depended on their ability to deal with their relationships with others. Some people interacted actively to make friends, while others refrained from interpersonal interaction to save trouble. If notions such as age hierarchy, harmony, cooperation, consideration and endurance functioned well, interpersonal relationships among residents would run smoothly and a supportive network would form. When these norms were violated, conflicts would arise.

Supportive sources such as family and friends were also important in institutional life. Individuals who received visits, calls and presents from their families regularly, or who had many friends in the community were obviously happy with their institutional life. However, since quite a number of residents in Sazanka and Akashia came from broken families, support from their families was less visible than in Aoba. Alienation from their families was one of the sources of some residents' loneliness and dissatisfaction.

Japanese institutional care can be characterised as 'being provided by private institutions in the form of receiving commission from public welfare administration'. Because of this characteristic, resident–staff relationships in Kotobuki could be characterised as a 'subordinate–superior' one. Staff members were generally respected by the residents. Residents' familiarity with staff members tended to increase as time went by. However, close resident–staff relationships were rarely observed.

Autonomy

In Kotobuki, except for a few residents in Sazanka and most residents in Aoba whose personal preferences were controlled under the institutional regime because of severe senility and physical disability, other residents in Sazanka and Akashia could create a schedule of their own around the home's routine. In addition to their attributed duties, some residents assumed their own responsibilities by volunteering to look after the flower garden, delivering meals and helping with confused persons. These roles not only gave the residents a sense that they were still able to carry out house-keeping tasks but also enabled them to feel useful and productive and to indirectly repay the home for its services.

Dealing with death

Death is an inevitable issue confronting every resident. Both the residents and the home performed rituals for death. Holding a farewell ritual when a resident died and conducting Buddhist memorial services on the spring and autumn equinoxes and at *Obon* were two ways the home tried to relieve anxiety about death for the residents and to make peace with the deceased. The home also held funerals for childless and homeless elderly when they passed away, and their ashes were interred in the public grave that the Tokyo Metropolis built for all elderly without a family. This gave such residents a sense of reassurance about their post-mortem status in the other world.

The residents also had their own rituals to prepare for death. Elderly people without children or families and homeless elderly put aside money for their funeral services. For the repose of their soul, some purchased 'eternal care' in advance. Female residents carried out a daily ancestor memorial service to get a sense of security that they would rejoin their family in the next world. However, few male residents conducted such rituals as often as women do. This suggests that, like other domestic tasks such as nurturing children, managing housework and caring for old parents, taking care of one's ancestors remains a female's domain.

The ability to prepare for death both psychologically and strategically ensured the residents a sense of self-control. Whether or not an individual could deal with his/her own death properly had major impact on their psychological satisfaction with life in the home.

Limitations of institutional care

The lack of privacy and choice in selecting a room-mate is one of the main problems for residents in Sazanka. Although most residents were considerate towards each other and restrained themselves in order to maintain a smooth relationship with their room-mates, this peaceful surface was achieved at the expense of suppressing their own emotions. Deep friendships could be found between room-mates, but latent tension as well as hostility was also ubiquitously concealed under the surface of harmony. When privacy was not ensured, conflicts between room-mates could not be avoided.

Accommodating mental patients together with ordinary elderly persons in Sazanka and Akashia caused another problem in institutional care. Prejudice towards mental illness and staff members' lack of professional knowledge in dealing with mental patients meant they could not create a therapeutic environment for these patients to lead an easy life. Some residents with mental illnesses were alienated and ostracised.

In Aoba, there are also problems such as lack of self-control, and staff members' wishes taking priority over those of the residents. These problems could lead to lower satisfaction with institutional life on the part of the residents.

Social policy

Social policy towards elderly persons also has an impact on institutional management and the lives of the residents. With the deterioration of the national finances due to the collapse of the bubble economy, the social security structure – which includes the welfare system for the elderly – has been under reform since the late 1980s. As the budget for social services has decreased, public subsidies for welfare institutions for the elderly have been cut year by year. This, of course, has an impact on the quality of life of the institutionalised elderly.

Substantial changes have occurred in long-term care facilities with the enactment of the LTCI policy. *Tokuyō* homes now operate on resources collected through care insurance benefits and co-payment by the clients rather than public subsidies. Such homes are now facing big challenges: whether they can accumulate enough capital to keep them operating, whether they can survive the competition from other care service businesses, and whether they can provide satisfactory services for the elderly under the new management. With this fundamental transition in governmental policy, the lives of the residents in institutions have greatly been affected.

Attitudes towards welfare and institutionalisation

A significant finding of my research was that perceptions about welfare and institutionalisation were different among different categories of people and different generations. This indicates that Japanese people's attitude towards social services is undergoing a transition.

As Kinoshita and Kiefer (1992) have pointed out, the word 'welfare' has an ambiguous meaning in Japan, reflecting changing and uncertain attitudes. On one hand, welfare traditionally means public support for the needy, those who cannot take care of themselves. As welfare is regarded as favour or charity bestowed by the government, a strong stigma is attached to marginal people who are 'on welfare'. In this context, welfare recipients tend to be submissive to public administration.

On the other hand, welfare also has the newer, less disparaging and more general meaning of 'public well-being', the welfare of a 'welfare society'. Both meanings have been reflected in Japanese social policies. Especially, the reforms in the eight laws related to welfare in the early 1990s, social policy for the elderly developed since the later 1980s, and the newly established LTCI policy have stipulated clearly that it is people's right to receive not only long-term care services for the elderly but also home care services for the elderly. And to advocate the newer sense of 'welfare' as everyone's right, concepts such as self-responsibility and contract have been introduced in the LTCI system. This means that insurers' contribution premium into the programme and personal payment for services justify their right to choose and buy services. In addition, when the LTCI is fully implemented, private welfare non-profit organisations and corporations will for the first time be able to enter the social service sector to form a consumer-oriented service market for the elderly. As such, the structure of the Japanese welfare state, according to Misa Izuhara, is moving towards 'welfare pluralism', or in a sense, is moving closer to the American model of a 'liberal-residual' welfare state, where welfare services are not granted freely and universally by the state, the family and the corporations, but are increasingly based on contracts between the clients and various service providers (Izuhara 2000: 83).

These two meanings of 'welfare' have been reflected in people's attitudes towards institutionalisation and their participation in voluntary activities. And there is a tendency that the older the generation, the more they think that welfare is public relief measures for the people in need and the stronger the sense of social stigma towards institutionalisation; the younger the generation, the more they endorse the idea that it is everyone's right to receive welfare services. With an enhanced awareness of welfare rights, people now realise that one's welfare needs will never be met by depending only on services provided by the government and that they need to find solutions to their ageing problems them-selves. Regarding home care services as a way to help the elderly in their communities, old relatives in their own families, and themselves in the future, a number of volunteers and staff members in Kotobuki described in Chapter 4 and Chapter 5, are actively participating in voluntary activities to offer their expertise and enthusiasm. For instance, retiring from Aoba a couple years ago, both the dietician Mrs Yoshiwara and the matron Mrs Suzuki are engaging in non-profit service businesses, the former providing meals-on-wheels services, and the latter joining the mutual aid association in her community as a home-helper delivering nursing care services for elderly living in their own homes.

Regarding institutionalisation, those elderly persons (usually over 75 years old) who had been instilled with the *ie* ideology and held the ideal that old parents should be cared for by their children, did not think that a home was a place where old people ought to live. Living in an institution meant lower social prestige or being abandoned by one's children.

Younger residents (usually in their 60s), especially those in Akashia, tended to have a more positive view of institutionalisation. As residents entered the home on contract, they thought they had the right to receive institutional care. Their sense of welfare or institutionalisation was in some ways similar to the 'welfare on contract' perspective of the middle-class residents in the Fujino retirement community (Kinoshita and Kiefer 1992).

Having received the post-war democratic education, been influenced by the mass media, become accustomed to their life as a consumer, and understood what a home life was like, most employees, family members of the residents and volunteers tended to regard institutions, especially the *tokuyō* home, as a good resource for security in later life. They believed that people's attitude toward institutions had changed a lot, with an increasing sense of basic rights. The LTCI system would reinforce people's sense of basic rights in relation to welfare services, so institutionalisation would become a kind of consuming activity rather than a social stigma. Staff members' criticism about the unfairness of the current welfare system actually implied their premise that welfare services should be provided for every elderly citizen. College students took it for granted that it was everyone's right to receive institutional care.

When it came to the issue of whether they would like to be institutionalised in their old age, people's attitudes tended to be ambivalent. Some preferred to live with their children, some wanted to manage by themselves, and others would like to live in an institution. As a tendency, people preferred a *tokuyō* home or a *yūryō* home or a Care House to a *yōgo* home if they had to enter a facility when becoming bedridden or senile. This indicates that institutionalisation because of severe physical or mental disabilities is reasonable, but less preferable when reasons are largely social ones. A negative image of *yōgo* homes for the elderly as relief facilities still persists.

The above discoveries tell us that although the negative image of welfare institutions is still retained in the larger society, it has faded over the years, especially in big cities. Institutionalisation has become an acceptable choice or one's basic right when one becomes impaired. This also suggests that cultural assumptions that govern the social contract between the states and individuals in elderly care has been moving from 'obligation' (filial obligation of children and responsibility of the state) to 'entitlement' (rights of the individual), two critical terms Hashimoto uses to distinguish the ways in which the elderly are considered to deserve to receive care in Japan and the US (Hashimoto 1996). This transition in welfare consciousness in the general public, as well as differences in the attitudes towards institutionalisation among different generations will have significant impact on social policy-making and social service provisions. In the near future, Japan will become a society that regards social services for the elderly as a kind of commodity.

Working with the elderly

A majority of staff members had not planned to work in a welfare home for the elderly. Middle-aged women who had finished the task of childrearing constituted the majority of the direct care staff, whose job was seen as an extension of the traditional female domestic skills that did not need specific qualifications. Quite a number of them came to work in Kotobuki because of the necessity to make a living and at a time when caregiving jobs were regarded as one involving the 3Ks that few people wanted to take.

The increasing number of disabled elderly persons, the development of social services for the elderly and the economic depression in other businesses in recent years have made welfare institutions for the elderly a favourable career choice for both young adults and middle-aged women. The stable salary, relatively good work environment and welfare provisions, as well as work satisfaction were the main reasons that could account for the low job mobility of the staff members. Obtaining preliminary knowledge and skills in nursing care for one's own kin and a fondness for old people were also numbered as factors in staff members' career orientation.

Visitors brought different motives, backgrounds and feelings to their involvement in Kotobuki. Family members came to the home regularly to provide emotional support to their parents. They regarded their visits as opportunities to compensate for their regret at being unable to care for their parents at home. Some family members volunteered in Kotobuki in order to repay the debt they felt they owed to the home for the care their parents received. Reciprocity explains the motivation of these family members' visits to the home.

Volunteers came to work with the elderly for diverse reasons: some wanted to foster residents' morale in living in a facility; some volunteered because it gave them feelings of well-being and enjoyment; and others were working to gain relevant experience for a future career serving the elderly. Volunteers gained a lot of benefits from their volunteer activities. Their involvement with the elderly residents is a combination of both self-serving motivation and altruistic consideration.

Campbell (1998) claims that staff work satisfaction in Japanese welfare institutions is generally higher than in American ones. This is borne out in Kotobuki. Most employees felt that a job dealing with people was a highly rewarding one. Gratitude expressed by the residents and appreciation from the visitors gave staff members enormous satisfaction with their work and a strong sense of being useful. Working in a home also provided employees with opportunities to learn lessons from the lives of the residents and to think about their own later life. A democratic work atmosphere, relatively smooth collegial relationships, permanent work opportunity, well-organised cooperative teamwork as well as a reasonable salary also ensured satisfaction in their work life. Most employees strongly identified themselves with the institution. However, with the enactment of the LTCI programme, institutional work in *tokuyō* homes is undergoing some fundamental transitions including the wage system, staff structure and staff's customer awareness towards the clients.

Volunteers in Kotobuki also derived substantial pleasure and fundamental benefits from their work. They discovered the many meanings that volunteering had brought to their own life. The respect and appreciation shown by the residents made some volunteers feel they were important to the needy. Some regarded their volunteer activities as a valuable experience in getting to know other aspects of the society and having a chance to think about old age. And others were surprised to find that they sometimes acted as 'therapists' who could soothe the nerves of the elderly persons.

Employees also had a great deal of difficulty and dissatisfaction in their jobs. Stress or frustrations resulted from the problems of solving conflicts among the residents and the relationships with co-workers. Administrators were annoyed about the management difficulties caused by the LTCI programme. In Sazanka and Akashia, staff occasionally found it beyond their abilities to deal with mental patients and the problems they caused. In Aoba, what displeased caregivers most was being too swamped by nursing duties to look after clients' personal needs. Age differences, different work styles and assumptions, disagreement over care plans among different occupations, and different levels of hierarchy were another source of concern.

Volunteers were engaged in an enterprise that was thought of as being emotionally rewarding rather than costly. Yet now and then, some visitors experienced pressures in their involvement in Kotobuki. Some felt both burdened and guilty when they could not fulfil certain residents' expectations. Students felt it difficult to tolerate the demanding nature of care work and their inability to communicate with the old persons. Others were disgusted by confronting death, the decay of the human body and the horror of senility caused by old age.

Savishinsky (1991) and Foner (1994) found in their research on American nursing homes that female staff were in the majority, and at Kotobuki, too, life and work were overwhelmingly female-dominated. The predominance of women among residents, staff and volunteers reflects some facts of Japanese society: women who have traditionally been the caregivers in their families often become institutional care recipients when they are old and frail, or care providers in another kind of societal institution; female adults with less education and the necessity to support their families are likely to take the physically demanding service jobs in welfare institutions; and middle-aged middle-class women are encouraged to devote their time and energy to do good for both the society and themselves. The fact that most paid care workers are female while top administrators and welfare supervisors are male also reveals the widespread division of gender roles in health care organisations: caring is regarded as a natural activity for women, and management is an area for men.

That middle-aged women and single young women constitute the care labour force in Kotobuki also reflects the characteristic M-shape of the

Japanese female labour market (peak participation occurs after education and before child rearing; and after child rearing). However, a recent transition has been observed in the social service world: with the expansion of social services for the elderly, quite a number of young male workers have taken up the caregiving jobs previously dominated by female workers. How this transition to male participation in the care labour force and the job prospects for different sexes in welfare institutions will impact on institutional care remains an interesting topic for investigation.

Theoretical aspects of my findings

As mentioned in Chapter 1, a number of studies have demonstrated that old age in Japan is often perceived as a time when people can be legitimately differentiated from other groups and old parents can depend upon their children for co-residence, financial support and health care. Recognition of age differences and a cultural norm of dependency allow Japanese people to take a 'protective' approach to respond to the need of the elderly (Benedict 1946; Hashimoto 1996; Kinoshita and Kiefer 1992; Long 1996).

I investigated what cultural meanings the term 'dependency' has in the practice of old-age care in Kotobuki. As a whole, based on the facts that sick elderly are allowed to lie in bed all day long and weak residents are often helped with cleaning their rooms, we can say that the dependent status of the elderly is more noticeable in Japanese institutions than in US nursing homes where old patients are urged to maintain independence. With respect to the 'dependency' on indulgence (*amae*) of the elderly residents in Kotobuki, however, I assume that there are different levels of dependency based on the different physical and mental capabilities of the elderly as well as the extent of intimacy of the residents with their caretakers.

In Sanzanka and Akashia, most healthy residents said that they did not intend or were unable to presume on the kindness of staff members. This is because (1) they were healthy enough to lead an autonomous life so that they did not need help from staff; (2) they were indebted to the home and its staff members, so they needed to restrain themselves and not to trouble the home; and (3) after all, staff members were strangers (*tanin*) and not their families, so they could not depend on their goodwill. This explains why these elderly people seldom made demands and tried their best to maintain their autonomy and kept a polite and superficial relationship with their caretakers. This situation is quite similar to Kinoshita and Kiefer's (1992) finding in their study of a Japanese retirement community that the most important behaviour norm for the resident is the necessity to avoid imposing on other's comfort and freedom. I suppose, in relationships that involve social obligations, affective social bonds involving 'dependency on indulgence' are difficult to form.

But exceptions also exist. Old women who had worked in the bar and restaurant businesses and who were good at getting along with their caretakers reported that they could easily presume on the matrons' kindness. This demonstrates that these women have extraordinary skills in social interactions to play the role of dependent. Yet, they were trying their best not to be a burden on their caretakers.

The mentally retarded elderly and demented elderly, on the other hand, could easily receive care from staff members. The former, whose intelligence and behaviour tended to remain at the level of a child, were often characterised by the staff members as 'cheerful and easy to deal with'. They made demands like children, accomplished tasks like children under the command of their mothers, and received attentive care from the matrons. The latter, who had gradually degenerated into behaving like children, could also always get attention from their caretakers. The relationship between these two groups of elderly residents and their caretakers could be identified with that between children and their family caretakers.

In Aoba, the home regime requires that staff should attempt to maintain maximum independence of the residents, so residents are encouraged to stay away from their bed as long as possible. However, the role of the elderly as sick people provides a social occasion for offering and accepting sympathetic care (Caudill 1962). And the tendency for the caregivers to compare the residents to their own old relatives enables the disabled elderly to accept sympathetic care from the staff. A number of staff members in Aoba said it was unnecessary to confine old persons over 80 years to their wheelchairs, and that the home should allow these old sick residents to *amaeru* as they did in their own families. In fact the strategy of using children's language, familiar language and different tones in nursing care indicates staff members' inclination to create a family-like relationship between themselves and the elderly. In this relationship, the sick or disabled elderly are allowed to depend on indulgence. This is why many Japanese care workers regard 'infantilisation' in nursing homes as 'affection, warmth, nurturance and liking' (Traphagan 2000: 105) rather than a serious problem of infringing upon human rights of the elderly as caregivers do in Western societies.

Staff members in Kotobuki said, 'I don't think elderly clients in Sazanka and Akashia are able to depend on our goodwill' and 'Residents in Aoba are presuming on our indulgence.' The closeness of interpersonal relationship between residents and their caretakers and Japanese people's cultural perception about illness decide the level of dependency of the elderly residents. Dependency on indulgence basically occurs among family members and close friends, but it could also be found in relationships between sick elderly and their caretakers, especially when they had established fictitious familial relationships over time. The sick role as well as staff members identifying the old person as a 'helpless and innocent child' made it possible for the elderly to receive total care.

Thus the interplay between 'presuming on goodwill' and maintaining independence is a complex one. It is true that in fact there are residents who do not want or feel able to *amaeru*. They want to maintain their independence. But residents' willingness to maintain independence and the feeling of being unable to *amaeru* are different issues. What I want to claim is that whether or not an elderly resident can *amaeru* to his/her caretakers depends on the closeness of the relationship between the elderly and the caretaker. Through the views of care workers and the residents as well as my analysis, I am making an assumption that contradicts Doi who claims that *amae* can be applied to all adult relationships. That is, *amae* is the feeling of attachment to another person. Basically it is limited to family relationships and close friendships where one can feel affection. In institutions for the elderly, as the care workers have authority over the residents, intimate relationships based on affection rarely form. So the elderly residents feel unable to presume on the care workers' goodwill. I also assume that whether or not an elderly can *amaeru* also depends on his or her physical and mental abilities as well as his caretaker's willingness to *amayakasu*. Disabled persons and demented elderly can easily receive total care from their care workers. Over a period of time, care workers tend to identify the residents as their fictive family members or friends, and are even occasionally indulgent to the elderly.

The large issues of dependency of the elderly and *amae*, in particular, have been regarded as unique Japanese cultural traits among Japanese studies specialists. My intention here, however, is to suggest that this is not unique in Japan and that we Chinese people also share similar culture of care for the elderly. In China, the rate of co-residence of the elderly with their children is probably higher than in Japan. The Confucian norm of filial piety still remains the core ethic that governs social support for the elderly in the private domain of the family. The old parents continuously accumulate credits by providing instrumental support for their children, taking care of grandchildren and so on in the expectation of receiving reciprocal care from the children in later life. We also have the empathic care pattern towards sick patients. We even have a Chinese word for *amae*. Thus, I advise that more cross-cultural studies be conducted to examine whether there is a universal culture regarding care for the elderly in Asian societies, and what kind of similarities and differences exist in the practice of elderly care.

In addition to the issue of dependency, I would like to briefly discuss disengagement theory and activity theory. The disengagement theory proposed by Cumming and Henry (1961) and developed by Havighurst (1968), and the activity theory suggested by Lemon *et al.* (1972), are two theories which posit a relationship between activity and the psychological well-being of elderly persons.

How do these two theories relate to the well-being of the institutionalised elderly persons? Staff in nursing homes believe that people have higher morale when they have enough to do, so they set up various kinds of recreational and rehabilitation programmes for the residents. A number of studies have examined the extent to which nursing home residents remain active and connected to the outside society. Gubrium noticed that residents who have regular family visitors or often 'step out' to visit relatives and friends not only enjoy higher morale, but also more power and prestige (Gubrium 1975: 99–104). Savishinsky (1991) pointed out that some of the regular programmes such as the pet therapy programme were effective in alleviating loneliness and promoting sociability. Of the few activities offered in Golden Mesa, Carobeth Laird (1979) felt that only the religious services gave her some sense of fulfilment. Kayser-Jones (1981b) found that the National Health Service home in Scotland had superior recreational programmes to that of Pacific Manor in California. The elderly people in Scotland were living near the town they had previously resided in, and not only did they go out more, but they also received more support from community members. These factors contributed significantly to the better quality of life that the residents enjoyed there. While in The Pines, Clough (1981) found that attempts to stimulate activities often failed. Residents were not willing to join in the singing, go on outings or exercise their legs, etc.

What about Kotobuki? Through observing the activities and interactions carried out by the residents in Kotobuki, I found that both theories had their justification and that we should take an eclectic approach in looking at the relationship between activity and psychological well-being of the elderly. In the social world of Kotobuki, old people's involvement in activity could be observed in their interaction with their peer residents, participation in clubs and recreational activities, and their interaction with outside society.

Generally speaking, Kotobuki's location near a bus stop and surrounded by many local shops was of some advantage in relation to residents' activity. It allowed the residents to go shopping and to venture out to the nearby railway stations to reach the wider outside society, and made it convenient for volunteers and families or friends from the area to visit. Monthly scheduled club activities and other recreational programmes were carried out regularly. Residents either lived a life according to their own schedules or became involved in activities the 'homes' planned for them.

There was a tendency for the amount of people's activity to diminish when their age advanced and their health declined. One example that could illuminate this trend was the attendance rate at the residents' club. Among the 15 clubs in Sazanka and Akashia, fewer than half of their members were attending activities regularly. New club members tended to be enthusiastic about club activities at the beginning and would continue their participation for several years. However, as time went by and their physical energy declined or their health deteriorated, these participants resigned from the clubs. Many residents who had lived in Sazanka and Akashia for more than ten years also began to disengage from recreational events such as day trips, overnight trips and eating outside, because of their back or feet ailments, their apprehension about falling down or their unwillingness to bother the staff members.

Residents also withdrew from socialisation with others. There was not as much social interaction among residents in Kotobuki as Bethel (1992a,b) had observed in the Aotani home. Many residents kept to themselves in their rooms, lying in bed or eating in bed or watching TV. Some stayed in the dayroom from morning to night, smoking, dozing and watching TV, without engaging in conversation with their peers. Others went less frequently to visit their families and friends. This lack of interaction indicates a tendency that when age advances, old people are more likely to cling to their own inner world.

On the other hand, however, some elderly persons were actively involved in activities and connected to the surrounding community. For example, Mrs Sugiyama had not only continued participating in clubs such as table tennis, gateball and painting for more than ten years, but was also actively involved in a local elderly group's activities. She said that she would participate in these activities as long as her health condition permitted, because activity brought a healthy body, a supportive network and, more important, a young spirit. Mr Nakajima rode on his bicycle nearly every day to the city's Central Park to do gateball exercise. Mrs Matsumoto was often seen to be chatting with her neighbours while knitting.

In Aoba, activity is an important factor that influences frail elderly persons' morale. Some residents regarded going to the rehabilitation room as their daily duty because doing exercise there not only maintained their physical functions but also provided fun through association with others. Coming to live in Aoba from Sazanka, some admitted that their enjoyment decreased because of the dramatic reduction in both recreational activities and social interaction with peers. Others looked forward to chances that the staff members would take them out for a walk. Some residents, like Mrs Nakamura, would keep on talking about their exciting day-trip experiences, in her case, as a news announcer in the NHK studio.

In short, it is obvious that some residents prefer to be by themselves, some dissociated, while others liked to participate and socialise. Whether or not an old person likes to take part in activities and interact with others largely depends on his or her physical stamina, health condition and personal character. We can hardly declare which theory, disengagement or activity, is superior in leading to greater life satisfaction, because each theory can only represent a part, and not the whole, of the entire elderly population. But one thing is definite, namely, appropriate participation in activities is good for the well-being of the old people. And it depends on an elderly person's own judgement to decide what activity to join in, and how much involvement is suitable. The 'home' administration should take both aspects of old people's activity preference into consideration to devise a wide range of recreational programmes suitable to individuals with different levels of physical functions.

Perspectives for the future

The QOL model I investigated in this study was mainly based on gerontological studies by Western scholars whose primary concerns were issues such as social environment, privacy, independence, self-determination, self-control, etc. Can these Western values be applied in Japanese welfare institutional care? I found that Japanese institutional care had its own characteristics.

In Japanese welfare services provision, welfare institutional care for the elderly has been regulated by the public administration. Elderly persons are usually assigned to institutions to receive care by their municipality welfare offices rather than through their own choice. Private welfare institutions are assigned by welfare offices to provide care for the elderly in need with public funds. Because their care is funded by the 'public administration', clients are submissive to the institutional administration. They receive services passively and seldom make demands. While on the other hand, staff members are doing their jobs for the purpose of 'protecting clients' lives'. This 'bestowed' welfare, thus, has created a dependent elderly population and a superintendent institutional administration.

Residents pay a moderate monthly fee, but they receive three meals a day and articles for daily living free of charge, and money to purchase clothes. Also, they are provided with many subsidised recreational programmes. In receiving such kinds of services, residents think they are indebted to the institution and its staff members, and that they should avoid giving trouble and be cooperative with the home. So they are grateful, self-abnegated and obedient rather than justificatory, self-assertive and self-determined. Those who make trouble or always make demands are criticised as self-centred, selfish and ungrateful. Family members, thinking that they are indebted to the institution for the care their old relatives receive, seldom act as advocates to demand better care for their kin. This is in contrast to nursing homes in America, where patients' families are a strong force in advocating the rights of their old kin (Foner 1994: 110–18; Savishinsky 1991: 71–9). Residents and their families' strong indebtedness towards the public and institutional administrations is the reason for the lack of willingness to urge the provision of basic rights. Changes can be expected when client awareness is well nurtured under the LTCI policy in the future, however, the unfavourable situation for the families at present, that is, limited resources for long-term care, and unavailability of vacancies in nursing homes in big cities, have kept them in a situation where they are incapable of claiming rights.

The homogeneous composition of Kotobuki's workforce and residents has eliminated the grounds for racial and ethnic tension that were found in the Jewish home researched by Shield (1988) and the Crescent home by Foner (1994). In order to keep the homes operating efficiently and smoothly, virtues such as mutual concessions and modesty are encouraged to avoid conflicts. And the spirit of 'team work' is promoted among the employees to provide the best care for the clients. Compared with the problem of demoralization of staff found elsewhere by Vesperi (1983), Kotobuki's relatively democratic workplace atmosphere and quite well functioning senior–junior system have resulted in fewer disagreements regarding individual clients' care plans as well as less work pressure on the employees. Staff members have a strong sense of belonging. In a word, the cultural norms of harmony and cooperation have not only minimised conflicts among the residents but also ensured the cooperation of staff members in different occupations and age groups. They have also given Kotobuki a good reputation in the local community.

Not only did the staff members boast about the home's good reputation, but college students too admitted that Kotobuki was better than some other homes they had been to. The students mentioned institutions where staff relationships were extremely bad. I also think Kotobuki is a good home compared with other institutions I visited. It is one of the few early established welfare institutions that provide comprehensive long-term care for the elderly in Tokyo area. So it has accumulated considerable experience in long-term care. It has a democratic working atmosphere not found in some paternalistic institutions run by members of one family who fill its administrative posts. And as few hostile residents happened to live in Kotobuki, there were not as many clashes among the residents as in other homes. I am not intending to attribute everything good in Kotobuki to its cultural norms such as harmony and cooperation. I think every Japanese elderly institution promotes harmony and cooperation, but the differences between a good one and bad one lies in how the administration manipulates such cultural norms in its operation.

Every institution is unique in terms of its own mixture of residents, finances, policies, personnel and surrounding community. Yet it shares with other institutions many common features as well as problems in institutional care. What has been discovered about Kotobuki offers some useful perspectives for practitioners in social service areas.

Considering the conflicts generated between the room-mates and the psychological stress of getting a room-mate one dislikes in a double room, more private rooms should be available. However those in private rooms reported that they felt lonely and less secure, because in case of an emergency no one could help them. As with Kayser-Jones's (1981a) findings, quite a number of Kotobuki residents preferred four-person rooms to private or double rooms. Advantages listed by them included feeling less lonely and more secure. They also believed that the company of more persons would cut down the possibility of getting a room-mate they did not like. Taking into consideration the preferences of individuals, and the advantages and disadvantages of private rooms, a variety of types of rooms should be provided, so that residents can have a choice.

As residents tend to feel bored when club and recreational activities become stereotyped, creative and effective programmes need to be designed to attract those who are withdrawn. The provision of meals and other household-related services, on the one hand, has liberated the residents from the burden of household chores and enabled them to have more leisure time. But, on the other hand, it has also deprived them of their roles as housekeepers and reduced the stimulation in their life. As a result, they are leading an easy but over-dependent life without much motivation.

Many relatively young elderly residents in their 60s said that their life in Kotobuki was meaningless, and that they hoped they would be able to get a job to do. A resident admired her friend in a *yōgo* home in Atami, a resort city in the Izu Peninsula, because she had plenty to do there. As Atami is a resort city, businesses prosper by selling souvenirs and special products, and need hands to make the boxes, do the wrapping, etc. The *yōgo* homes there take on such jobs, so their residents can earn some pocket money. As a result, the elderly are not only highly motivated but also enjoy their institutional life.

In the current Japanese welfare system, only workshops for mentally retarded persons have been established in local communities. The government might consider constructing some workshops for the elderly in institutions as well, in order to have them lead a productive later life. The homes might also find ways to help the elderly who want to work to get employment opportunities or obtain some part-time jobs to do.

Not only Kotobuki but also other institutions I visited are facing the dilemma caused by admitting mental patients: both the principle of 'welfare' and financial necessity have forced welfare institutions to accept more such patients; meanwhile, the various troubles caused by the patients, the persistent prejudice towards mental patients and the homes' lack of professional psychiatrists have made it one of the most difficult problems for the homes to cope with. This is not just a problem for a single institution or the whole welfare field, but a structural problem in the mental health care system. It further involves people's attitudes towards mental illnesses and those who suffer from them. In order to improve the living environment for mental patients, reform and cooperation in the mental health care system and welfare system are needed. It is also necessary for people to know more about mental illnesses and reduce their prejudice towards mental patients.

Despite the fact that institutions for the elderly have gradually become socialised into the local communities, the elderly residents are still isolated from the wider society. Except for the volunteer teachers in various clubs, volunteer activities by other groups and individuals are few in Kotobuki. Although the main purpose of volunteer teachers is to use their specific skills to help the elderly residents enjoy their institutional life, their regular visits also provide chances for the residents to increase their interpersonal interactions. The home administration should be aware that volunteers' meaning for the residents lies not just in the programmes they run, but also in the personal contacts they provide for the residents. It should not let the volunteers feel they are isolated from the residents. The home should encourage volunteer activities by students and local citizens, and it might also consider the possibility of recruiting its retired care workers as volunteers.

Application to China

In contrast to Japan, where the capacity of the family to take care of the elderly has been declining during the tremendous transformation in family structure and norms of filial piety in the process of industrialization, China is a developing country where agriculture remains the major industry. Although family structure is tending towards nuclear families in major cities and coastal areas, as pension systems and health care programmes are only provided in urban areas and the Confucian norm of filial piety is still deeply rooted in Chinese society, old parents mainly depend on their families for elderly care.

However, China is moving towards a market economy. With the breakdown of public-owned entities, many welfare functions of these enterprises such as pensions systems, health care, services for children and retired persons have been transferred to the society and the communities where old people live. How to reform the social security system and how to develop community-based health care and social services industries for the elderly have become the focus of a heated discussion among government agencies and academia. In this regard, I think we should learn from the experiences of Japan, not only in public policy-making for the elderly but also the on-the-ground practice in providing services.

On the policy-making level, I think China should learn from both Japan's failures and successes. China should develop its own policies and programmes based on its own cultural traditions, economic capacity and social transitions in the society. The most important thing for China to do first, I think, is to establish a nationwide pension system and health care insurance scheme for all citizens. At the same time, it is necessary to develop social services to meet the expanding social demands of elderly people, especially in big cities such as Shanghai and Beijing where ageing problems have already become prominent.

In fact, in recent years, a number of residential homes for the elderly have been established in Beijing and Shanghai. And some nursing homes based on international cooperation, for example, the International Nursing Home operated by the Sino-Japan Friendship Hospital in Beijing, have been built to provide long-term care for Chinese elderly. There remain many unsolved challenges in such settings, such as how to recruit residents, how to develop programmes to enrich residents' later life, how to create a familiar atmosphere in the institutions, and how to create a Chinese-style institutional culture while adopting care management models from foreign countries. We can borrow some useful experiences from Japanese institutional care.

An important point of this volume is how to facilitate a productive later life for elderly persons. Comparing the elderly in Kotobuki and in a home in my hometown in China, I found that although the living standard of the elderly in China was far lower than in Japan, the Chinese elderly were more healthy and active in associating with people in the local community while the Japanese elderly were more inactive and isolated. The social stigma of living in a home for the elderly and the tendency towards inactivity with ageing may account for the alienation of the elderly from society, but I think a more important factor is that the institutions in Japan are so well equipped, and there are so many services for the residents that they rarely have the chance to do something by themselves. Some elderly are young and healthy enough to be able to work, yet there are no employment chances for them. They have nothing to do in the home but watch TV, do some reading and chat with others.

In China, by contrast, the elderly help the staff members raise chickens and pigs and plant vegetables to supply their food. They even sell some of the surplus produce to the local market. Also, they have wide connections with the local people, so their social life is more productive. Thus it is important for institutions not only to provide services and programmes for the elderly to lead a comfortable and secure life, but also to provide opportunities for those who want to be productive in their later life to perform their working roles.

Appendix 1
The mechanism of the LTCI

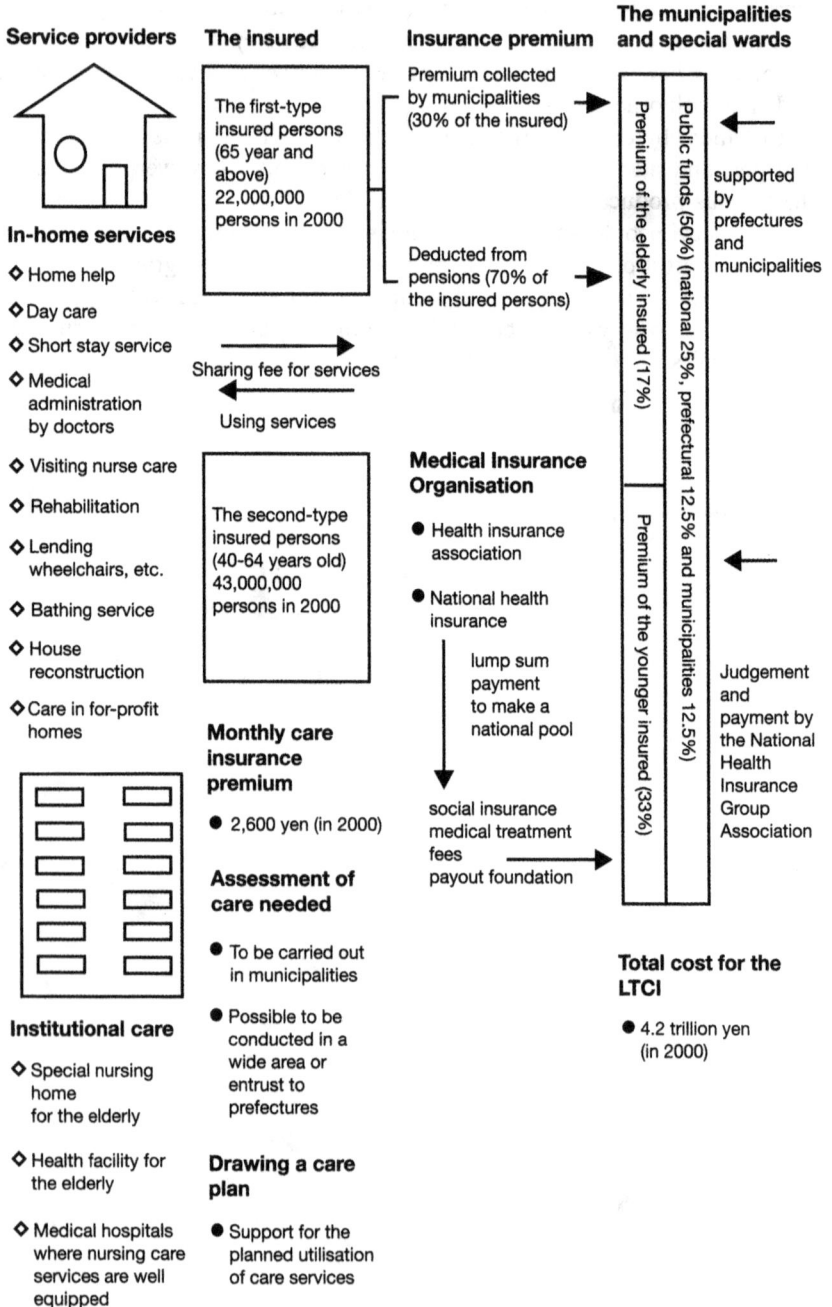

Service providers

In-home services

◇ Home help

◇ Day care

◇ Short stay service

◇ Medical administration by doctors

◇ Visiting nurse care

◇ Rehabilitation

◇ Lending wheelchairs, etc.

◇ Bathing service

◇ House reconstruction

◇ Care in for-profit homes

Institutional care

◇ Special nursing home for the elderly

◇ Health facility for the elderly

◇ Medical hospitals where nursing care services are well equipped

---

The insured

The first-type insured persons (65 year and above) 22,000,000 persons in 2000

Sharing fee for services →

Using services ←

The second-type insured persons (40-64 years old) 43,000,000 persons in 2000

Monthly care insurance premium

● 2,600 yen (in 2000)

Assessment of care needed

● To be carried out in municipalities

● Possible to be conducted in a wide area or entrust to prefectures

Drawing a care plan

● Support for the planned utilisation of care services

Insurance premium

Premium collected by municipalities (30% of the insured) →

Deducted from pensions (70% of the insured persons) →

Medical Insurance Organisation

● Health insurance association

● National health insurance

lump sum payment to make a national pool

↓

social insurance medical treatment fees payout foundation →

The municipalities and special wards

Premium of the elderly insured (17%)

Public funds (50%) (national 25%, prefectural 12.5% and municipalities 12.5%)

supported by prefectures and municipalities ←

Premium of the younger insured (33%)

Judgement and payment by the National Health Insurance Group Association ←

Total cost for the LTCI

● 4.2 trillion yen (in 2000)

Appendix 2

Physical layout of Kotobuki
(each floor)

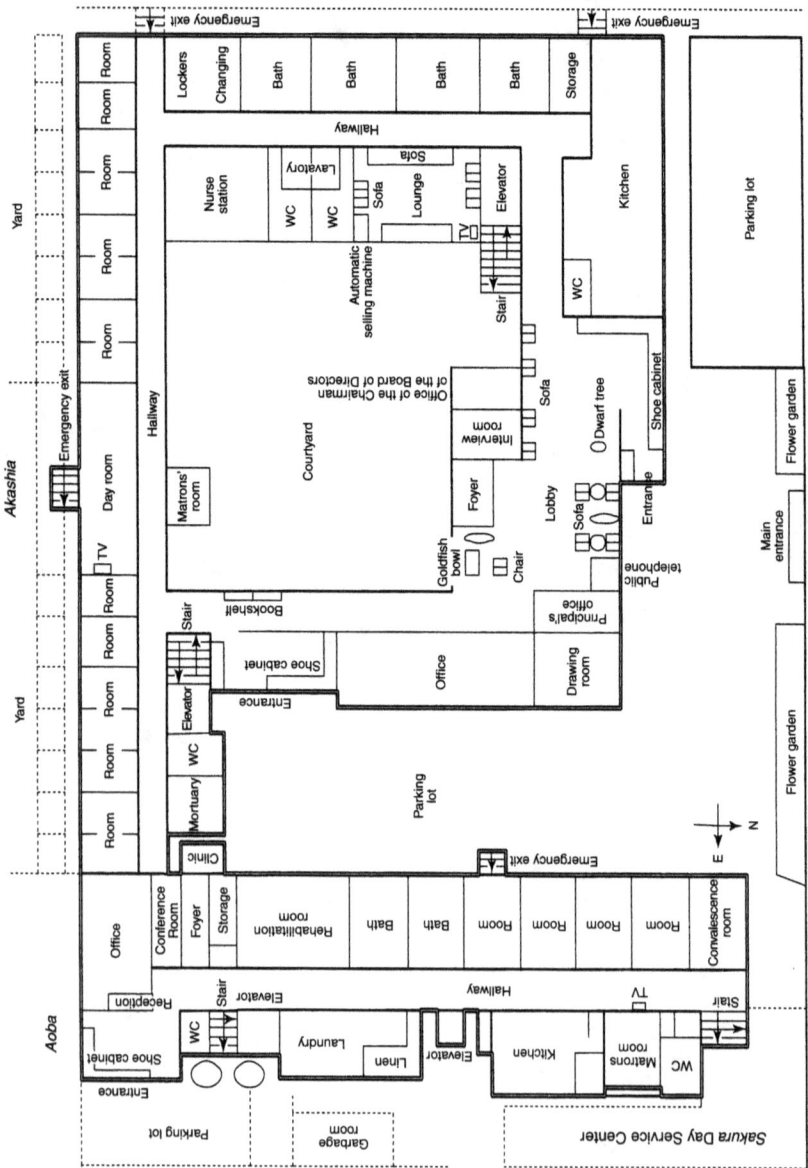

First floor

Akashia

Aoba

Sakura Day Service Center

Emergency exit

Room · Room · Room · Room

Lockers

Changing

Bath

Bath

Bath

Bath

Storage

Hallway

Nurse station

Lavatory

WC · WC

Sofa

Lounge

Sofa

Elevator

TV

Automatic selling machine

Stair

Kitchen

WC

Courtyard

Office of the Chairman of the Board of Directors

Sofa

Dwarf tree

Shoe cabinet

Interview room

Foyer

Lobby

Sofa

Entrance

Goldfish bowl

Chair

Public telephone

Principal's office

Parking lot

Flower garden

Main entrance

Flower garden

N
E

Emergency exit

Matrons' room

Bookshelf

Emergency exit

Hallway

Day room

TV

Room

Stair

Elevator

WC

Mortuary

Clinic

Shoe cabinet

Entrance

Office

Drawing room

Yard

Room · Room · Room · Room · Room · Room · Room

Yard

Office

Conference Room

Foyer

Storage

Rehabilitation room

Bath

Bath

Room

Room

Room

Room

Convalescence room

Reception

Stair

Elevator

Hallway

TV

Stair

WC

Entrance

Shoe cabinet

Laundry

Linen

Elevator

Kitchen

Matrons room

WC

Parking lot

Garbage room

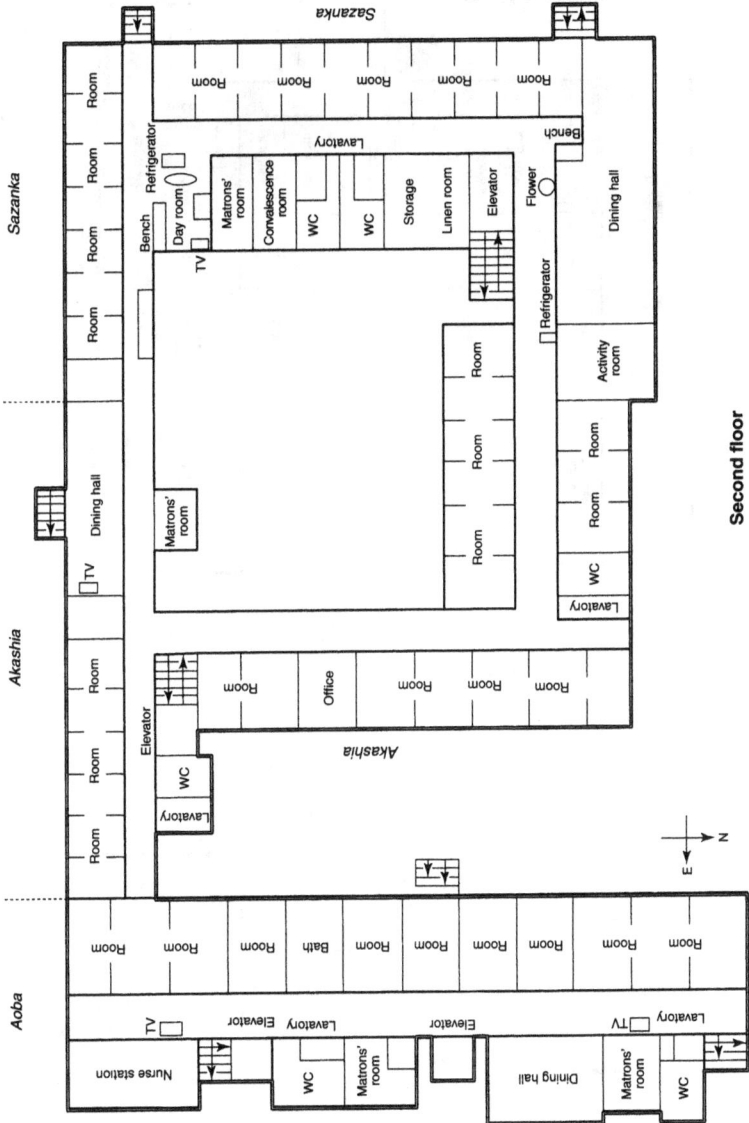

Sazanka

Sazanka

Akashia

Aoba

Second floor

Room Room Room Room Room

Refrigerator
Day room
Bench
TV
Matrons' room
Convalescence room
WC
WC
Storage
Linen room
Elevator
Lavatory
Bench
Flower
Refrigerator
Dining hall
Activity room

Dining hall
TV
Matrons' room

Room
Room
Room
Room
Room
Room
Room
WC
Lavatory

Elevator
WC
Lavatory
Room
Office
Room
Room
Room
Akashia

N
E

Room Room Room Bath Room Room Room Room Room Room

TV
Elevator
Lavatory
Elevator
TV
Lavatory

Nurse station
WC
Matrons' room
Dining hall
Matrons' room
WC

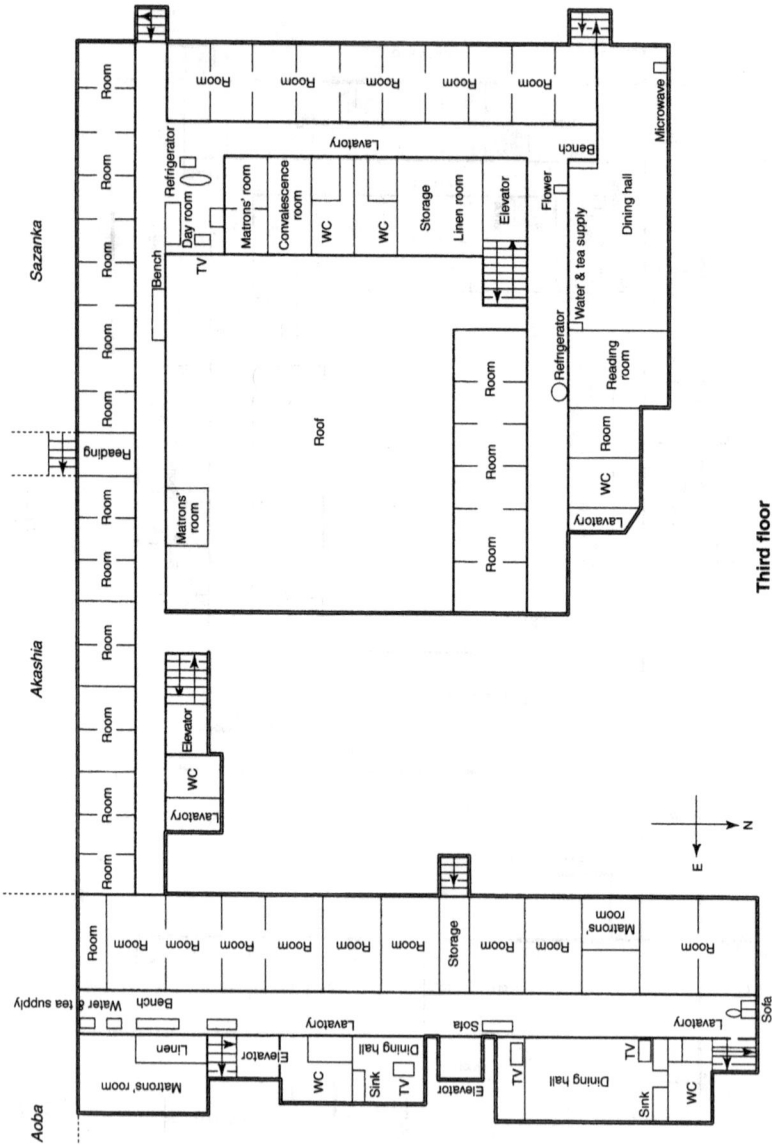

Third floor

Sazanka

Akashia

Aoba

Room (×multiple, along top corridor)

Refrigerator
Day room
TV
Bench
Matrons' room
Convalescence room
WC
WC
Lavatory
Storage
Linen room
Elevator
Flower
Water & tea supply
Microwave
Dining hall

Refrigerator
Reading room
Room
WC
Room
Room
Room
Lavatory

Roof

Matrons' room
Reading

Elevator
WC
Lavatory

Room

Storage
Matrons' room

Water & tea supply
Bench
Sofa

Lavatory
Sofa
Linen
Elevator
WC
Dining hall
Sink
TV
Elevator
TV
Dining hall
Sink
WC
Lavatory

N
E

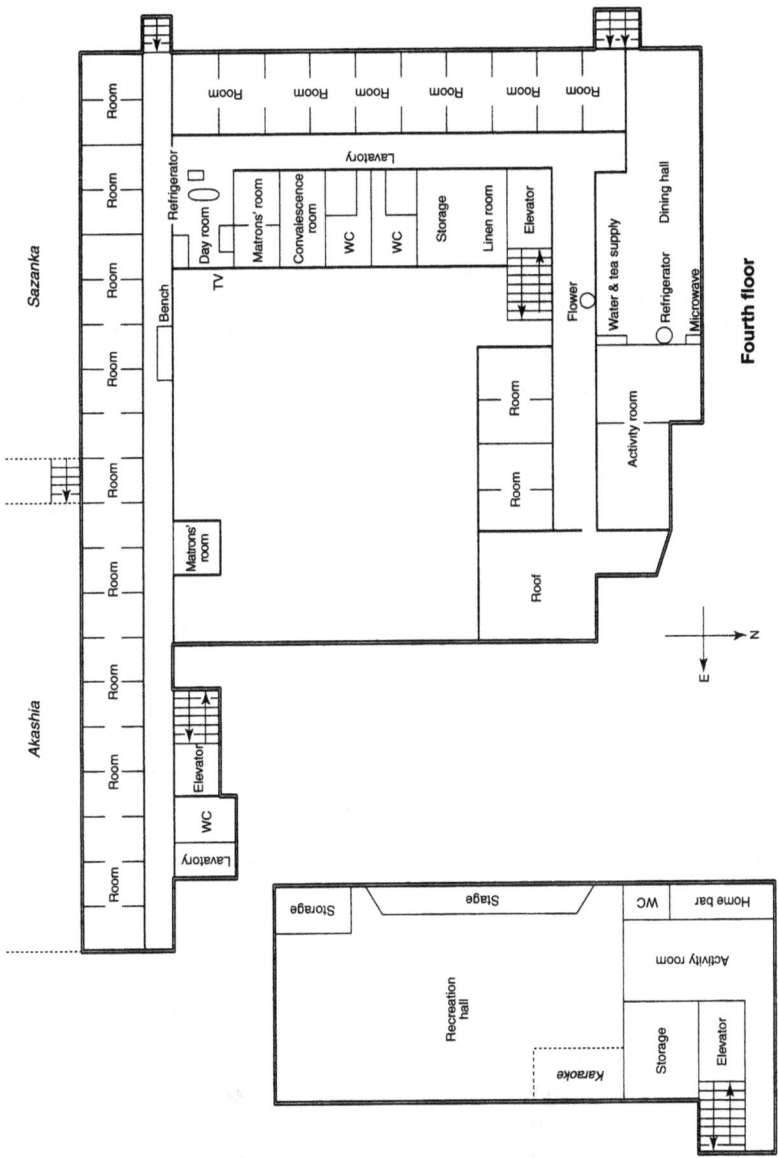

Sazanka

Akashia

Room | Room | Room | Room | Room | Room | Room | Room | Room | Room | Room | Room

Matrons'
room

Bench

Lavatory
WC
Elevator

Refrigerator

Day room
TV

Matrons' room

Convalescence
room

WC

WC

Storage

Linen room

Elevator

Flower

Water & tea supply

Refrigerator

Microwave

Lavatory

Room | Room | Room | Room | Room | Room

Room

Room

Activity room

Roof

Dining hall

Fourth floor

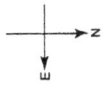

N
E

Storage

Stage

WC

Home bar

Recreation
hall

Karaoke

Storage

Activity room

Elevator

Fifth floor

Bibliography

Adachi, Kiyoshi (2000) 'The Development of Social Welfare Services in Japan', in Susan O. Long (ed.) *Caring for the Elderly in Japan and the US*. London, New York: Routledge.

Akiyama, Hiroko, Toni C. Antonucci and Ruth Campbell (1990) 'Exchange and Reciprocity among Two Generations of Japanese and American Women', in Jay Sokolovsky (ed.) *The Cultural Context of Aging*. New York: Bergin and Garvey.

Arnold, Sharon B. (1991) 'Measurement of Quality of Life in the Frail Elderly', in J.E. Birren, J.E. Lubben, J.C. Rowe and D.E. Deutchman (eds) *The Concept and Measurement of Quality of Life in the Frail Elderly*. San Diego: Academic Press.

Asano, Hitoshi (1992) 'Public Policies for the Elderly in Japan', in *Aging in Japan*, Material Information Centre/ International Publication Series No. 2: 55–74. Tokyo: Japan Aging Research Centre.

Asano, Hitoshi (ed.) (1994) *Kōreisha no Sōsharuwāku Jissen: Kazoku no Mondai to QOL ni Motozuku Gihō no Tenkai* (Social Work Practice for the Elderly: Technique Development Based on Problems of the Family and QOL). Tokyo: Kawashima Shoten.

Asano, Hitoshi (1995) *Kōreisha Fukushi no Jisshō-teki Kenkyū: Yutaka na Kōreiki ni mukete* (Practical Research on Welfare for the Elderly: Towards a Rich Later Life). Tokyo: Kawashima Shoten.

Asano, Hitoshi and Sōji Tanaka (eds) (1993) *Asu no Kōreisha Kea 5: Nihon no Shisetsu Kea* (Tomorrow's Elderly Care: Institutional Care in Japan). Tokyo: Chūō Hōki.

Atsumi, Reiko (1989) 'Friendship in Cross-cultural Perspective', in Yoshio Sugimoto and Ross E. Mouer (eds) *Constructs for Understanding Japan*. London, New York: Kegan Paul International.

Batson, C.D., J. Fultz and P.A. Schoenrade (1987) 'Distress and Empathy: Two Qualitatively Distinct Vicarious Emotions with Different Motivational Consequences', *Journal of Personality*, 55: 175–81.

Befu, Harumi (1977) 'Social Exchange', *Annual Review of Anthropology*, 6: 225–81.

Befu, Harumi (1986) 'Gift-giving in a Modernizing Japan', in T. Lebra and W. Lebra (eds) *Japanese Culture and Behavior*. Honolulu: University of Hawaii Press, pp. 158–70.

Befu, Harumi (1990) 'Four Models of Japanese Society and their Relevance to Conflict', in S.N. Eisenstadt and Eyal Ben-Ari (eds) *Japanese Models of Conflict Resolution*. London, New York: Kegan Paul International, pp. 213–36.

Benedict, Ruth (1946) *The Chrysanthemum and the Sword: Patterns of Japanese Culture.* London: Routledge and Kegan Paul.

Bethel, Diana Lynn (1992a) 'Alienation and Reconnection in a Home for the Elderly', in Joseph J. Tobin (ed.) *Re-made in Japan.* New Haven, CT: Yale University Press.

Bethel, Diana Lynn (1992b) 'Life on Obasuteyama, or, Inside a Japanese Institution for the Elderly', in T. Lebra (ed.) *Japanese Social Organization.* Honolulu: University of Hawaii Press.

Campbell, John Creighton (1992) *How Policies Change: The Japanese Government and the Aging Society.* Princeton, NJ: Princeton University Press.

Campbell, John Creighton (2000) 'Changing Meanings of Frail Old People and the Japanese Welfare State', in Susan O. Long (ed.) *Caring for the Elderly in Japan and the US.* London, New York: Routledge.

Campbell, John Creighton and N. Ikegami (eds) (1999) *Long-term Care for Frail Older People: Reaching for the Ideal System.* Tokyo, Berlin, Heidelberg, New York: Springer Verlag.

Campbell, John Creighton and N. Ikegami (2000) 'Long-term Care Insurance Comes to Japan', *Health Affairs*, 19(3): 20–39.

Campbell, Ruth (1998) 'Nursing Homes and Long-term Care in Japan', in Edward R. Beauchamp (ed.) *Japanese Society since 1945.* New York, London: Garland Publishing.

Campbell, Ruth and Berit Ingersoll-Dayton (2000) 'Variation in Family Caregiving in Japan and the US', in Susan O. Long (ed.) *Caring for the Elderly in Japan and the US.* London, New York: Routledge.

Caudill, William (1961) 'Around the Clock Patient Care in Japanese Psychiatric Hospitals: The Role of the Tsukisoi', *American Sociological Review*, 26: 204–14.

Caudill, William (1962) 'Patterns of Emotion in Modern Japan', in R.J. Smith and K. Birdseye (eds) *Japanese Culture: Its Development and Characteristics.* Chicago: Aldine.

Clipp, Elizabeth C. (1996) 'Quality of Life', in George L. Maddox (ed.)*The Encyclopedia of Aging: A Comprehensive Resource in Gerontology and Geriatrics.* New York: Springer Publishing Company.

Clough, R. (1981) *Old Age Homes.* London: George Allen and Unwin.

Cook, A.S. (1981) 'A Model for Working with the Elderly in Institutions', *Social Casework*, 62(7): 420–25.

Coons, Dorothy and Nancy Mace (1996) *Quality of Life in Long-term Care.* New York: The Haworth Press.

Cumming, Elaine and William Henry (1961) *Growing Old: The Process of Disengagement.* New York: Basic Books.

Cumming, John and Elaine Cumming (1962) *Ego and Milieu: Theory and Practice of Environmental Therapy.* New York: Atherton Press.

Curtin, Sharon (1972) *Nobody Ever Died of Old Age.* Boston: Little, Brown.

De Vos, George A. (1992) *Social Cohesion and Alienation: Minorities in the United States and Japan.* Boulder, CO: Westview Press.

Doi, Takeo (1962) '*Amae*: A Key Concept for Understanding Japanese Personality Structure', in R.J. Smith and R.K. Beardsley(eds) *Japanese Culture: Its Development and Characteristics.* Chicago: Aldine.

Doi, Takeo (1971) *Amae no Kōzō* (The Structure of *Amae*). Tokyo: Kōbundo.

Doi, Takeo (1973) 'The Japanese Patterns of Communication and the Concept of *Amae*', *Quarterly Journal of Speech*, 59(2), April.

Doi, Takeo (1992) 'On the Concept of *Amae*', paper presented at 12th International Congress of Child and Adolescent Psychiatry, WAIPAD Symposium 'Attachment and Dependency', 18 July 1990. *Infant Mental Health Journal*, 13(1), spring.

Eijingu Sōgō Kenkyū Sentā (eds), Ageing Comprehensive Research Centre (1998) *Kōrei Shakai no Kiso Chishiki: Nijūisseiki e no Kii-wādo* (Basic Knowledge for Ageing Society: Keywords for the 21st Century). Tokyo: Chūō Hōki.

Erikson, Erik H. (1959) *Identity and the Life Cycle: Selected Papers*. New York: International Universities Press.

Erikson, Erik H. (1970) *Childhood and Society*. Harmondsworth: Penguin Books.

Foner, Nancy (1994) *The Caregiving Dilemma: Working in an American Nursing Home*. Berkeley: University of California Press.

Foner, Nancy (1995) 'Relatives as Trouble: Nursing Home Aides and Patients' Families', in J. Neil Henderson and Maria D. Vesperi (eds) *The Culture of Long-term Care – Nursing Home Ethnography*. Westport, CT: Bergin and Garvey.

Freed, Anne O. (1993) *The Changing Worlds of Older Women in Japan*. Manchester, CT: Knowledge, Ideas and Trends, Inc.

Fukazawa, Shichiro (1964) *Narayama Bushikō*. Tokyo: Shinchō Bunko.

George, Linda K. and Lucille B. Bearon (1980) *Quality of Life in Older Persons*. Human Sciences Press.

Goffman, Erving (1961) *Asylums: Essays on the Social Situation of Mental Patients and Other Inmates*. Garden City, NY: Doubleday.

Gouldner, Alvin (1960) 'The Norm of Reciprocity', *American Sociological Review* 25(2): 161–78.

Gubrium, Jaber F. (1975) *Living and Dying at Murray Manor*. New York: St Martin's.

Gubrium, Jaber F. (1993) *Speaking of Life: Horizons of Meanings for Nursing Home Residents*. Hawthorne, NY: Aldine De Gruyter.

Harding, T.W., J. Schneider, H.M. Visotsky and C.L. Graves (1985) *Human Rights and Mental Patients in Japan*. Geneva: The International Commission of Jurists and the International Commission of Health Professionals.

Hashimoto, Akiko (1996) *The Gift of Generations: Japanese and American Perspectives on Aging and the Social Contract*. Cambridge, New York, Melbourne: Cambridge University Press.

Hashimoto, Yasuko (1998) 'Kaigo Hoken to Shakai Fukushi' (Long-term Care and Social Welfare), *Shakai Fukushi Kenkyū* (Social Welfare Research), 72: 2–10.

Havighurst, R.J., B.L. Neugarten and S.S. Tobin (1968) 'Disengagement and Patterns of Aging', in Bernice L. Neugarten (ed.) *Middle Age and Aging: A Reader in Social Psychology*. Chicago: University of Chicago Press.

Higashimurayama-shi Kaigo Hoken-ka (Department of Nursing Care Insurance, Higashimurayama City) (eds) (1999) *Kōreisha Tōkei-hyō* (Statistical Tables of Elderly Persons).

Itō, Arthur K. (1975) 'Keirō Nursing Home: A Study of Japanese Cultural Adaptations', in E. Percil Stanford (ed.) *Minority Aging*. Institute Proceedings, San Diego: Center on Aging, School of Social Work, San Diego State University.

Izuhara, Misa (2000) *Family Change and Housing in Post-war Japanese Society: The Experience of Older Women*. Aldershot, Burlington USA, Singapore, Sydney: Ashgate.

Japan Aging Research Center (1996) *Aging in Japan*. Tokyo: Japan Aging Research Center.

Kayser-Jones, Jeanie (1981a) *Old, Alone and Neglected: Care of the Aged in Later Life.* New York: New American Library.

Kayser-Jones, Jeanie (1981b) *Old, Alone and Neglected: Care of the Aged in Scotland and the United States.* Berkeley: University of California Press.

Kayser-Jones, Jeanie (1981c) 'Quality of Care for Institutionalized Aged: A Scottish–American Comparison', in Christine L. Fry (ed.) *Dimensions: Aging, Culture, and Health.*New York:Praeger.

Keith, Jennie (1988) 'Participant Observation', in K.W. Shaie, R.T. Campbell, W. Meredith and S.C. Rawlings (eds) *Methodological Issues in Aging Research.* New York: Springer Publishing Company.

Kiefer, Christie W. (1987) 'Care of the Aged in Japan', in Edward Norbeck and Margaret Lock (eds) *Health, Illness, and Medical Care in Japan: Cultural and Social Dimensions.* Honolulu: University of Hawaii Press.

Kiefer, Christie W. (1990) 'The Elderly in Modern Japan: Elite, Victims, or Plural Players?', in Jay Sokolovsky (ed.) *The Cultural Context of Aging: Worldwide Perspectives.* Westport, CT: Bergin and Garvey.

Kinoshita, Yasuhito and Christie W. Kiefer (1992) *Refuge of the Honored: Social Organization in a Japanese Retirement Community.* Berkeley: University of California Press.

Koncelik, Joseph A. (1976) *Designing the Open Nursing Home.* Stroudsburg, PA: Dowden, Hutchinson and Ross.

Kono, Shigemi (1996) 'Demographic Aspects of Population Ageing in Japan', in Japan Aging Research Center (eds) *Aging in Japan.* Tokyo: Japan Aging Research Center.

Kōseishō (1995) *Kokumin Seikatsu Kiso Chōsa* (Basic Survey of National Life). Tokyo: Kōseishō Daijin Kanbō Tōkei Jōhō-bu (MHW: The Minister's Secretariat Statistics and Information Bureau).

Kōseishō (1996) *Kanja Chōsa* (Inpatient Survey). Tokyo: Kōseishō Daijin Kanbō Tōkei Jōhō-bu (MHW: The Minister's Secretariat Statistics and Information Bureau).

Kōseishō (1997a) *Jinkō Dōtai Tōkei* (Statistics of Population Trends). Tokyo: Kōseishō Daijin Kanbō Tōkei Jōhō-bu (MHW: The Minister's Secretariat Statistics and Information Bureau).

Kōseishō (1997b) *Shakai Fukushi Shisetsu Tō Chōsa* (Survey of Social Welfare Institutions, etc.). Tokyo: Kōseishō Daijin Kanbō Tōkei Jōhō-bu (MHW: The Minister's Secretariat Statistics and Information Bureau).

Kōseishō (1997c) *Rōjin Hoken Shisetsu Chōsa* (Survey of Health Care Facilities for the Elderly). Tokyo: Kōseishō Daijin Kanbō Tōkei Jōhō-bu (MHW: The Minister's Secretariat Statistics and Information Bureau).

Krauss, Ellis S., Thomas P. Rohlen and Patricia G. Steinhoff (eds) (1984) *Conflict in Japan.* Honolulu: University of Hawaii Press.

Kyōgoku, Takanobu (1996) *Kaigo Kakumei – Rōgo wo Machitooku suru Kōteki Kaigo Hoken Shisutemu* (Care Revolution: Public Care Security System for Old Age). Okayama: Benesse Corporation.

Laird, Carobeth (1979) *Limbo: A Memoir about Life in a Nursing Home by a Survivor.* Novato, CA: Chandler and Sharp Publishers.

Lawton, M. Powell (1983) 'Environment and Other Determinants of Well-being in Older People', *The Gerontologist* 23: 349–57.

Lawton, M. Powell, (1991) 'A Multidimensional View of Quality of Life in Frail Elders', in J.E. Birren, J.E. Lubben, J.C. Rowe and D.E. Deutchman (eds) *The Concept and Measurement of Quality of Life in the Frail Elderly.* San Diego: Academic Press.

Lebra, T. Sugiyama (1976) *Japanese Patterns of Behavior.* Honolulu: University of Hawaii Press.

Lebra, T. Sugiyama (1984) 'Nonconfrontational Strategies for Management of Interpersonal Conflicts', in Ellis S. Krauss, Thomas P. Rohlen and Patricia G. Steinhoff (eds) *Conflict in Japan.* Honolulu: University of Hawaii Press.

Lebra, T. Sugiyama and William P. Lebra (eds) (1986) *Japanese Culture and Behavior: Selected Readings,* revised edn. Honolulu: University of Hawaii Press.

Lee, Gary (1985) 'Theoretical Perspectives on Social Networks', in W. Sauer and R. Coward (eds) *Social Support Networks and the Care of the Elderly.* New York: Springer.

Lemon, B.W., V.L. Bengtson and J.A. Peterson (1972) 'An Exploration of the Activity Theory of Aging: Activity Types and Life Satisfaction among In-movers to ...', *Gerontology* 27(4): 511–23.

Linhart, Sepp (1997) 'Does *Oyakōkō* Still Exist in Present-Day Japan?', in Susanne Formanek and Sepp Linhart (eds) *Aging: Asian Concepts and Experiences, Past and Present.* Vienna: Verlag Der Österreichischen Akademie der Wissenschaften.

Long, Susan O. (1987) *Family Change and the Life Course in Japan,* East Asia Papers, No. 44. Ithaca, NY: Cornell University.

Long, Susan O. (1996) 'Nurturing and Femininity: The Ideal of Caregiving in Postwar Japan', in Anne E. Imamura (ed.) *Re-imaging Japanese Women.* Berkeley: University of California Press.

Long, Susan O. (ed.) (2000) *Caring for the Elderly in Japan and the US.* London and New York: Routledge.

Maeda, Daisaku and Nakatani, Youmei (1992) 'Family Care of the Elderly in Japan', in Jordan I. Kosberg (ed.) *Family Care of the Elderly: Social and Cultural Changes.* Newbury Park, CA: Sage Publications.

Maeda, Daisaku (1996a) 'Social Security, Health Care, and Social Services for the Elderly in Japan', in Japan Aging Research Center (eds) *Aging in Japan.*Tokyo:Japan Aging Research Center.

Maeda, Daisaku (1996b) *Kōreisha no QOL Kenkyū no Genjō to Kadai* (Current Research Condition and Topics on QOL for the Elderly). Tokyo: Annual Report of the Social Work Research Institute of Japan College for Social Work, No. 32.

Maeda, Daisaku (2000) 'The Socioeconomic Context of Japanese Social Policy for Aging', in Susan O. Long (ed.) *Caring for the Elderly in Japan and the US.* London, New York: Routledge.

Martin. Linda G. (1989) 'The Graying of Japan', *Population Bulletin,* 44(2), July (Washington, DC: Population Reference Bureau.)

Maslow, Abraham H. (1954) *Motivation and Personality.* New York: Harper and Row.

Masuda, Koh (ed.) (1974) *Kenkyusha's New Japanese–English Dictionary.* Tokyo: Kenkyusha.

Matsuda, M. (1959) *Kenkyusha's New Pocket Japanese–English Dictionary.* Tokyo: Kenkyusha.

McLean, Athena and Margaret Perkinson (1995) 'The Head Nurse as Key Informant: How Belief and Institutional Pressures Can Structure Dementia Care', in J. Neil Henderson and Maria D. Vesperi (eds) *The Culture of Long-term Care: Nursing Home Ethnography.* Westport, CT: Bergin and Garvey.

Mineruva Shobō Henshūbu (eds) (1997) *Shakai Fukushi Shō Roppō* (Six Small Laws for Social Welfare). Kyoto: Mineruva Shobō.

Ministry of Health and Welfare, (1998) White Paper. Tokyo: Gyōsei.

Miura, Fumio (1996) *Zusetsu Kōreisha Hakusho 1996*. Tokyo: Zenkoku Shakai-fukushi Kyōgikai.

Mouer, Ross E. and Yoshio Sugimoto (1986) *Images of Japanese Society*. London, New York: Kegan Paul International.

Munakata, Tsunetsuka (1986) 'Japanese Attitudes toward Mental Health', in T.S. Lebra and W.P. Lebra (eds) *Japanese Culture and Behavior: Selected Readings*. Honolulu: University of Hawaii Press.

Myers, David G. (1988) *Social Psychology*, international edn. New York: McGraw-Hill.

National Census (1997) *Transition of Young-old Elderly and Old-old Elderly Persons*. Tokyo: Management and Coordination Agency Statistics Bureau.

Neugarten, Bernice Levin (1973) 'Personality Change in Late Life: A Developmental Perspective', in Carl Eisdorfer and M. Powell Lawton (eds) *The Psychology of Adult Development and Aging*. Washington, DC: American Psychological Association.

Nishio, H.K. (1994) 'Japan's Welfare Vision: Dealing with a Rapidly Increasing Elderly Population', in Laura K. Olson (ed.) *The Graying of the World: Who Will Care for the Frail Elderly?* New York: Haworth Press.

Norbeck, Edward (1953) 'Age-grading in Japan', *American Anthropologist*, 55: 373–83.

Ogawa, N. and Robert D. Retherford (1990) 'Care of the Elderly in Japan: Changing Norms and Expectations', *Journal of Marriage and the Family*, 55(3): 585–97.

Ōhashi, Kensaku (1999) *Chiiki Fukushi* (Community Welfare). Tokyo: Hōsō Daigaku Kyōiku Shinkō-kai.

Ōkuma, Kazuo (1990) *Anata no Oi wo Dare ga Miru* (Who Will Care for Your Old Age?). Tokyo:Asahi Bunko.

Ōkuma, Kazuo (1992) *Haha wo Kukuranaide Kudasai* (Please Don't Bind My Mother). Tokyo: Asahi Bunko.

O'Leary, James S. (1993) 'A New Look at Japan's Honorable Elders', *Journal of Aging Studies*, 7(1): 1–24.

Palmore, Erdman (1975) *The Honorable Elders: A Cross-cultural Analysis of Aging in Japan*. Durham, NC: Duke University Press.

Plath, David W. (1972) 'Japan: The After Years', in Donald O. Cowgill and Lowell D. Holmes (eds) *Aging and Modernization*. New York: Appleton-Century-Crofts, Meredith Corporation.

Reilly, Michele (1996) 'Human Rights in the Japanese Mental Health System', in Roger Goodman and Ian Neary (eds) *Case Studies on Human Rights in Japan*. Richmond, Surrey: Japan Library.

Ryff, Carol D. (1995) 'Psychological Well-being', in James E. Birren (eds) *Encyclopedia of Gerontology: Age, Aging and the Aged*, vol. 2. San Diego: Academic Press.

Sakurai, Keiichi and Keisō Imura (eds) (1991) *Shakai Fukushi wo Manabu, Kaitei-ban* (Study Social Welfare, revised edn). Tokyo: Gakubun-sha.

Sasaki, Yuji (1986) 'Nonmedical Healing in Contemporary Japan: A Psychiatric Study', in T.S. Lebra and W.P. Lebra (eds) *Japanese Culture and Behavior: Selected Readings*, revised edn. Honolulu: University of Hawaii Press.

Savishinsky, Joel S. (1991) *The Ends of Time: Life and Work in a Nursing Home*. New York: Bergin and Garvey.

Shibata, Yoshihiko (1998) *Nihon no Shakai Hoshō* (Social Security of Japan). Tokyo: Shin-nihon Shuppan-sha.

Shield, Renee Rose (1988) *Uneasy Endings: Daily Life in an American Nursing Home.* Ithaca, NY: Cornell University Press.

Shimizu, Yutaka and Junko Wake (1994) 'The Formal Services for the Elderly in Japan', in Jordan I. Kosberg (eds) *International Handbook on Services for the Elderly.* Westport, CT: Greenwood Publishing Group.

Shimizu, Yutaka, Hitoshi Asano and Akio Miyazaki (eds) (1994) *Rōjin Fukushi: Seisaku – Shogū-no Shiten to Hōhō, Daisan-ban* (Social Welfare Services for the Elderly: Concepts and Methods in Policy and Practice, 3rd edn). Tokyo: Kaiseisha.

Shokuhin Ryūtsū Jōhō Sentā (ed.) (2002) *Shōshi Kōrei Shakai Sōgō Tōkei Nenpō 2002 nenban* (Statistical Data of the Decline in the Number of Births and Aged Society, 2002 version). Tokyo: Shokuhin Ryūtsū Jōhō Sentā.

Smith, Robert J. (1974) *Ancestor Worship in Contemporary Japan.* Stanford, CA: Stanford University Press.

Sodei, Takako (1994) 'Care of the Elderly: A Women's Issue', in Kumiko Fujimura-Fanselow and Atsuko Kameda (eds) *Japanese Women: New Feminist Perspectives on the Past, Present and Future.* New York: Feminist Press at the City University of New York.

Sodei, Takako (1999) 'Role of Family in Long-term Care', in J. Creighton Campbell and N. Ikegami (eds) *Long-term Care for Frail Older People: Reaching for the Ideal System.* Tokyo, Berlin, Heidelberg, New York: Springer Verlag.

Sōmuchō (General Management and Coordination Agency) (1992) *Rōjin no Seikatsu to Ishiki* (Life and Attitude of the Elderly), Report on International Comparative Studies on People's Public Opinion. Tokyo: Ōkura-shō Insatsu-kyoku.

Sōmuchō (General Management and Coordination Agency) (eds) (1999) *Kōrei Shakai Hakusho* (Aging Society White Paper). Tokyo: Ōkura-shō Insatsu-kyoku.

Sōmuchō Tōkei-kyoku (General Management and Coordination Agency [GMCA], Statistics Bureau) (1992) *Rōgo no Seikatsu to Kaigo-ni kansuru Chōsa* (Survey on Life and Care in Old Age). Tokyo: Ōkura-shō Insatsu-kyoku.

Stevens, Carolyn S. (1997) *On the Margins of Japanese Society: Volunteers and the Welfare of the Urban Underclass.* London: Routledge.

Stewart, A. and A. King (1994) 'Conceptualizing and Measuring Quality of Life among the Older Population', in Ronald P. Abeles, Helen C. Gift and Marcia G. Cry (eds) *Aging and Quality of Life.* New York: Springer.

Thang, Leng Leng (2001) *Generations in Touch: Linking the Old and Young in a Tokyo Neighborhood.* Ithaca, NY and London: Cornell University Press.

Tochimoto, Ichisaburo (1999) 'Long-term Care Policy in Japan: Background and Basic Concepts of the Long-term Care Insurance Law', paper presented at the Japan–Germany Symposium on Nursing Care for Elderly People, Japan College of Social Work 14–15 February.

Townsend, Claire (1971) *Old Age: The Last Segregation.* New York: Bantam.

Traphagan, John W. (1998) 'Localizing Senility: Illness and Agency among Older Japanese', *Journal of Cross-cultural Gerontology* 13.

Traphagan, John W. (2000) *Taming Oblivion: Aging Bodies and the Fear of Senility in Japan.* Albany: State University of New York.

Vesperi, Maria (1983) 'The Reluctant Consumer: Nursing Home Residents in the Post-Bergman Era', in Jay Sokolovsky (ed.) *Growing Old in Different Societies: Cross-Cultural Perspectives.* Belmont, CA: Wadsworth, pp. 225–37.

Ware, J.E. (1984) 'Methodological Considerations in the Selection of Health Status Assessment Procedures', in N.K. Wenger, M.E. Mattson, C.D. Furberg and J. Elinson (eds) *Assessment of Quality of Life in Clinical Trials of Cardiovascular Therapies.* New York: Le Jacq Publishing Inc.

Ware, J.E. (1987) 'Standards for Validating Health Measures: Definitions and Contents', *Journal of Chronic Diseases* 40: 473–80.

Yamanoi, Kazunori (1991) *Taiken Ripō: Sekai no Kōreisha Fukushi.* Tokyo: Iwanami Shinsho.

Yamanoi, Kazunori and Yayoi Saitō (1994) *Taiken Ripō: Nihon no Kōreisha Fukushi.* Tokyo: Iwanami Shinsho.

Young, Richard and Fukui Ikeuchi (1997) 'Religion in the Hateful Age: Reflections on *Pokkuri* and Other Geriatric Rituals in Japan's Aging Society', in Susanne Formanek and Sepp Linhart (eds) *Aging: Asian Concepts and Experiences, Past and Present.* Vienna: Verlag Der Österreichischen Akademie de Wissenschaften.

Index

For Product Safety Concerns and Information please contact our EU
representative GPSR@taylorandfrancis.com
Taylor & Francis Verlag GmbH, Kaufingerstraße 24, 80331 München, Germany

www.ingramcontent.com/pod-product-compliance
Lightning Source LLC
Chambersburg PA
CBHW070404270326
41926CB00014B/2693

*9 7 8 0 4 1 5 5 4 6 0 5 8 *